ISBN 978-1-5285-2566-4
PIBN 10898729

1 MONTH OF
FREE
READING

at
www.ForgottenBooks.com

By purchasing this book you are eligible for one month membership to ForgottenBooks.com, giving you unlimited access to our entire collection of over 1,000,000 titles via our web site and mobile apps.

To claim your free month visit: www.forgottenbooks.com/free898729

English
Français
Deutsche
Italiano
Español
Português

www.forgottenbooks.com

Mythology Photography **Fiction**
Fishing Christianity **Art** Cooking
Essays Buddhism Freemasonry
Medicine **Biology** Music **Ancient**
Egypt Evolution Carpentry Physics
Dance Geology **Mathematics** Fitness
Shakespeare **Folklore** Yoga Marketing
Confidence Immortality Biographies
Poetry **Psychology** Witchcraft
Electronics Chemistry History **Law**
Accounting **Philosophy** Anthropology
Alchemy Drama Quantum Mechanics
Atheism Sexual Health **Ancient History**
Entrepreneurship Languages Sport
Paleontology Needlework Islam
Metaphysics Investment Archaeology
Parenting Statistics Criminology
Motivational

CULTURAL LANDSCAPE REPORT

FOR

WEIR FARM

NATIONAL HISTORIC SITE

Volume 1: Site History and Existing Conditions

CULTURAL LANDSCAPE REPORT

For

WEIR FARM

NATIONAL HISTORIC SITE

CULTURAL LANDSCAPE REPORT FOR WEIR FARM NATIONAL HISTORIC SITE

by
Child Associates, Inc.
Landscape Architecture
240 Newbury Street
Boston, MA 02116

Cynthia Zaitzevsky, Ph.D.
Cynthia Zaitzevsky Associates
31 Elm Street
Brookline, MA 02146

CULTURAL LANDSCAPE PUBLICATION NO. 6

Olmsted Center for Landscape Preservation
National Park Service
U.S. Department of the Interior

1996

This report is part of the Cultural Landscape Publication Series produced by the Olmsted Center for Landscape Preservation. This series includes a variety of publications designed to provide information and guidance on landscape preservation to historic site managers and other preservation professionals.

Cover illustration: J. Alden Weir, "Upland Pasture," oil on canvas, ca. 1905 (National Museum of American Art, Smithsonian Institution, Gift of William T. Evans, 1909).

Library of Congress Cataloging-in-Publication Data

Cultural landscape report for Weir Farm.
        p. cm.
1. Weir Farm National Historic Site (Conn.) 2. Ridgefield
(Conn.)--Buildings. structures. etc. 3. Wilton (Conn.)--Buildings.
structures. etc. 4. Julian Alden, 1852-1919--Homes and
haunts--Connecticut--Ridgefield Region.
F104.R5C85 1996
974.6'9--dc20   96--33426
                                                    CIP

Publication credits:

CONTENTS

LIST OF ILLUSTRATIONS

CHAPTER II

CHAPTER III

CHAPTER IV

APPENDIX

FOREWORD

Weir Farm is a very special place where the cultivated landscape and the built features upon it have evolved hand-in-hand with a thriving artistic tradition. It is perhaps the only place where an important nineteenth-century American artist's domestic and creative milieu survives virtually intact, including a significant portion of the landscape that was integral to the artist's vision. This might be appropriately termed a vernacular rural landscape with an added cultural dimension, as host to intense, ongoing artistic activity for over a century.

We wish to thank Child Associates, Inc., and Cynthia Zaitzevsky Associates for the work contained in this report, which marks an important step in recording the landscape in all its details and defining the compelling character of the whole that continues to draw artists to it today. The report will serve as a baseline for future planning and will provide site managers with a valuable reference manual for maintaining as well as interpreting the cultural landscape to visitors. This report is also the point of departure for developing detailed treatment plans for restoring the character of the landscape familiar to the Weirs and Youngs.

Restoration of the landscape is prescribed in the General Management Plan, which was prepared simultaneously with the Cultural Landscape Report (CLR). As information was generated for the CLR, it was also used by the general management planning team. At the same time, reports were developed that specifically address the structures throughout the site and the historic interiors of the main house and the art studios—Historic Structures and Historic Furnishings Reports, respectively. All of these reports form an important beginning library for the park. The painting location plan contained herein is a first of its kind and a significant beginning in charting the locations of hundreds of landscape paintings executed by Weir.

We have been fortunate, indeed, to conduct so much research at the beginning of the site's new role as a national park area. In spite of the thoroughness of the research in this report, additional documentation is almost sure to emerge as families that hold additional pertinent records become aware of the site and its importance. We can expect, too, that physical evidence will continually emerge as we stabilize and make repairs to built features throughout the site. It is important that we dedicate ourselves to building on the excellent foundation laid in this report by incorporating new information as it appears.

Sarah Olson, Superintendent
Weir Farm National Historic Site

ACKNOWLEDGMENTS

The publication of this report would not have been possible without the generous contributions of many individuals. In particular we are indebted to Nora Mitchell, Director of the Olmsted Center for Landscape Preservation of the National Park Service. Katy Lacy and Lauren Meier, Historical Landscape Architects, of the Olmsted Center for Landscape Preservation, have also contributed generously during the preparation of this report.

The staff of the National Park Service and the Weir Farm Heritage Trust at the Weir Farm National Historic Site were of great assistance throughout the project. In particular we wish to thank Sarah Olson, Superintendent, Robert Fox, Facility Manager, and Gay Vietzke, Museum Technician at Weir Farm NHS, who provided guidance, information on the site, and made many helpful recommendations to the consultant team. A special commendation goes to Gay Vietzke for the identification of painting sites and for responding cheerfully to numerous research inquiries and requests for documents.

Several Weir and Young family members and friends kindly provided personal recollections that gave us invaluable information on the Weir Farm landscape. These include Mahonri Sharp (Bill) Young, Anna Weir Ely Smith, Charles Burlingham, and Doris and Sperry Andrews.

Thanks are also due to the staffs of the Lee Library and Museum of Art at Brigham Young University, Provo, Utah, who were most helpful during a week-long research trip, and to the staff of the Fine Arts Department, Boston Public Library. We are most grateful to Phyllis Andersen, Landscape Historian, Arnold Arboretum, Jamaica Plain, Boston; Robert Brown, Director of the Archives of American Art, Smithsonian Institution, Boston; Susan Faxon, Curator, Addison Gallery of American Art, Andover, Massachusetts; and to Hildegard Cummings, Curator of Education, William Benton Museum of Art, Storrs, Connecticut.

Child Associates, Inc., of Boston, Massachusetts, and Cynthia Zaitzevsky Associates of Brookline, Massachusetts, composed the consultant team for this project. Cynthia Zaitzevsky served as the landscape historian and William A. Niering acted as ecological and natural history consultant. Contributors at Child Associates, Inc., included Susan Child, Robert Corning, John Grove, Jennifer Parker, and Lynn Wolff.

EXECUTIVE SUMMARY

The Weir Farm National Historic Site (NHS) was acquired by the National Park Service in 1990. As the home and workplace of J. Alden Weir (1852-1919), a noted American impressionist painter, the farm was the subject of many of Weir's significant paintings and is therefore of national historic importance. The fact that other American artists such as Childe Hassam and Albert Pinkham Ryder were also inspired by the farm for their work contributes to its value as a cultural landscape.

J. Alden Weir began painting as a boy under the guidance of his father and studied at the National Academy of Design in New York City and later at the Ecole des Beaux Arts in Paris. By 1882 Weir had established a reputation as an accomplished artist and was able to purchase a home on 153 acres in Ridgefield and Wilton, Connecticut. The following year he married Anna Dwight Baker and took an extended European honeymoon. Upon their return, the couple resided primarily in New York City, spending summers at the farm in Connecticut. Between 1884-1892 J. Alden and Anna Weir had four children. Their three daughters, Caroline, Dorothy, and Cora, all survived, but their son, J. Alden Weir Jr., died in infancy. Anna Weir died just after the birth of her daughter Cora in 1892.

One of Weir's first paintings of the farm is "Spring Landscape, Branchville," dated 1882. The farm landscape was the inspiration for many paintings and sketches by Weir and other artists.

During Weir's tenure at the farm a series of alterations were made to the main house and several outbuildings were added, including a studio constructed in 1885. The noted architect, Charles Adams Platt developed plans for renovation of the main house in 1900, and the firm of McKim, Mead and White designed a new dining room in 1911.

Weir added to his initial purchase of land over the years. In 1896 he purchased a 10-acre parcel of land on which he constructed a pond for fishing. Additional land purchases were made in 1900 and 1907, augmenting the property by 32 and 50 acres, respectively.

J. Alden Weir died in 1919. After her father's death, Dorothy Weir and her stepmother, Ella Weir, continued to spend summers at the farm until Ella's death in 1930. In 1931 Dorothy married sculptor Mahonri Young, and the couple spent a great deal of time at the farm. In 1932 Young built a studio suitable for large pieces of sculpture adjacent to Weir's studio. Young spent less time at the farm after Dorothy's death in 1947.

After Young's death in 1957, the farm was purchased by Doris and Sperry Andrews, fellow artists and friends of Mahonri Young. Through the efforts of many individuals, groups, and agencies such as the Andrews, Cora Weir Burlingham, The Trust for Public Land, The Weir Farm Heritage Trust, and the Connecticut Department of Environmental Protection, Weir Farm has been protected. Weir Farm was established as a National Historic Site in 1990 through legislation initiated by State Senator John Matthews and United States Senator Joseph I. Lieberman. The National Park Service is now charged with preserving this cultural legacy for the enjoyment of future generations.

INTRODUCTION

The Weir Farm National Historic Site in Ridgefield and Wilton, Connecticut, is a significant part of our national heritage. Established in 1990, it is the only national park dedicated to the stewardship of a property associated with an American painter. As the home and workplace of the eminent American impressionist painter J. Alden Weir (1852–1919), the landscape of Weir Farm has been captured in many of his paintings and sketches. Other American artists such as Albert Pinkham Ryder, John Twatchman, and Childe Hassam also found inspiration for paintings and sketches at the farm. In addition, Weir's daughter Dorothy painted at the farm while her husband, Mahonri Young, made many sketches of the landscape and had a sculpture studio on the premises. The 153-acre property was acquired by Weir in 1882. Subsequent land purchases added to the property, which totaled 238 acres at Weir's death. The farm remained under the ownership of Weir's descendants until 1957. Doris and Sperry Andrews, fellow artists and friends of Mahonri Young, owned and cared for the property from 1958 to 1990, when it was acquired by the Trust for Public Land and subsequently the National Park Service. A site chronology from ca. 1779 to the present is included in this report, with the most detailed site history covering the years of the J. Alden Weir ownership (1882–1919).

The purpose of this Cultural Landscape Report is to thoroughly document and interpret the evolution of the site. It is intended to aid the National Park Service in the planning and management of the Weir Farm property. Detailed information relating to historic structures can be found in the Historic Structures Reports (Cardon, Crisson, Phillips, NPS), which are underway at the present time. Information on historic furnishings is available in the Historic Furnishings Report (Wallace, NPS).

Methodology

This report is divided into chapters based on the various periods of ownership of Weir Farm. Period plans were developed by Child Associates, Inc., and Cynthia Zaitzevsky Associates for the years 1919 and 1947, corresponding to the deaths of J. Alden Weir and Dorothy Weir Young, respectively. A discussion of the methodology and the specific sources used in the preparation of specific period plans can be found prior to each period plan. Some landscape features, such as the Victory Garden, were created and lost between the dates of the period plans and therefore do not appear on either of the plans. However, these features are discussed in the text.

Cynthia Zaitzevsky, Principal, of Cynthia Zaitzevsky Associates, conducted the research and wrote the site history chapters, with the exception of the sections dealing with the period plans. Archival sources for the site history have included correspondence (the J. Alden Weir, Weir Family, and Mahonri M.

Young papers); Weir, Young, and Burlingham family photographs dating from ca. 1884 through the early 1960s; aerial photographs from the 1940s and 1950s; J. Alden Weir's works of art (paintings, etchings, drawings, and pastels) which have the farm as subject; similar works of art by Weir's friends (Hassam, Ryder, etc.); and the works of art, principally drawings, by Mahonri M. Young. Secondary sources included Dorothy Weir Young's *The Life and Letters of J. Alden Weir;* interviews with Weir and Young descendants, as well as with Doris and Sperry Andrews; and the draft reports of General Management Plan, Historic Structure Reports, Historic Furnishings Report, and the National Park Service's Olmsted Center for Landscape Preservation report on the secret garden. Since all of these reports were being done concurrently with the Cultural Landscape Report, we have also benefited from discussions with many of the authors.

Although this source material is very rich and provides a vivid picture of life at Weir Farm in the late 19th and early 20th centuries, portions of the site, especially the areas used for farming, have been difficult to document because of the lack of certain kinds of records. Before this project began, there had never been an engineering survey made of the property. Therefore, there was no baseline of information that covers the entire site, or even its core area, at some earlier point in its history. (Early 20th-century surveys are available for other properties such as the Saint-Gaudens and Frederick Law Olmsted National Historic Sites and for the core area of the Vanderbilt Mansion National Historic Site.) Also, with the exception of the Burlingham sunken garden, there are no surviving design plans for the site, since the Weir and Young families appear not to have used professional landscape architects or designers. In addition, the property was never photographed by professional photographers, and the bulk of the family photographs, while extremely helpful, are generally concerned with areas near the houses or studios. The Weir and Young works of art are also an invaluable source, but some locations remain impossible to identify with certainty. One can also not rule out the possibility that both artists at times used artistic license.

The sources for the site history are listed in full in the bibliography and endnotes. In the endnotes, whenever possible, our method has been to group sources together to avoid an inordinate number of endnotes. All sources for a given paragraph will be included under one or more notes for that paragraph, so there is not necessarily a note number at the end of each sentence.

PROLOGUE: THE BEERS AND WEBB FARMS BEFORE WEIR
CA. 1745–1881

As yet, no photographs have been located that illustrate the pre-1882 landscape of either the Beers Farm or the Webb Farm, nor has any written documentation been found concerning the pre-Weir landscape at either location. However, extensive deed research has been done on both properties, so that the chain of ownership can be easily traced. Additionally, recent thorough research and physical investigation have brought to light considerable information about the early history of the houses on both farms.

In 1745 the Ridgefield Proprietors granted three parcels of land in the sixth 20–Acre Division of the town to Matthew Benedict, Benjamin Burt, and jointly to Joseph Northrup and Henry Whitney. The first mention of a house on the Beers property, which was the farm acquired by Weir for his own residence in 1882, occurs in a deed dated 1781, when Joseph Jackson sold the second parcel to James Abbott. This deed refers to a dwelling house on the northwest corner of Nod Hill Road and Pelham Lane.[1] On the basis of structural investigations, architectural materials, stylistic evidence and historical records, the authors of the 1995 Historic Structures Report prepared by the National Park Service for the site and the Weir complex suggest an initial construction date for house of between 1760 and 1779.[2] In 1789 Anthony Beers purchased the first two parcels of land, including the one with the dwelling house, and in 1797 he acquired the third parcel. When Anthony Beers died in 1821, the deed or probate record transferring the property to his heirs indicated that, on the northwest corner of Nod Hill Road and Pelham Lane, there was now a dwelling house, a barn, a necessary house, and a wagonshed. By 1836 Lewis Beers had inherited or purchased all three parcels of land as well as two additional parcels.[3] The house appears to have been remodelled in the Greek Revival style at an undocumented date, probably ca. 1830.[4]

Lewis Beers' will, dated 1860–1861, provides more information about the Beers farm. It includes a detailed inventory, which lists all of the structures then on the land. On the northwest corner of Nod Hill Road and Pelham Lane (present site of Weir Farm core area), there was now a dwelling house, barn and cow houses, a wash house, and a hog house "by the house." Additionally, there was another barn and cow houses "up north of the homestead." On the southeast corner, there was now a small dwelling house and a carriage house. Assorted livestock and furniture are also listed.[5] The small dwelling house on the southeast corner of Nod Hill Road and Pelham Lane must be the caretaker's house. Since this was not mentioned in Anthony Beers' 1821 inventory, it would seem probable that the caretaker's house was built sometime between 1821 and 1861.

In the case of the Webb property, which was purchased by Weir in 1907, there is also considerable information about early land ownership. In 1748 the Proprietors of Ridgefield (Wilton had not yet been set off from Ridgefield) granted 41 acres out of 2200 acres of common land known as Rockhouse Woods to John Belden and an adjacent parcel of 9 acres to Samuel Brimsmade and John Reed. (Rockhouse Woods was named for an outcropping of a large, flat rock apparently used for shelter by the Indians and early settlers. It is located on the ridge at the foot of Olmsted Hill.) In 1782 a deed transferring the property from Joshua Chase to Colonel Stephen St. John mentions a small dwelling house. In 1832 Jared Webb bought the 9–acre parcel, and in 1843 he purchased the 41–acre parcel, at the same time transferring partial rights in the latter parcel to William Webb, presumably his son. The deeds for the 1843 transactions mention buildings, probably referring to, at the least, the house and barn on the site. According to Volume III of the Weir Farm Historic Structures Report, which deals with the Burlingham property, the existing Webb/Burlingham barn was probably built before 1835 and may have been constructed even earlier, since the nails in the extant roof sheathing have characteristics of cut nails manufactured between ca. 1815 and 1835.[6] At Jared Webb's death in 1847, William Webb inherited the remaining rights to the 41–acre parcel, while the 9–acre parcel was left to other heirs. By 1855 William Webb had acquired the 9–acre parcel as well.[7] Physical evidence, such as the position of the ridgepole paralleling Nod Hill Road and the muntin profiles, suggests that the Webb-Burlingham house was probably built around 1775.[8]

On plate 37 of *Atlas of New York and Vicinity*, published by F. W. Beers et al. in 1867, a house belonging to Mrs. Beers is indicated in Ridgefield and one owned by W. Webb is shown just over the line in Wilton (figure 1). On plate 40 of the same atlas, Mrs. Beers' house is again shown, along with the cemetery and a house to the north of it belonging to W. B. Beers (figure 2). Today, the cemetery still contains stones dated from 1820 to 1886 and inscribed with names of members of the Beers family.[9] The caretaker's house does not appear on plate 37, although the house was probably built by 1867. As noted above, it may be the "small dwelling house" referred to in the Beers inventory of 1861. Unfortunately, the 1867 atlas is not sufficiently detailed to show the footprints of the houses or the lines of drives or paths. Outbuildings, including the several mentioned in the Beers Inventory, also do not appear.

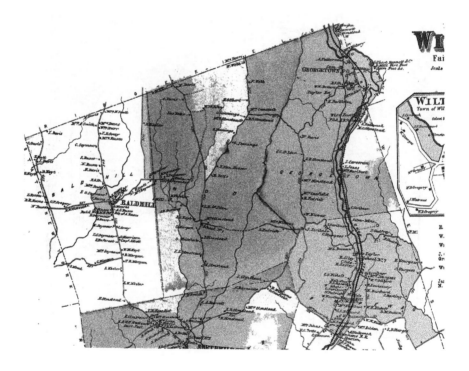

Figure 1   Locations of W. Webb and Mrs. Beers houses, 1867 (From F. W. Beers, *Atlas of New York and Vicinity*, 1867, plate 37, Harvard College Map Room).

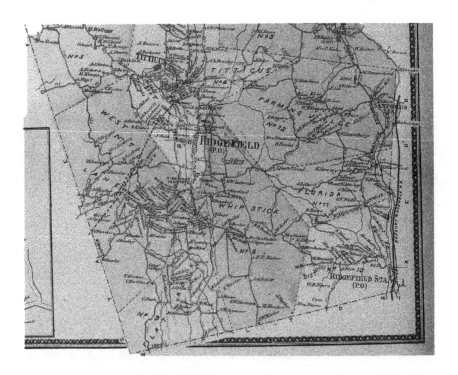

Figure 2   Locations of Mrs. Beers and W. B. Beers houses and cemetery (From F. W. Beers, *Atlas of New York Vicinity,* 1867, plate 40, Harvard College Map Room).

ENDNOTES TO PROLOGUE

1.   This is a deed conveying the property from James Burchard to Daniel Whitlock, Jr. and Nathan Whitlock in 1778. (Deed research August 1995 by Gay Vietzke and Richard C. Crisson.) See also Marie L. Carden and Richard C. Crisson, "Weir Farm Historic Structures Report, Weir Farm National Historic Site, Wilton, Connecticut". Volume I: "The Site and the Weir Complex" (Lowell, Massachusetts: Building Conservation Branch, Cultural Resources Center, Northeast Region, National Park Service, U. S. Department of the Interior, 1995), 42.

2.   Ibid., 42-46. The National Register form for the property contains some dates and other information that, in the light of more recent research, do not seem to be accurate. (See David F. Ransom, Consultant, "National Register of Historic Places Inventory-Nomination Form for the J. Alden Weir Farm in Ridgefield, Connecticut," Edited by John Herzan, National Register Coordinator, January 16, 1983. Copy at Weir Farm National Historic Site.)

3.   Ellen Paul, CGRS, History and Documentation of Weir Farm" (1990), Weir Farm National Historic Site, 1-2.

4.   Carden and Crisson," Weir Farm Historic Structures Report," Volume I, 47.

5.   Will of Lewis Beers, Probate Court, Fairfield County Courthouse. Notes by Gay Vietzke, December 21, 1992, Weir Farm National Historic Site. Maureen K. Phillips, "Weir Farm Historic Structure Report. Volume II, Caretaker's Buildings," Draft (Boston: Building Conservation Branch, Cultural Resources Center, North Atlantic Region, National Park Services, U.S. Department of the Interior, 1994), 3-5.

6.   Maureen K. Phillips, "Weir Farm Historic Structures Report, Weir Farm National Historic Site, Wilton, Connecticut." Volume III: "Burlingham Complex" (Lowell, Massachusetts: Building Conservation Branch, Northeast Cultural Resources Center, National Park Service, U. S. Department of the Interior, 1995), 187.

7.   Ibid., 3-4; Paul, "History and Documentation," 6, 10–11. For the derivation of the name "Rockhouse Woods," David Herman Van Hoosear, *Annals of Wilton,* Vol. I (Wilton, Connecticut: Wilton Historical Society, 1940), page 27 is cited.

8.   Memorandum from Maureen Phillips to Gay Vietzke, May 9, 1994, Weir Farm National Historic Site. This may mean that Joshua Chase built the house.

9.   Weir Farm National Register Form, under Criterion C.

CHAPTER I: THE J. ALDEN WEIR OWNERSHIP, PART I: 1882–1900

YOUTH, STUDIES, EARLY CAREER

Julian Alden Weir was born on August 30, 1852, the son of Robert Walter Weir (1803–1889), a drawing professor at the United States Military Academy, West Point, New York, and his second wife Susan Martha Bayard Weir. Julian Alden Weir began painting as a boy, with his father as his first teacher. His elder half-brother John Ferguson Weir (1841–1926), was an artist as well. In the late 1860s and early 1870s, Julian frequently visited his brother in New York City and also used his studio at the Tenth Street Studio Building. Between 1869 and 1872, he studied during the winters at the National Academy of Design in New York City. As Julian's exceptional talent emerged, John Ferguson Weir (hereafter referred to as John) became convinced that his brother needed an extended period of study in Europe, which the family could not afford. In 1873 John persuaded a family friend, Mrs. Bradford R. Alden, who was also the widow of Julian's godfather, to finance Julian's European education.[1] Weir was always called Julian by his family and friends, and in early life he signed his name Julian A. Weir. In 1874, however, he changed his professional signature to J. Alden Weir in recognition of Mrs. Alden's kindness.[2]

Between 1873 and 1877, Weir studied in Paris at the École des Beaux-Arts. His practical experience was in the atelier of Jean-Léon Gérôme. As an advanced student, Weir won awards and exhibited at the Paris Salon. During this period, he also traveled in Brittany, Belgium, Holland, Spain, and England, where he met the American expatriate painter James Abbott McNeill Whistler.[3]

Shortly after his return to the United States in October 1877, Weir joined the new Society of American Artists and the Tile Club. Fellow members of the Tile Club included the architect Stanford White, the sculptor Augustus Saint-Gaudens, and painters Winslow Homer, William Merritt Chase, and John Henry Twachtman, who became one of Weir's closest friends. In 1878, Weir began teaching at the Cooper Union and Art Students League, as well as taking private pupils, and in 1880 he began exhibiting at the American Watercolor Society. In the summers of 1878, 1880, and 1881, he returned to Europe, again spending most of his time in France. In the summer of 1881, he also travelled to Dordrecht in Holland with his brother, John, where they joined Twachtman and his new bride, Martha, on a successful and memorable sketching trip. Weir's reputation continued to grow, especially in the areas of portraiture, still life, and genre painting. Stylistically, his work was firmly rooted in realism, until about 1890, when he turned to Impressionism and became one of its foremost American practitioners.[4]

9

1882–1890

By 1882 Weir had become sufficiently successful to consider both marriage and a home in the country. In January, Weir took on a new drawing student, Anna Dwight Baker, with whom he fell immediately in love (a "coup de foudre," in the words of Anna's friend Ernestine Fàbbri). Three weeks later, the two were engaged.[5]

Weir first explored the possibility of a summer home and studio in the Adirondacks, where he purchased several parcels of contiguous land in Keene Valley just south of Lake Placid in Essex County, New York. During a visit of about three weeks in August 1882 to Keene Valley, Weir wrote almost daily letters to Anna, in which he enthusiastically described this property and his plans for it. In addition, he brought Stanford White up to Keene Valley to discuss the design of his projected Adirondacks house.[6] Construction began on this house in October 1882, but it is unclear whether it was ever completed.[7] These plans appear to have been dropped by late 1883, since there is little further mention of the Adirondacks property in the Weir/Anna Baker correspondence.[8]

There are two possibilities why this may have occurred. First, the Adirondacks plan may have been contingent on having Twachtman build nearby or on the same land. In a letter of July 1882, Weir wrote to Anna: "I shall begin to pack up my sketching things today, ready for my trip and hope that Mr. Twachtman will be on, for it was partially by agreement that I saw to the land in the Adirondacks during the month of July. . . ."[9] But Twachtman, whose financial resources were slim, eventually settled year round in Cos Cob, part of Greenwich, Connecticut, which, of course, was much more accessible by train to New York City. Twachtman appears to have begun renting in Cos Cob in the summer of 1886, although he did not purchase property there until 1890–1891, when he bought a house with 16 acres of land.[10] The second reason might have been Anna's strong ties to Connecticut, where her parents had a home in Windham, in the eastern part of the state.[11] Weir found Connecticut appealing as well. In early spring 1882, Weir visited Windham with Anna and later wrote:

> No hour of the day passes but what I recall those few hours we had in the charming little village of Windham, this is really the first Connecticut village that I have really ever known, & now I feel that a charm is connected with all villages, such as I have never before appreciated.[12]

Ultimately, it may have seemed impractical to maintain two summer places, and Connecticut, being closer to both New York City and Windham, had clear advantages.

Having decided on Connecticut, the reasons why Weir chose Ridgefield over Windham or Greenwich and why he bought this particular property are not recorded, but it may have been simply the happy chance of being offered a very good deal. In the summer of 1882, while he was still actively pursuing his Adirondacks plans, Weir purchased 153 acres in Branchville (the name for this part of Ridgefield and Wilton) from art collector Erwin Davis for $10.00 and a painting that Weir had just purchased for $560.00.[13] A few days later, Weir decided to go up to look at the Branchville property to see if it was habitable: ". . . if so we might have that as a sort of a hunting lodge for part of the season. . . .I hear that there is good hunting & fishing near the place & if that is the case it will serve to keep on hand. . . ."[14] Unfortunately, Weir never described the Branchville property, or his plans for it, with the same kind of enthusiastic detail that he had used in writing about the Adirondacks land. However, the Weir Farm Heritage Trust has recently acquired a watercolor that must have been painted during Weir's first visit to his new Connecticut farm in June 1882: "Spring Landscape, Branchville," dated 1882 (figure 3). See also Exhibits 1 and 2, the Painting Location Plans prepared for this report, which show this and all other works of art by Weir for which it has been possible to identify locations at the site today. The watercolor shows an open pasture typical of those on the farm, with a stone wall and trees in new leaf. Since the open pastures of 1882 are now heavily overgrown, the exact location of the painting is difficult to determine.[15]

After his somewhat casual purchase, Weir began to make repairs and improvements to the house.[16] By the time he dropped the Adirondacks project, Weir had stopped regarding the Connecticut land merely as a place for an occasional hunting lodge. Instead, he began developing the property as a working farm. Never, apparently, did he intend it to be an highly ornamental "country place." By October 1882, Weir was deeply involved in his agricultural plans and had arranged to have Alderney cattle brought in.[17]

On April 24, 1883, Weir and Anna Dwight Baker were married at the Church of the Ascension in New York City.[18] Immediately after the wedding, they went up to Branchville for a few days of rest before leaving on their European honeymoon.[19] While on his honeymoon, Weir still had the improvement of the Branchville place on his mind. From Nuremberg, he wrote to his brother John, who was staying on the property while he was away, telling him that he planned to "set out willow trees about the moist land. This will add to the beauty and . . . if trimmed as they do here, which gives a very interesting character to the landscape."[20] In August, John wrote to Julian:

> I tinker about the premises and hold the reins over the work which is needful. . . . My dear fellow, may your 'corn and wine and oil increase.' . . .We often speak of you as we sit on the pleasant porch in the evening twilight. I imagine you and Anna, seated in your two armchairs, sitting in these twilights in future summers. Hang on to this place, old boy, a 'lonesome lodge' which is a pleasant place of retreat in storm and drought . . . keep it trim and untrammelled and you will find it a haven of refuge.[21]

11

Figure 3   J. Alden Weir, "Spring Landscape, Branchville," watercolor, 1882 (Weir Farm
                  Heritage Trust).

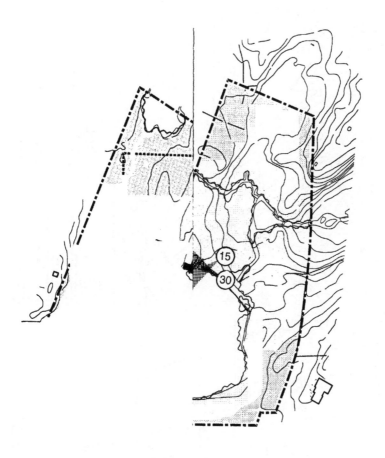

United States Department Of The Interior
National Park Service North Atlantic Regional Office

WEIR FARM NATIONAL HISTORIC SITE

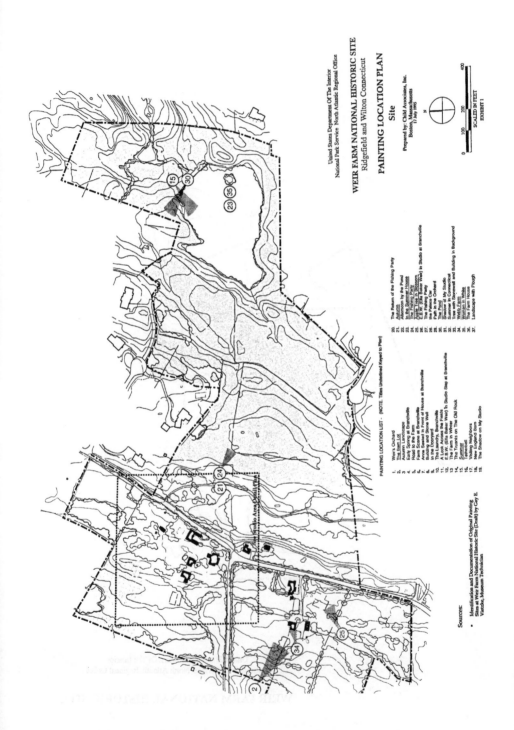

United States Department Of The Interior
National Park Service North Atlantic Regional Office

WEIR FARM NATIONAL HISTORIC SITE
Ridgefield and Wilton Connecticut

PAINTING LOCATION PLAN
Site

Prepared by: Child Associates, Inc.
Boston, Massachusetts
17 July 1995

N

SCALED IN FEET
0   100   200   400

EXHIBIT 1

PAINTING LOCATION LIST -   (NOTE: Titles Underlined Keyed to Plan)

1.   Weir's Orchard
2.   The Barn Lot
3.   Autumn Landscape
4.   Early Spring at Branchville
5.   Road to the Farm
6.   Farm Scene at Branchville
7.   Area Seated In Front of House at Branchville
8.   Building and Stone Wall
     in the Dooryard
9.   The Laundry, Branchville
10. The Laundry, Branchville
11. A Look Across the Fields
12. E.B.W. (Ella Baker Weir) In Studio Step at Branchville
13. The Farm in Winter
14. The Trysts on The Old Rock
15. Summer
16. Twilight
17. Visiting Neighbors
18. New England Barn
19. The Shadow on My Studio

20. The Return of the Fishing Party
21. Autumn
22. Afternoon by the Pond
23. In the Summer House
24. The Fishing Party
25. Apple Tree in Blossom
26. E.B.W. (Ella Baker Weir) in Studio at Branchville
27. The Fishing Party
28. the Plateau Car
29. Path in the Orchard
30. The Pond
31. Shadow of My Studio
32. Summer in Connecticut
33. Tree with Stonewall and Building in Background
34. Web Farm
35. Woman in White
36. The Farm House
37. Landscape with Plough

Sources:

•   Identification and Documentation of Original Painting
    Sites at Weir Farm National Historic Site (Draft) by Guy E.
    Vietzke, Museum Technician

PAINTING LOCATION LIST (NOTE: Titles Underlined Keyed to Plan)

1. Weir's Orchard
2. The Barn Lot
3. Autumn Landscape
4. Early Spring at Branchville
5. Road to the Farm
6. Farm Scene at Branchville
7. Anna Seated In Front of House at Branchville
8. Building and Stone Wall
9. In the Dooryard
10. The Laundry, Branchville
11. A Look Across the Fields
12. E.B.W. (Ella Baker Weir) In Studio Step at Branchville
13. The Farm In Winter
14. The Truants on The Old Rock
15. Summer
16. Tetherball
17. Visiting Neighbors
18. New England Barn
19. The Shadow on My Studio
20. The Return of the Fishing Party
21. Autumn
22. Afternoon by the Pond
23. In the Summer House
24. The Fishing Party
25. Apple Tree in Blossom
26. E.B.W. (Ella Baker Weir) In Studio at Branchville
27. The Fishing Party
28. the Palace Car
29. Path in the Orchard
30. The Pond
31. Shadow of My Studio
32. Summer In Connecticut
33. Tree with Stonewall and Building in Background
34. Webb Farm
35. Woman in White
36. The Farm House
37. Landscape with Plough

Sources:

* Identification and Documentation of Original Painting
  Sites at Weir Farm National Historic Site (Draft) by Gay E.
  Vietzke, Museum Technician

United States Department Of The Interior
National Park Service ,North Atlantic Regional Office

WEIR FARM NATIONAL HISTORIC SITE
Ridgefield and Wilton Connecticut

PAINTING LOCATION PLAN
Studio Area Detail Plan
Prepared by: Child Associates Inc.
Boston, Massachusetts
17 July 1995

N

0   50   100   200

SCALED IN FEET
EXHIBIT 2

Legend:

- Structures
- Tree Cover
- View Shed
- ⓝ Painting Location

PAINTING LOCATION LIST (NOTE: Titles Underlined Keyed to Plan)

1. Weir's Orchard
2. Burlen Lot
3. Autumn Landscape
4. Early Chancery at Branchville
5. Road to the Farm
6. Farm Scene at Branchville
7. Farm Scene in Front of House at Branchville
8. Afternoon and Snow Wall
9. U's Vineyard
10. The Laundry, Branchville
11. The Fishing Party
12. E.B.W. (Ella Baker Weir) in Studio Step at Branchville
13. The Farm in Winter
14. The Fourth on The Old Rock
15. Summer
16. Farmhead
17. Visiting Neighbors
18. Weir Original Studio
19. The Shadow on My Studio
20. E.B.W. (Ella Baker Weir) in Studio at Branchville
21. Autumn
22. Afternoon by the Pond
23. In the Summer House
24. The Fishing Party
25. Apple Tree in Blossom
26. The Fishery Party
27. The Pond
28. Path in the Orchard
29. Pond
30. The Pond
31. Shadow of My Studio
32. Summer in Connecticut
33. Summer in Connecticut and Building in Background
34. Webb Farm
35. Woman in White
36. The Farm House
37. Landscape with Pond

Sources:

- Identification and Documentation of Original Painting Sites at Weir Farm National Historic Site (Draft) by Gay E. Vietzke, Museum Technician

United States Department Of The Interior
National Park Service North Atlantic Regional Office

WEIR FARM NATIONAL HISTORIC SITE
Ridgefield and Wilton Connecticut

PAINTING LOCATION PLAN
Studio Area Detail Plan

Prepared by: Child Associates Inc.
Boston, Massachusetts
17 May 1995

N

SCALED IN FEET
0   50   100   200

EXHIBIT 2

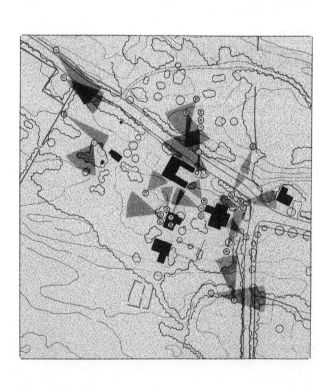

In the same letter, John wrote: "Here will we rest and call Content our Home," apparently a quotation and a motto that Weir liked so much he later had Stanford White paint it over the front door of the house.[22] In a more practical vein, John went on:

> Your crops are doing finely. The barn is full of hay, and the potatoes and corn are in fine shape ... You must get this place in such running order that it supports itself, and you can another year. But you must not leave it all to Holsten ... When·you get back I must have a good talk with you about your farm and its management.[23]

(Holsten was apparently the tenant farmer.) John was also supervising the improvements and construction that were ongoing at the farm and paying bills for Weir.[24]

While abroad, Weir had occasional spells of homesickness for Connecticut. In July he wrote to his mother-in-law: "We often recall the modest Branchville and think it would be very nice to be there."[25] The following month, he wrote her again: ". . . so you can see we are not overcome by the fascination of a wandering life but long for the quiet, plain little house among the rocks . . ."[26]

In September 1883, Weir cut short his honeymoon. Rumors of a depressed American art market had reached him and made him decide to return home to "hammer at portraits." For their winter quarters in New York City, he and Anna at first settled into an apartment on East 10th Street close to his studio in the Benedict Building in Washington Square. In 1886, however, they moved into a townhouse at 11 East 12th Street, where Weir would remain until 1907.[27]

By the end of 1883, renovations and repairs to the caretaker's house, which, as noted in the Prologue, was probably an existing building on the property, had been completed. Holsten, the tenant farmer, was probably its first occupant under Weir's ownership.[28] On March 24, 1884, Weir's and Anna's first child Caroline (Caro) Alden Weir was born. It was a successful year professionally for Weir, also: he had his first solo exhibition of watercolors at Doll and Richards, and he was elected to the American Water Color Society.[29] The summer of 1884 was spent in Branchville, where Weir painted some of the farmhouse rooms himself, and he and Anna took long country drives, sometimes at night. Nevertheless, the late 1880s were difficult years for American artists, since both "artistic" photography and paintings by European artists sold better than their work.[30] This may have been why, in 1886, Weir mortgaged the

Branchville property to the Ridgefield Savings Bank.[31] In March 1885, Weir gave notice to Holsten, who had proved unsatisfactory:

> You will be surprised to hear this, my noble gardener goes April 1st, having let all our celery freeze, some 500 heads . . . I think I have a good man this time, an old soldier from West Point who is glad to take the place for $20 and his wife to make butter and help with the washing . . .[32]

In the summer of 1885 Weir's studio was completed.[33]

From the outset of his career, Weir, a man of warm friendships and convivial habits, liked to work with other artists. This trait was very marked even during his student days in Paris, when he shared a studio with Albert Edelfelt, a Finnish artist. After Weir's return to the United States, Edelfelt wrote him praising "ton enthusiasme, ton coeur généraux" (French was apparently their only common language), adding that other friends sent Weir their best wishes: "Tous nos amis te serrent la main. Nous parlons souvent de toi. On ne manque jamais de dire, quand on prononce ton nom: 'Quel brave ami, quel grand coeur, quel chic garçon!'"[34] At home, Twachtman was Weir's preferred painting companion, but he also invited others, including the withdrawn and somewhat eccentric Albert Pinkham Ryder, his friend since 1870, to paint with him at Branchville.[35] Possibly the first work of art by another artist to be painted at Weir Farm is Ryder's painting "Weir's Orchard" (figure 4), which can be dated only to the period ca. 1885–1890. It is an evocative and slightly eerie interpretation of a rural subject, in this case the orchard at the rear of Weir's property not far from the cemetery boundary.

In the spring and summer of 1886, there are several references to gardening. In May, Weir wrote to Anna's sister Ella Baker: "The garden is all planted and the vegetables up, and the trees out in leaf, so that we are beginning to long for the old farm."[36] He followed this with another letter to Ella in June:

> We will miss you here this summer, as we have gotten things a little better arranged. . . . Our garden is looking finely and this has been a remarkable season for grass, having had more rain and showers (they say) than we have had in thirty years.[37]

In 1886 Anna Weir planted a flower garden, but by July, when Weir wrote again to Ella, who was apparently an experienced gardener, it became obvious that it was not a success:

18

Figure 4   Albert Pinkham Ryder, "Weir's Orchard," oil on canvas, ca. 1885–1890
                           (Wadsworth Athenaeum, Hartford. The Ella Gallup Sumner and Mary Catlin
                           Sumner Collection Fund).

19

> We are also glad to tell you that we are enjoying our garden this year, having plenty of vegetables, but alas, Anna's flower garden does not look (well?) nor have any of them bloomed yet. There is considerable art required to have a good flower garden, and unless the seeds are planted at the right time, things never seem well. I wish you could have given us a little counsel when we planted the bed.[38]

After the watercolor done in spring 1882 (figure 3), dated works of art by Weir showing his farm and the adjacent Webb Farm do not appear until 1887. Weir had, of course, been painting in Branchville from the beginning, especially after his studio was completed in 1885, and he had painted interior scenes of the house. However, not all the art created at Weir Farm necessarily had the farm as its subject. Until about 1889, portraits and figure studies continued to dominate Weir's work, in spite of the early interest in landscape shown in the 1882 watercolor. By the late 1880s, Weir had turned increasingly to landscape.[39] Weir also seemed to need to live with a landscape for a while before committing it to canvas:

> One of my best landscapes was a clump of old trees standing down in the corner of my place in Connecticut. Now I had seen those old trees year after year until they had become a part of me, so to speak. One day the impulse seized me to paint them, and the picture instantly "caught on." This proves to my mind that you must make a subject a part of yourself before you can properly express it to others.[40]

An 1887 painting possibly of Pelham Lane near the farm is "Lengthening Shadows" (figure 5). In the late 1880s, Weir also began experimenting with etching. However, most of his etchings are of the nearby Webb Farm and will be illustrated in chapter V. What is probably the earliest photograph of the Weir house is illustrated in figure 6. This shows the south side of the house before 1887–1888, when the first story was extended to the west. In this photograph, a single vine-covered trellis leans against the house, and some planting, probably flowers, is visible against the foundation.[41]

In February 1888, J. Alden Weir, Jr., was born.[42] A beautiful studio photograph of Anna and her infant son is shown in Figure 7. Another photograph of Anna with the baby near the Weir barn (figure 8) was probably taken in the summer of 1888.[43] As Weir wrote in July 1888, this summer brought him a new farmer and a plentiful harvest as well as the completion of the addition to the house:

> The garden is full of vegetables and the fields are heavy with grass and grains . . . I am delighted with our farmer and wife. They are by far the best we have ever had. They are Scotch and thrifty, tidy people . . . We made a great effort to get settled with unknown all about us and are only now coming to a terminus and hope by Friday to finish our addition. Then alas comes the reckoning, as usual the bills are twice what we expected . . .[44]

Figure 5   J. Alden Weir, "Lengthening Shadows," oil on canvas, 1887 (Private Collection).

21

Figure 6   Weir House. Photograph, ca. 1886–1887 (WFNHS-HP No. 5).

Figure 7   Anna Baker Weir with J. Alden Weir, Jr. Photograph by G. C. Cox, entitled
                                  "Mother and Child," n.d. (1888) (Lee Library, Special Collections, Brigham
                                  Young University, Provo, Utah).

23

Figure 8   Anna with baby by the Weir barn. Photograph, ca. summer 1888 (WFNHS-HP
                  No. 70).

24

It has been tentatively concluded by the author of Volume I of the "Weir Farm Historic Structure Report" that ca. 1888 the first story of the house was expanded westward, making the center part of the house 54 feet deep. The sun porch was also extended.[45]

1888 was also a productive year in terms of art and friendship. Weir had begun to etch the previous summer, but in the summer of this year, Twachtman rented a house in Branchville, and the two experimented with Weir's new press and painted, fished, and walked together. For Weir, it was the last happy summer for some time.[46]

Between 1888 and 1890, Weir painted two major Branchville landscapes. One, called "Autumn Landscape" (figure 9), shows Weir's stone wall and the silhouette of his barn. In figure 10 we see one of Weir's most interesting paintings of the farm: "Early Spring at Branchville," a wonderfully expressive image painted in golden tones, with the road just hinted at by the curve of the stone wall to the left. The point of view is from the north side of Weir's property looking toward his house. "Early Spring at Branchville" is also an object lesson, illustrating the caution that should be taken before one interprets Weir's paintings as literal representations of a scene: Weir has eliminated his barn from the painting to create a more open view toward his house.

In the spring of 1889, Weir suffered first the death of his infant son, from diphtheria, and then of his father. After the death of Julian, Jr., John Ferguson Weir attempted to comfort his brother, a role he took again a few years later when Anna Weir died. Of the baby boy, John F. Weir wrote:

> I am glad you will not yield to the inclination to avoid anything that recalls the dear one to you, even in these painful days; and I hope you will be able to go up to Branchville with Anna some bright day, and let all the holy influence pour in upon you.[47]

In April 1889, the exemplary Scots farmer and his wife left.[48] In June, Weir and Anna, hoping for healing from the death of their son, sailed for four months in England, where they spent most of their time on the Isle of Man and in Derbyshire, leaving Caro with Anna's mother and the farm in John's charge. Weir worked on an important series of etchings on the Isle of Man.[49]

In 1889 a series of cyanotypes was taken, showing family members, friends, and pets near the Weir house and at other locations on the grounds. These cyanotypes, which also include at least one view of the Roscoe Farm located further south down Nod Hill Road, appear to be, with the exceptions of

25

Figure 9   J. Alden Weir, "Autumn Landscape," oil on canvas, 1888–1890 (Private
                  Collection).

Figure 10   J. Alden Weir, "Early Spring at Branchville," oil on canvas, 1888–1890 (Private
                   Collection).

figures 6 and 8, and possibly figures 27 and 28, the earliest dated or datable photographs located thus far of Weir Farm.[50] To judge from the full foliage on the trees and from people's attire, all of the photographs seem to have been taken in midsummer. Since Weir and Anna were in Europe, the people in the cyanotypes must be John's family and friends.[51]

Figures 11 through 14 were all taken in the immediate vicinity of the house. In figure 11 (WFNHS-HP No. 233, 1889), two women, two men, and four children are sitting or standing near the front steps. Very close to the house, the trunk of a tree can be made out. This is a Canada hemlock (*Tsuga canadensis*), which still stands today and has reached an impressive height and girth. A shrub is also visible close to the house, and a portion of the barn and some farm equipment can be glimpsed to the right. Figure 12 (WFNHS-HP No. 230, 1889) shows two adults, two children, and a dog grouped near the open, awninged porch that shaded the rear portion of the south facade of the house. Comparison with figure 6 (WFNHS-HP No. 5) clearly shows that the south facade at the first-floor level and the porch have now been extended to the west, so that the awning no longer fits. The changes to the living room windows (three new multipaned windows) and a new placement of the door on this side, have not yet been made.[52] In front of the porch, there are three trellises propped up against the house, but nothing appears to be growing on them. What may be a line of washing is visible to the left.

Figure 13 (WFNHS-HP No. 231, 1889) must have been taken on the same day as figure 11, since it shows some of the same people wearing the same clothes (for example, the woman with a black bow at her neck). This time they are grouped under the porch awning. Beyond the people may be seen the early wooden boundary fence on Nod Hill Road and a very large tree, possibly an oak, between the fence and the road. In figure 14 (WFNHS-HP No. 232, 1889), a woman (apparently the same one as in figure 12), a man, two children, and two dogs are in the Webb field (later part of the Burlingham property) across Pelham Lane from Weir's farm. In the background, Weir's boundary fence along Pelham Lane and his barn are visible, in addition to the south facade of the house. Pelham Lane itself cannot really be seen. In the Webb/Burlingham field (lower left corner of the photograph) sumac may be seen. Sumac may well have grown spontaneously in all of the Weir Farm fields, as it does in most places in New England. In an 1891 letter to Weir, John described a field overgrown with sumac.[53] Two other photographs in this series (WFNHS-HP No. 228, 1889, and WFNHS-HP No. 234, 1889) may well have been taken on the farm, but the locations cannot be identified. The original fence around the Weir property and the large oak that show up in figure 13 may also be seen in the undated photograph illustrated in figure 15 (WFNHS-HP No. 90). As will be seen in some of the photographs in the next chapter, this early fence was replaced by a more rustic wooden fence at an undocumented date before about 1915 and possibly as early as 1890.[54]

Another early photograph of Weir Farm is illustrated in figure 16 (WFNHS-HP No. 19). This shows a team of oxen pulling a cart with a load of hay past the caretaker's house on Nod Hill Road. The

Figure 11   Group of people near front steps of Weir house. Cyanotype, 1889 (WFNHS-
                   HP No. 233, 1889).

Figure 12   People sitting on grass near south side of Weir house. Cyanotype, 1889
                     (WFNHS-HP No. 230, 1889).

Figure 13   Group of people under awning, Weir house. Cyanotype, 1889 (WFNHS-HP
                   No. 231, 1889).

Figure 14   Group of people in field opposite south side of Weir house. Cyanotype, 1889
                     (WFNHS-HP No. 232, 1889).

Figure 15   Fence along Nod Hill Road in front of Weir's house. Photograph, before ca.
                   1915 (WFNHS-HP No. 90).

Figure 16.   Oxen and cart with a load of hay on Nod Hill Road at caretaker's house. Photograph, after 1883 (WFNHS-HP No. 19).

photograph was probably taken around 1890, when repairs, were completed on the caretaker's house, which probably included the hip-roof porch, had been completed for several years. The oxen appear to be the type used by Weir on the farm. The photograph also shows a rustic wooden fence to the left (north) of the caretaker's house, which Weir installed around 1890, and a stone wall extending some distance parallel to Nod Hill Road on the right (south) of the house.[55] The area behind the stone wall appears to be open and was probably an open field or a vegetable garden. Nod Hill Road at this time seems to be a very narrow dirt road.

By the time the Weirs returned home from Europe, they were expecting the arrival of their second daughter, Dorothy, who was born on June 18, 1890.[56] During the previous fall, their new farmer, Paul Remy, had worked hard to remove rocks from the fields, "held down to terra firma by rocks and boulders," an activity that continued into the winter months of 1889–1890.[57] Remy, seen in an undated portrait by Weir (figure 17), was a native of Alsace (then part of Germany), who had studied to become a priest and then ran away to the United States. He stayed with the Weirs for many years as their farmer and probably lived in the caretaker's house.[58] By the autumn of 1890, Weir was painting in his "Palace Car," a portable outdoor studio, which had been built with Paul's help. The Palace Car, seen in Weir's painting of the same name (figure 18), was built on runners so that it could be pulled by oxen to whatever spot Weir wanted. It had windows on all four sides and was heated by an oil stove so that he could work no matter how cold it became.[59] In November 1890, Weir wrote to his sister-in-law: "I have been painting outdoors in a little house I have had made with windows . . ."[60] Weir apparently used the Palace Car for a number of years, but at some point the children turned it into a playhouse.[61]

Important paintings of Weir Farm dating from about 1890 include "Road to the Farm" (figure 19), which Weir shows the approach to his property but again simplifies the scene, eliminating buildings. "Farm Scene at Branchville" (figure 20) shows the view from the north side of Weir's house toward the orchard, with the side of the barn to the right.

891–1900

In the summer of 1891, Weir worked hard at establishing a lawn, "to try and make the grass grow as it should . . ."[62] The family also enjoyed native strawberries.[63] Weir wrote to his brother about his new farmer, Paul: "We have good hands on the farm and so we have peace."[64] In the fall John F. Weir again stayed on the farm and supervised it, writing to Julian about work on the farm:

> Today I had my last sweat in working about the place . . . after a hard tug at the rocks during the season. Everything is in good shape, and the place looks trim and lovely. Paul gets on well, has the big field nearly all ploughed. It was a rough job, so overgrown with sumach. . . . This

35

Figure 17   J. Alden Weir, "Paul Remy," n.d. (ca. late 1890s) (Private Collection).

Figure 18   J. Alden Weir, "The Palace Car," n.d. (ca. 1890) (Museum of Art, Brigham
                     Young University, Provo, Utah).

37

Figure 19   J. Alden Weir, "Road to the Farm," oil on canvas, 1890 (Private Collection).

38

Figure 20   J. Alden Weir, "Farm Scene at Branchville," oil on canvas, ca. 1890 (Collection
                   unknown).

afternoon we all walked down to the field where Paul is ploughing to watch him. Paul's grin as he shied over the rocks with the plough was worth seeing.[65]

John also recommended that Weir enlarge and dredge the existing pond and offered advice on landscape improvements and the opening up of vistas:

If my time had been longer I would have extended your drive-way through the woods down back of the house, bringing it around through another part of the woods. I surveyed the route and find it could be done without much cutting. I would like to cut down one of the cherry trees across the road, and a lot of those distant bushy chestnuts, to open the view from the front of the house—it would be fine, showing the trees and ledge where you once talked of putting a house, with the expanded view beyond. I would even cut it low enough to show that pretty field of millet, which would make a middle-ground. You are too much shut in by trees.[66]

In this letter, John wrote much more explicitly about landscape improvements done for purely aesthetic reasons than Weir ever did, to judge from the surviving letters. It also opens up the possibility that John may have played a significant role himself in the landscaping of Weir Farm. Unfortunately, there appears to be no documentation about whether Weir actually carried out the improvements suggested by John. Figure 21 illustrates Weir's painting "Midday," done in 1891, and probably showing Weir Farm.   A related work, also dating from the early 1890s, is the pastel illustrated in figure 22, "Feeding the Chickens, Branchville," which shows the original Weir chicken house. This chicken house was located near the present Young studio and appears in later photographs that will be illustrated in chapter II. Figure 23, "The Grey Trellis," was also painted in 1891 and appears to be the earliest work of art of the farm that depicts an arrangement of lattices and a birdhouse on a pole. Although the exact location is difficult to determine, a rustic wooden fence and a flowering fruit tree may be seen in the background. This painting raises the possibility that the more finished wooden fence seen in figures 13 and 15 may have been replaced by the rough-finished rustic fence as early as 1890 or 1891.

On January 3, 1892, Weir wrote one of his most beautiful letters to his young godson Alden Twachtman:

I received your poem on "the Brook" which I like very much. It brings to my mind very vividly the running water; but what charms me most is that you are looking at these beautiful things which God has given us to enjoy with your own eyes, and beginning early to love this little stream that runs by your home.

There is another, a greater stream which this little one will teach you much about—the stream of life—home is the starting place and love the guide to your actions. . . .[67]

40

Figure 21   J. Alden Weir, "Midday," oil on canvas, n.d., (Private Collection).

Figure 22   J. Alden Weir, "Feeding the Chickens, Branchville," pastel on paper mounted on
                   canvas, early 1890s (Private Collection).

42

Figure 23   J. Alden Weir, "The Grey Trellis," oil on canvas, 1891 (Private Collection).

Only a few weeks later, Weir's home was disrupted, and he suffered a blow from which he did not fully recover for at least two years. On January 29, his third daughter, Cora, was born, and on February 8, Anna died of puerperal fever. In his grief, Weir left his figure paintings, most of which included Anna, unfinished.[68] He stayed away from Branchville altogether, leaving the farm in his brother's care. John and his wife, Mary, tried to comfort Weir, telling him that Anna was still present in spirit: "All here is bright and sacred, and I hope you will always keep it as a place to refresh your spirit . . ."[69] John reported regularly about activities on the farm, telling him in August that Paul was clearing a field for sowing and that the new lawn mower made "the lawn look like velvet."[70] In September, Nod Hill Road was repaired in front of the house so that it would drain properly, and Paul ploughed the rough field beyond the rye using oxen.[71]

In August 1893, seven poplars that had been planted by Anna were blown down in a storm. Weir heard about it at second hand from a letter written by Paul to John:

> This has given me the blues, and I dread to see that mark, which I hoped would have lasted, as
> Anna took so much pleasure in the planting of them and to me they were so closely identified with
> her.[72]

In October 1893, John was back at Branchville. He recommended to Weir that he have Paul build a poultry house for the ducks and turkeys (presumably in addition to the existing chicken house), and added: "I wanted to walk about your place with you and talk over its possibilities . . ."[73] On October 29, 1893, in Boston, Weir married Ella Baker, Anna's sister, who had kept house for him, taken care of the children, and been a source of companionship and support for Weir ever since Anna's death. Twachtman was his best man.[74]

Numerous important paintings and drawings of the farm were created by Weir between about 1893 and 1895. These include two drawings: "Building and Stone Wall," an ink wash scene from the opposite side of Nod Hill Road looking toward the barn (figure 24) and "A Look Across the Fields," a sweeping view toward the Webb barn, drawn in a stippled technique reminiscent of the Japanese prints that Weir had begun collecting in the 1880s (figure 25).[75] Dating from the same period is "The Laundry, Branchville," one of Weir's best known paintings, showing the house from the rear with long lines of laundry (figure 26). There are two historic photographs dating from 1888–1890 that show the house from a similar point of view (figures 27 and 28). The well near Pelham Lane below the Weir House is shown in figure 29. Figure 30, "The Farm in Winter," is an impressionistic view of the barn, painted in 1895.

44

Figure 24   J. Alden Weir, "Building and Stone Wall," ink wash on paper, ca. 1894 (Private Collection).

Figure 25   J. Alden Weir, "A Look Across the Fields," ink and brush on paper, ca. 1894
                 (Brigham Young University, Provo, Utah).

Figure 26   J. Alden Weir, "The Laundry, Branchville," oil on canvas, ca. 1894 (Weir Farm Heritage Trust).

47

Figure 27   Weir house from the rear. Photograph, ca. 1888–1890 (WFNHS-HP No. 235).

Figure 28   Weir house from the rear. Photograph, ca. 1888–1890 (WFNHS-HP No. 236).

Figure 29   Well below the Weir house. Photograph, after 1893 (WFNHS-HP No. 16).

Figure 30   J. Alden Weir, "The Farm in Winter," oil on canvas, 1895 (Private Collection).

In 1895 Weir wrote to Ella: "... there are plenty of lima beans and tomatoes and the sweet peas are in abundance."[76] Another painting dating from 1895 was "The Truants" or "The Old Rock" (figure 31). It was this picture that won a $2,500 prize at the Boston Art Club exhibition in 1896. With the prize money, Weir purchased ten acres of land and constructed the "Boston Art Club Pond," probably the most significant change in the Weir landscape since his original purchase.[77] While Weir certainly had the improvement of the landscape in mind, his chief aim was to have a pond on his own property so that he could more easily enjoy his favorite recreation—fishing (figure 32). The pond and some of the landscape features related to it appear in several other photographs, including one showing a woman crossing a small wooden bridge leading toward a gate in a stone wall (figure 33).

Among the Weir family records, five herbarium pages have survived from what may once have been a larger collection. All of the specimens—one shrub, one vine and three perennials—are labelled Branchville and are dated either May or June 1895: *Viola obliqua* (blue violet); *Aquilegia canadensis* (American or common columbine); *Lonicera sempervirens* (scarlet honeysuckle, now referred to as trumpet honeysuckle); *Pedicularis canadensis* (wood betony or common American lousewort); and *Potentilla canadensis* (five fingers, common name now cinquefoil).[78] All five of the plants are native to the northeastern United States and were probably collected in the field on Weir's farm. (The collecting of plant specimens from the wild is the usual purpose of an herbarium.) Although the handwriting on the herbarium pages has not yet been identified, it must be either Weir's or Ella's.[79] The Weir correspondence includes no references to this herbarium or the collecting of wild plants.

An extant landscape feature that dates from the childhood of Weir's daughters is the stone picnic table underneath the large tree to the southwest of the house. This table has been inscribed with a chisel with the names of Weir and his three daughters. The table is not mentioned in correspondence and does not appear in photographs, although it does appear in an 1894 painting by Weir.[80]

1896 was the beginning of a happy and productive period in Weir's life. As his daughter Dorothy wrote:

> Weir's summers at Branchville during the nineties helped him come to terms with himself and his art. In the peace of the warm, lazy evenings and the exhilaration of tramps through the hills his zest for living revived completely after the sorrow of his wife's death. ... That summer [1897] his painting progressed smoothly. His work seemed at once easier and more confident; and such major canvases as "Noonday Rest," "The Factory Village, and "The Sand Pit" reflected a mood of acceptance.[81]

Figure 31   J. Alden Weir, "The Old Rock," oil on canvas, 1895 (Private Collection).

Figure 32   J. Alden Weir fishing from boat on the pond. Photograph, after 1896 (WFNHS-
                   HP No. 22).

Figure 33   Woman crossing bridge. Photograph, after 1896 (WFNHS-HP No. 2).

From 1897 through 1901, Weir held art classes at Branchville in June and July.[82] Many artists visited him. Some even stayed at the farm when Weir was away, as did Ryder, who was recuperating from an illness. In May 1897, Ryder wrote thanking Weir:

> I feel it my duty to drop you a line to let you know what good your kind interest and brotherly friendship have done for me. I sleep nights, Mr. and Mrs. Remy are as kind as possible; I like the domestic noise and bustle of their dwelling, and the busy planning of the garden which comes on apace.

> I have never seen the beauty of spring before; which is something to have lived and suffered for. The landscape and the air are full of promise. That eloquent little fruit tree that we looked at together, like a spirit among the more earthy colors, is already losing its fairy blossoms, showing the lesson life; how alert we must be if we would have its gifts and values.

> My little guide Carl Remy waits in the morning to see what I would do; and is altogether a sweet and amiable little lad and his brother also.[83]

During this same period, Weir's daughters kept gardens and hunted for wild strawberries, and his asparagus and peas were prized.[84] A Branchville painting from 1898 is Weir's "Ploughing for Buckwheat" (not illustrated); Weir's customary oxen appear in this painting, but the field cannot be located precisely.[85] In 1900 Weir bought 32 acres of land "west of the homestead" from Ann Eliza Smith.[86] This was presumably the $25 lot, on which John and Paul labored to remove rocks.[87] In June 1900 the art patron C. E. S. Wood gave Weir an abundance of practical advice, recommending that he have Paul:

> . . . cut those dead trees down, remove the flag staff, shingle the chicken house, hang the gates, move the front gate and make a new walk, put up a good boundary stone, clear off the $25. lot, paint those steps on the walk. . . . Keep the weeds down and the flowers going, fork over and manure and salt the asparagus bed—and see that the potatoes and vegetables are kept clean.[88]

In a less critical tone, Wood later wrote to Weir: "I often think of . . . Paul and the sauerbeans and cider, and the peacefulness of your stony farm."[89] Figure 34 shows Weir standing with his palette next to the house about 1900.

We have little in Weir's own words about the landscaping of his Branchville property. Fortunately, Joseph Pearson, a student at the summer classes, wrote vividly of the pleasure that Weir took in improving his land:

Figure 34   J. Alden Weir with palette near house. Photograph, ca. 1900 (WFNHS-HP No. 37).

Few artists of character I have known have escaped the diverting effect of the purchase and development of run down property. It charmed him. He gave much thought, time and energy to its improvement. How he enjoyed clearing vistas, trimming trees well up from the ground revealing beautiful notes and things unseen before. The making of level places for tennis, working with his men who used great red oxen to haul the boulders to one side; the building of the pond with prize money, some of which was generously shared with employees; piling brush here and there and making a bon-fire now and then when the boy in him suggested it. That all of this was not diverting only may be readily understood when one recalls the pictures "Building the Pond," "Noonday Rest," and "The Coon Hunt." The things made by the faithful Paul found a place in his pictures: sapling fences, rustic arbors and bridges as well as hen runs, and informal gardens . . ."[90]

SUMMARY

Between his acquisition of the Beers farm in 1882 and 1900, Weir, with the aid of his brother, John, repaired and remodelled the house, built his studio, established his own working farm on the property, and built a pond. His wife, Anna, planted a flower garden as early as 1886, but its exact location is not known. The earliest photographs of the site, for example, figures 6, 8, and 11 through 16, show a fairly modest landscape treatment, with shrubs and trellises next to the house and a wooden fence along Nod Hill Road. Weir's paintings depict the same sort of setting and include many agricultural subjects as well. As Pearson's account indicates, Weir enjoyed working on the property and was constantly improving it.

From the beginning, Weir found the landscape of his farm to be a powerful inspiration for his art, as did his many artist friends who came to visit and paint with him. Family was also extremely important to Weir. Although he suffered terrible personal blows during these years—the deaths of his infant son and young wife—Weir, in time, was able to resume a happy life with his second wife, Ella, and his three daughters. The next chapter will discuss Weir's continued improvements to the landscape of Weir Farm during the remaining years of his life.

ENDNOTES TO CHAPTER I

1.   Dorothy Weir Young, *The Life and Letters of J. Alden Weir* (New York: Kennedy Graphics, Inc., Da Capo Press, 1971), 1–18;   Doreen Bolger Burke, *J. Alden Weir: An American Impressionist* (Newark: University of Delaware Press, 1983), 23–111, and "Chronology," 293–299.

2.   Julian A. Weir to his mother from Paris, March 1, 1874, in Young, *Life and Letters,* 31.

3.   Young, *Life and Letters,* 19–136. Whistler had been a student of Weir's father, Robert Walter Weir.

4.   Ibid., 137–162;   and Burke, "Chronology," 293–299. The chronology of Weir's life in *J. Alden Weir: A Place of His Own* (Storrs, Connecticut: The William Benton Museum of Art, The University of Connecticut, Storrs, 1991), 97–98, is also useful.

5.   Young, *Life and Letters,* 150–152.

6.   Weir to Anna Dwight Baker, June 27, August 4, 5, 6, 7, 8, 9, 10, 11, 13, 16, 17, 18, 19, 20, 22, and 26, 1882, typed transcripts (probably made by Dorothy Weir Young) in the Lee Library, Special Collections, Brigham Young University, Provo, Utah (hereafter BYU). Many of these letters are on microfilm at the Archives of American Art (hereafter AAA), and some are reproduced in Young, *Life and Letters.* The *Life and Letters* also includes some letters that do not appear in either the BYU or AAA collections.

        A letter in the Dorothy Weir Young scrapbooks (privately owned) includes a sketch elevation and plan of the proposed Adirondacks house. (The Weir Farm National Historic Site owns a complete copy of this scrapbook collection.)

7.   On October 4, 1882, Weir wrote to Anna that "Mr. Shurtleff wrote to me from the Adirondacks that they were at last at work on the house, and I trust now that all will go on well and smoothly." On October 11, 1882, he wrote to her that the Adirondacks house was under construction but that mortar couldn't be laid until spring. Construction costs apparently ran three times as much as the architect thought. Both of these letters are on AAA, Reel 125, but are not at BYU.

        A complete catalogue of the work of McKim, Mead and White does not exist, but the Weir project (which would be an early one for White) is not mentioned in the most complete study to date of the architects: Leland M. Roth, *McKim, Mead and White, Architects* (New York: Harper and Row, 1983). However, McKim, Mead and Bigelow designed a house for Mrs. Anna C. Alden in Cold Spring Harbor on Long Island in 1879-1880, and McKim, Mead and White designed one for R. Percy Alden in Cornwall, Pennsylvania, in 1880–1884 *(Roth, McKim, Mead and White,* 52–53, 70). These were probably Weir's patron and her son.

        Another McKim, Mead and White scholar, Professor Richard Guy Wilson of the University of Virginia, also has no knowledge of a Weir commission.

8.   There are two references to the Adirondacks property in July 1883, when Weir and Anna were on their honeymoon. See Anna Baker Weir to Ella Baker, July 18, 1883, and J. Alden Weir to Mrs. Baker, July 22, 1883, AAA, Reel 125.

Weir apparently kept the property until 1890 or 1891 when he sold it to a Mr. Mendonca, who was the United States Ambassador to Brazil. By 1906 Mr. Mendonca had assembled three parcels of land and built a large house. There is also a cottage on the property that is known locally as the Weir studio, but from the description, this does not sound like a studio. Information courtesy of Mr. Howard Bushman-Kelly, current owner of the property ... and Mr. Robin Pell, who lives in the cottage. Richard Plunz, Professor of Architecture at Columbia University, is writing a book on Keene Valley, New York, which should clarify these issues.

9.   J. A. Weir to Anna Dwight Baker, July 11, 1882, Weir Family Papers, Lee Library, Brigham Young University, and AAA, Weir Papers, Reel 125. For mention of Twachtman's role, see also the letters from Weir to Anna dated August 22 and 26, 1882, in the same collections.

10.   Alfred Henry Goodwin, in "An Artist's Unspoiled Country Home," *Country Life in America,* vol. 8, no. 6 (October 1905) 625–630, describes Twachtman's Cos Cob home and its setting. The article also includes photographs by Henry Troth. See also Susan Larkin, "The Cos Cob Clapboard School," in *Connecticut and American Impressionism* (Storrs, Connecticut: The William Benton Museum of Art, The University of Connecticut, Storrs, 1980), 89.

11.   It should be noted that Anna was always very supportive of Weir's enthusiasm for the Adirondacks, even though she had never seen the area. See Anna D. Baker to Weir, August 13, 1882, AAA, Reel 125.

12.   Weir to Anna Dwight Baker, May 16, 1882, BYU, also AAA.

13.   Hildegard Cummings, "Home Is the Starting Place: J. Alden Weir and the Spirit of Place," in *J. Alden Weir: A Place of His Own,* 15–23; Weir to Anna Dwight Baker, June 15, 1882, AAA. See also Young, *Life and Letters,* 159.

The deed recording Weir's purchase of the farm does not mention the painting and states only that he paid $10.00 for the farm (Deed, Weir Farm National Historic Site).

An apocryphal version of the story of the transaction by art dealer Frederic Newlin Price, who was not born until 1884, asserts that the painting was a still life by Proctor. See Frederic Newlin Price, *Goodbye Ferargil* (New Hope, Pa.: The Hufnagle Press, 1958), np. No American artist by the name of Proctor, active 1882, has been identified.

14.   Weir to Anna Dwight Baker, June 17, 1882, AAA, Reel 125.

15.   Although it is difficult today to find the exact location of Weir's 1882 watercolor, the fields to the south and west of the Burlingham barn and woodshed remain open and suggest the same kind of landscape that appears in the watercolor. See "Weir Farm Historic Painting Sites Trail" (Ridgefield and Wilton, Connecticut: Weir Farm Heritage Trust and National Park Service, 1994), Site 1. Weir must have made this painting when he was visiting Branchville just before purchasing the property. It is therefore unlikely that he would be exploring the back fields of the Webb farm, which was not the one he was planning to buy.

16.   Weir to Anna Dwight Baker, July 10, 11, and 12, and August 11 and 19, 1882, AAA, Reel 125.

'.   Weir to Anna Dwight Baker, October 22, 1882, BYU and AAA, Reel 125.

:.   Young, *Life and Letters,* 158–159. Among Weir's ushers were Stanford White, Elliott Roosevelt, and illiam Merritt Chase, and guests at the wedding included Charles F. McKim and Augustus Saint-Gaudens. (Weir d wanted Saint-Gaudens to make a medallion of Anna, but this was never done.)

Weir's mother noted in her journal for April 24, 1883: "Tuesday a dark rainy day for dear Julian's wedding. e had a good start so that everything might go smoothly. Julian had a letter from dear Charlie." (Susan Martha Bayard Weir Journal, Weir Family Papers, BYU. This was her entire entry for the day.)

19.   Young, *Life and Letters,* 159.

20.   Weir to John F. Weir from Nuremberg, July 1, 1883, AAA, Reel 125.

21.   John F. Weir to Weir, August 2, 1883, AAA, Reel 125.

22.   Ibid., and Young, *Life and Letters,* 161.

23.   John F. Weir to Weir, August 2, 1883, AAA, Reel 125.

24.   Ibid.

25.   Weir to Mrs. Baker, July 22, 1883, AAA, Reel 125, Frame 292.

26.   Weir to Mrs. Baker, August 26, 1883, AAA, Reel 125, Frame 313.

27.   Young, *Life and Letters,* 162, 168; Cummings, "Home Is the Starting Place," 23.

28.   In August 1883, John wrote to Weir that "Benton is finishing off the Dutchman's house yesterday and today —and I have planned this to reduce expense to a minimum." (John F. Weir to J. A. Weir, August 2, 1883, AAA, Reel 529, Frame 1086.) Benton, apparently a local carpenter or contractor, was paid $86.00 for this work. "The Dutchman" probably refers to Holsten.

29.   *J. Alden Weir: A Place of His Own,* 97.

30.   Young, *Life and Letters,* 163–165.

31.   Ellen Paul, CGRS, "History and Documentation of Weir Farm" (1990), 7, 12. The mortgage was paid off in 1907.

32.   Weir to John F. Weir, March 22, 1885, AAA, Reel 125.

33.   Weir to Ella Baker, July 7, 1885, AAA, Reel 125.

34.   Albert Edelfelt to J. Alden Weir, January 22, 1878, BYU. Portions quoted in Susan G. Larkin, "A Curious Aggregation: J. Alden Weir and His Circle," in *J. Alden Weir: A Place of His Own,* 60.

The section quoted in this paragraph can be translated as follows: "All our friends send greetings. Whenever your name is mentioned, we never fail to say: 'What a wonderful friend, what a goodhearted, fine

61

fellow!'"

35.   Larkin, "A Curious Aggregation," 71–73. See also Larkin, "The Cos Cob Clapboard School," 89.

36.   Weir to Ella Baker, May 3, 1886, AAA, Reel 125.

37.   Weir to Ella Baker, June 26, 1886, AAA, Reel 125.

38.   Weir to Ella Baker, July 14, 1886, AAA, Reel 125.

39.   Larkin, "A Curious Aggregation," 62–63.

40.   J. Alden Weir, quoted in J. Walker McSpadden, *Famous Painters of America* (New York: Dodd, Mead and Co., 1916), 388–389.

41.   What may be another very early photograph of the Weir House is WFNHS-HP No. 27, which definitely shows the house before the Platt changes were made and probably before the 1888 westward addition.

42.   Young, *Life and Letters,* 169.

43.   There is a possibility that figure 8 was taken in 1891 rather than 1888 and that it shows Anna with Dorothy, who was born in June 1890, rather than Alden. If so, the photograph might have been taken by Weir, who first purchased a camera in 1891. Ella seems to have been the first person in the family to take up photography. On November 24, 1890, Weir wrote to Ella, "I wish you all were here to spend Thanksgiving with us, the country is very beautiful and I know you would find many little bits for photographing. . . ." (AAA, Reel 125, Frame 481.) On June 3, 1891, Weir wrote again to Ella, "I have not told you about the camera which I have enjoyed very much, but with none of the success that you have. . . . all of those of Anna and the baby did not come out. . . ." (AAA, Reel 125, Frame 493.)

     Judging from the light clothing worn by both mother and child, the photograph in figure 8 was taken in warm weather, which could mean anything from late spring to early fall. The baby in the photograph is sitting up and appears to be between six months and a year old. This baby could be Alden in late summer 1888, but it could also be Dorothy, who, as documented above, was photographed by her father with Anna in late spring 1891. Babies of both sexes wore dresses in those days.

44.   Weir to John F. Weir, July 1888, AAA, Reel 125.

45.   Marie Carden, Coordinator, Historic Structure Report, "Summary Chronology of Weir House," August 5, 1994, 1. This and all other issues relating to the Weir House will be thoroughly examined in Volume I of the "Weir Farm Historic Structure Report," which is forthcoming.

46.   Young, *Life and Letters,* 169, 179.

47.   John F. Weir to Weir, March 13, 1889, AAA, Reel 125; Young, *Life and Letters,* 170.

48.   Weir to John F. Weir, April 18, 1889, AAA, Reel 125.

49.   Young, *Life and Letters,* 170–171.

50.   All of the photographs are from the Weir Family Scrapbooks, Blue, "1884–1891 - Pages," Weir Farm Heritage Trust.

51.   Ten people (total) are shown in these cyanotypes. Not all can be identified. One of the cyanotypes not used to illustrate this chapter (WFNHS-HP 228, 1889) shows four adults, a little girl, and a dog sitting on the ground in a field. The adults are identified, presumably by one of Weir's daughters, as "Aunt Annie," "Uncle Charlie," "Grandmother Weir," and "Aunt Carrie." These are Weir's mother, brother, and two sisters. Except for Aunt Carrie, who may be the woman in figures 12 and 14 (WFNHS-HP 230, 1889, and WFNHS-HP 232, 1889), these people do not appear in the other cyanotypes.

         The question also arises as to who took these cyanotypes, which are good but don't appear to be of professional quality. It might have been John, although there are no references to him as a photographer. Mrs. Baker (Weir's mother-in-law) was taking care of Caro this summer, presumably at Windham, but she might have visited the John Ferguson Weirs at Branchville. Ella, who as discussed in note 43 had taken up photograph no later than 1890, might have gone with her. No other immediate Weir family member is mentioned as a photographer until 1910, when Dorothy was taking "Kodaks" of Weir's paintings (Weir to Wood from Windham, November 13, 1910, AAA, Reel 125, Frame 1160). The 1889 cyanotypes could also, of course, have been taken by an unidentified family member or friend.

52.   These issues of chronology are discussed in the completed Volume I of the "Weir Farm Historic Structure Report," which is forthcoming..

53.   John F. Weir to Weir, September 26, 1891, AAA, Reel 125.

54.   Ibid.

55.   Maureen K. Phillips, "Weir Farm Historic Structure Report, Weir Farm National Historic Site, Wilton, Connecticut." Volume II-B: "Weir Farm Outbuildings: Caretaker's House. Caretaker's Garage" (Lowell, Massachusetts: Building Conservation Branch, Northeast Cultural Resources Center, National Park Service, U.S. Department of the Interior, 1995), 8-10.

56.   Young, *Life and Letters,* 172–173.

57.   Weir to Mrs. Baker, December 13, 1889, AAA, Reel 125.

58.   Young, *Life and Letters,* 173; Notations, probably in Dorothy Weir Young's hand, on the painting of Remy by her father, WFNHS, Scrapbooks - Blue - 3A - Pages, 249B.

         Originally a province located in the northeastern part of France, Alsace and the neighboring province of Lorraine were annexed to Germany after the Franco-Prussian War of 1871. They were restored to France after World War I. Remy probably "ran away" because of political or religious unrest.

59.   Young, *Life and Letters,* 173.

60.   Weir to Ella Baker, November 24, 1890, AAA, Reel 125.

61.   Young, *Life and Letters,* 173.

62.   Weir to Ella Baker, June 8, 1891, AAA, Reel 125.

63.   Ibid.

64.   Weir to John F. Weir, August 23, 1891, AAA, Reel 125.

65.   John F. Weir to Weir, September 26, 1891, AAA, Reel 125.

66.   Ibid.

67.   Weir to Alden Twachtman, January 3, 1892, in Young, *Life and Letters,* 176–177.

68.   Young, *Life and Letters,* 180; Burke, *J. Alden Weir,* 196–200.

69.   John F. Weir to Weir, August 28, 1892, AAA, Reel 529.

70.   John F. Weir to Weir, August 28, 1892, and Mary Weir to Weir, September 1, 1892, AAA, Reel 529.

71.   John F. Weir to Weir, September 21, 1892, AAA, Reel 529.

72.   Weir to Ella Baker, August (28?), 1893, AAA, Reel 125.

73.   John F. Weir to Weir, October 2, 1893, AAA, Reel 125.

74.   Young, *Life and Letters,* 186.

75.   Young, *Life and Letters,* 186–187.

76.   Weir to Ella, August 14, 1895, AAA, Reel 125.

77.   Young, *Life and Letters,* 188; F. W. Benson to Weir, January 10, 1896; John F. Weir to Weir, February 1897; Clipping from an unidentified magazine, ca. 1911, AAA.

       Weir purchased this land from Abram H. Gilbert, although the deed seems to be dated 1895. See Paul, "History and Documentation," 4.

78.   Weir Farm National Historic Site. Information on the columbine, honeysuckle, wood betony and potentilla may be found in Liberty Hyde Bailey, *The Standard Cyclopedia of Horticulture* (New York: MacMillan, 1928 edition), 340–341, 1911, 2524, and 2771–2775. Phyllis Andersen of the Arnold Arboretum located this information for us.

79.   The study of botany was very popular among American women and girls in the 19th century. See Elizabeth Keeney, *The Botanizers: Amateur Scientists in 19th-Century America* (Chapel Hill, North Carolina: University of North Carolina Press, 1992), Chapter 5: "Gender and Botany." This source was brought to my attention by Phyllis Andersen of the Arnold Arboretum.

80.   The painting is "In The Dogwood," oil on canvas, 1894 (Private Collection. Information from Weir Farm National Historic Site).

81.   Young, *Life and Letters,* 194.

.   Young, *Life and Letters*, 192.

.   Ryder to Weir, May 5, 1897, BYU and AAA. Also quoted in Young, *Life and Letters*, 188–189.

.   A. P. Ryder to Weir, June 16, 1897, BYU and AAA; Erskine Wood to Weir, August 1, 1899; AAA, Reel 5. There are no other references to the asparagus and peas and no indication of where they were planted.

.   "Ploughing for Buckwheat" is illustrated in Burke, *J. Alden Weir*, figure 5.34, 221.

.   The first deed for this parcel was from the Proprietors to Richard Olmsted in 1745. Ann Eliza Smith's sband, Henry, purchased the 32 acres from William W. Beers in 1871. See Paul, "History and Documentation,"

.

7.   John F. Weir to Weir, September 11 and 15, 1899, AAA, Reel 529.

8.   C. E. S. Wood to Weir, June 13, 1900, AAA, Reel 125.

9.   Wood to Weir, November 29, 1900, AAA, Reel 125.

0.   Joseph Pearson to Dorothy Weir Young, quoted in Young, *Life and Letters*, 193–194. No painting called Building the Pond" has been located. There is also no other documentation of tennis courts at Weir Farm; they ould have been grass courts at this period, not involving anything in the way of construction except levelling of e ground.

CHAPTER II: THE J. ALDEN WEIR OWNERSHIP, PART II
1901-1919 (1921)

In January 1899, Weir was able to give up his winter teaching in New York City permanently and vote all his time and energy to painting. He sent new work each year to the exhibitions of The Ten and e National Academy. He was also now able to stretch the summer season at Branchville from May to ecember, and even more than in earlier years the farm became his home and "starting place."[1]

Probably because he was now spending so much more time in the country, Weir decided, about 00, to commission Charles Adams Platt to design major additions and alterations to his house. While e core of the ca. 1780 house was left intact, as well as its ca. 1840 Greek Revival front (east) elevation d the enlargements made by Weir ca. 1888, Platt changed the structure significantly. His design, for hich blueprints survive, extended the depth of the house to its present 54 feet, as well as adding a dlumned porch measuring 10 by 28 feet to the south elevation, which became the primary entry. Platt so designed a one-story, shed-roofed addition 9 feet wide that extended the full length of the north evation of the house and increased the width of its first story to 28 feet. The south facade was also ctended to the full length of the house, and dormers were added.[2]

Unfortunately, no Platt/Weir correspondence has been located that relates to this commission, but ere is no mystery about Weir's choice of Platt as architect: both men moved in the same artistic circles. harles Adams Platt (1861-1933) was an artist well before he became an architect and landscape designer. s a young man, Platt quickly made a name for himself in the New York City art world. The "boy- cher," as some referred to him, joined the New York Etching Club and produced his first print in 1880, veral years before Weir. In 1882 Platt left for five years study in Paris, where he eventually enrolled the Académie Julian, which was popular among Americans. Upon his return to New York in 1887, e joined the Society of American Artists, of which Weir had been a early member, and exhibited at the ational Academy of Design and the New York Etching Club.[3]

Beginning in 1889 with his own house and garden in Cornish, New Hampshire, Platt shifted into chitectural and landscape design, eventually becoming one of the most noted practitioners of his period. lis houses and his gardens were classically inspired, the latter derived from his visit to Italy and the

67

resulting book, *Italian Gardens,* published in 1894. Artists, including the sculptor Augustus Saint-Gaudens, his neighbor in Cornish, were among Platt's closest friends, and many of them became his clients. (As noted in chapter I, Saint-Gaudens was also a close friend of Weir.) By 1900, the time of the Weir commission, Platt's architectural and landscape designs included the Miss Annie Lazarus house and garden in Cornish, New Hampshire (1890–1891), the Herbert Croly house and garden also in Cornish, and the elaborate Tuscan-inspired gardens of Faulkner Farm, the Charles F. Sprague residence in Brookline, Massachusetts (1897–1898).[4] All of these were on a much larger scale than the modest Weir project. The Weir house alterations seem to have been one of Platt's first commissions in Connecticut. Other Connecticut projects designed by Platt around 1900 or a bit later include several houses or gardens for the Cheney family in Manchester; several for the Maxwell family in Rockville; and "Glen Elsinore," the Randolph M. Clark estate, in Pomfret. All of these commissions were also on a large scale.[5]

Weir and his brother appear to have supervised the construction themselves, suggesting that Platt may have had little to do with the project other than providing plans. Not only is there no correspondence between Platt and Weir about this commission (there is only one later letter), but references in other letters are sparse.[6] In September 1900, Weir wrote to Ella that "Things are going on well. . . . They have just set up the new fireplace and have it wrongly placed and I discovered it just in time to have them change it and do it right."[7] In January 1901, C. E. S. Wood wrote to Weir, sending him a clipping from a French antique dealer and recommending that he buy "stalls of the period" and use them "during improvements at Branchville."[8] Finally, John F. Weir wrote to his daughter in March 1901: "Yesterday I went to Branchville, meeting your Uncle Julian at South Norwalk. . . . The workmen are still in the house but the improvements are really fine."[9] The date and designer for the terraced garden area at the rear (west) of the house have not yet been determined. At the earliest, these terraces must date from after Platt's addition and could be considerably more recent, perhaps from the Young ownership.[10]

Weir and his family spent the summer of 1901 in Europe. They spent most of their time in London, where they visited John Singer Sargent and James A. M. Whistler, and in Paris, where they visited Jean-Léon Gérôme, Weir's old teacher.[11] Upon his return to Branchville in October, Weir wrote: "no one was more happy to return to a place than I was to America. Europe palls on me. For some there is no place like home."[12] Increasingly, other painters came to visit Weir during his extended summer stays. Among them were, of course, old friends Twachtman, Childe Hassam, and J. Appleton Brown, but also Edmund Tarbell, Frederic Remington, and Frank Millet. Weir enjoyed even late autumn in the country. In November 1902, he reported himself in good shape "after all my walks and climbing stone walls, and how many beautiful things I have seen in these tramps . . ."[13] Unfortunately, Weir's circle of friends was diminished when Brown and Twachtman both died in 1902.[14] In the summer of 1903, Wilfred Von Glehn, a young English artist, visited Weir and wrote him after moving on to the Adirondacks:

> I write you—as from a different country, so great is the change here after the quiet, peaceful and
> pastoral Branchville—that will always represent for me, when I return to England—the peace loving

'intime' America and very dear to think of—I'm glad to come back to you and am looking forward to it. . . .

I can't tell you how I enjoyed those good days with you all—the fields—the woods—the fishing— silent hours, the peaceful times at night looking up into the stars . . .[15]

Another old friend was C. E. S. Wood, mentioned previously, whom Weir had known at West Point. In 1897 Wood came to New York and resumed the close friendship with Weir that had begun fifteen years earlier. At some point, Wood left the army and took up practice as a lawyer in Portland, Oregon, where he tried to introduce the work of Weir and other eastern artists, including Hassam and Ryder, to collectors on the West Coast. He also collected the work of these painters and was himself an amateur artist.[16] Wood, one of whose letters was quoted on page 16 near the end of chapter I, visited Weir Farm frequently and, like John F. Weir, seems to have occasionally taken a hand in supervising it. In June 1903, Weir wrote to Wood that: ". . . as we have nothing but rain, fog and cold weather, nothing grows but weeds and we will have to buy hay I fear this winter unless we have a let up."[17] Wood wrote Weir wistfully: "My wouldn't I like to loaf under the beeches around the pond at Branchville."[18]

Other letters have survived from the summer of 1903. Early in August, lightning struck Weir's house ripping out a column from the porch, tearing up the pavement and splitting a huge maple tree.[19] When he heard this, Ryder wrote: "I am sorry enough for your fright and damage, especially the splendid maple; still I hope it may come around."[20] About a month later, Ryder visited the Weirs, but at Windham, not Branchville, where he fell asleep at the dinner table after having made the unaccustomed effort of catching an early morning train from New York.[21] A delightful painting from this period is "Visiting Neighbors," also known as "After the Ride," which shows Cora standing with a donkey next to Nod Hill Road, with the rustic wooden fence and part of the Weir tack house to her left and behind her (figure 35). At Cora's feet is a clump of orange daylilies, similar to those that still grow in this location today.[22]

Summer 1904 was a fine one for Weir's farm and garden. In June, Ryder wrote him: "You will be in prime condition after hazing the hay. . . . I suppose your barns are bursting with the good results of good grass weather."[23] John Weir and his family spent considerable time at the farm that year, enjoying the pond and its summerhouse:

We often go on the pond, and over to the summerhouse for tea, and stroll about the fields which never looked more beautiful . . . We have had a lot of rain. Nevertheless Paul has got all the hay in—the barn is about full. He says he won't have to buy hay next winter. They cut the grain, but it has been too wet to bring in. The garden is in good shape—Willie seems to have done well with it. We are careful not to interfere with the regular work in any way . . .[24]

69

Figure 35   J. Alden Weir, "Visiting Neighbors," or "After the Ride," oil on canvas, ca.
                       1903. (The Phillips Collection, Washington, DC)

another letter, John wrote:

> This place is certainly a paradise. You have developed it all so wisely and well, without marring its character. May and I never cease to comment on it and praise the judgment with which everything has been planned and carried out. . . . Paul works as steadily in the field as the rain will allow. He cut the oats today. The barn is full and he has made a haystack at the back. Willie keeps the gardens and the grounds in good order. He is a good worker—at it from morning till night. It looks as if Willie would eventually fill Paul's place here, while Carl would grow into similar office at Windham.[25]

Carl was Remy's son. Willie is not identified anywhere but may have been another Remy son.)

In September 1904, Ryder again wrote to Weir, concluding with the following blessing:

> That the fish will thrive, and there will be no more 25 lb. turtles. Almost a sea monster, wasn't it.

> That your work will answer.

> And your farms too, and haystacks grow, and rocks disappear, and everything be as you wish.[26]

Paintings done by Weir and others at the farm in 1905–1906 include Weir's "New England Barn" in the Phillips Collection (figure 36), a painting that is impressionistic and yet reveals the form and details of the barn in considerable detail. Flowers may also be seen along the wall in front of the barn, although it is impossible to tell what kind they are. Dating from 1905 and painted in a similar style is Weir's "The Shadow of My Studio" (figure 37). Besides this painting, there are three additional sketches for "The Shadow of My Studio." About one of them, Dorothy Weir Young wrote: "Moonlight —The shadow of the studio falls over the flower garden at Branchville."[27] The painting and the sketches are of particular interest because they show an enclosed garden smaller in size and simpler in design than the one that appears in several ca. 1915 photographs. The entire sequence of paintings and photographs of the enclosed garden will be discussed later in this chapter.

About 1905, the Danish-born artist Emil Carlsen (1853–1932), who frequently visited the Weirs at Ella's family home in Windham in the early 1900s, painted "Weir's Tree" (figure 38), in which a magnificent sycamore is silhouetted against a cloudy sky. Although the tree is depicted in close detail, the surrounding landscape is hazy, and it is difficult to place this splendid tree. (Since Carlsen, identified the sycamore as "Weir's," it is reasonable to assume that it was in Branchville, although by this time Ella had probably inherited the Baker family property in Windham. As noted above, Ryder, Carlsen, and other

Figure 36   J. Alden Weir, "New England Barn," oil on canvas, ca. 1904 (The Phillips
                   Collection, Washington, DC).

Figure 37   J. Alden Weir, "The Shadow of My Studio," oil on canvas, 1905 (Private
                   Collection).

Figure 38   Emil Carlsen, "Weir's Tree," oil on canvas, ca. 1905 (Collection, Diana and
                   Richard Beattie, New York City. Photograph, courtesy of the Cooley Gallery,
                   Old Lyme, Connecticut).

:iends often visited them in Windham as well as in Branchville.) Besides being a noted artist in his own
ght, Carlsen prepared Weir's canvases. The story goes that, on one occasion, Carlsen went to visit Weir
and found that he had hung the prepared canvases without painting anything on them, explaining: "Old
Carlsen, they were too beautiful."[28]

Another artist who frequently visited Weir in Branchville in the early 1900s was Childe Hassam
(1859–1935), who produced oils, pastels, and watercolors while at the farm.[29] In 1903 Hassam painted
a delightful watercolor titled "Weir's Garden" (figure 39). This does not seem to be the enclosed garden
that Weir painted in "The Shadow of My Studio" (figure 37), but instead Hassam's subject is a trellis and
a portion of a fence or gate set amidst low trees. In Weir's much earlier painting "The Gray Trellis"
(1891, figure 23), a trellis and stakes arranged in parallel lines, presumably to support beans or other
vegetables, appear. By contrast, Hassam's painting depicts a flower-covered, fan-shaped trellis with a
birdhouse perched above it and the gate construction off to the right. Unfortunately, in neither painting
is it possible to be completely sure of the locations of the trellises.[30] Hassam probably made another visit
to the farm in 1905, for the following year a few days after the fourth of July, Hassam wrote:

> Are you still thrashing that pond? I should have enjoyed seeing those fireworks as much as the
> children. I am sure they were as fine as their titles. Fiery Dutchman. Dauntless Dane. What are
> they anyway?[31]

(The use of the word "thrashing" in this context is unclear, but it might have been an obscure reference
to fireworks, which, for safety's sake, could have been set off near the pond.)

Hassam was a central figure of the Old Lyme, Connecticut, artists' colony, but he also spent
considerable time on Appledore Island in the Isles of Shoals, an isolated group of tiny islands off the coast
of Portsmouth, New Hampshire, where the poet Celia Thaxter and many other artists and writers
summered. In 1893 Hassam painted Thaxter's garden in a series of famous watercolors that were used
to illustrate the 1894 edition of her book *An Island Garden*.[32] Hassam probably paid Weir a visit in
Branchville in late July or early August 1906, as on August 14 he wrote to Weir from the Isles of Shoals:

> This place is pretty fine this year and I am thinking it would look better if you were here. Can
> you come up for a while? Come on! The water is fine! . . .

> How the summer is slipping underneath our feet. It seems only yesterday that I was with you in
> Branchville.[33]

Figure 39   Childe Hassam, "Weir's Garden," watercolor, 1903 (Hood Museum of Art, Dartmouth College, Hanover, New Hampshire; purchased through the Phyllis and Betram Geller 1937 Memorial Fund).

76

In 1909 Hassam even sent Weir a menu from the Appledore Hotel, along with a sample of lueberry pie, but there is no record that Weir ever went to the Isles of Shoals although Hassam continued) visit Branchville.[34] In 1910 Hassam painted "Road to the Land of Nod" (figure 40), which, although : shows the approach to the farm rather than the farm itself, is a wonderfully evocative depiction of the onnecticut countryside as it was then, with its irregular topography, snaking stone walls, and almost open ields.

A 1906 painting by Weir of the Weir Farm landscape is his "The Return of the Fishing Party" (figure 41), which shows fishermen, who, having come back from the pond, are approaching an opening in a stone wall, possibly the stone wall across from Weir's house.

In March 1907, Weir made the decision to purchase the 50-acre Webb Farm from the heirs of William Webb. He appears to have always admired the property since its fields and outbuildings were the subject of some of his early etchings and pastels. Why he decided to buy it at this particular time, however, is not recorded. However, he may have been planning to buy it for some time in order to protect his own farm against encroachment. When the property became available, Weir moved quickly: William Webb died in the fall of 1906, and his son William Foster Webb was appointed administrator of his father's estate in November of that year.[35] It is also possible that Weir was thinking ahead in order to provide at least two of his daughters with separate households in Branchville after his death. The development of the Webb/Weir/Burlingham property will be discussed in chapter IV of this report.[36]

Between about 1907 and 1910, Weir had trouble selling his paintings, as his many letters to Wood attest, and in addition, he had taken on heavy expenses by moving into a large duplex apartment at 471 Park Avenue during the winters.[37] At about this same time, Weir's devoted and hard-working farmer, Paul Remy, seems to have left (whether he moved on to other employment, retired, or was let go is unclear), throwing Weir back into his earlier chronic problem of trying to find a satisfactory replacement. In May 1907, he wrote to Wood: "I have had much trouble getting a man for Branchville. Am now trying to rent it for the first time but fear this is a bad year to turn a penny in any way."[38] More than three years later, Weir was still looking for a farmer for Branchville, and probably for Windham as well, writing to Wood in September 1910: "I wish the farms were deep down in the sea. I can't get a good man and you know what happens when it is all guess."[39] Two months later, he wrote again to Wood from Windham:

> We will probably stay here until after Thanksgiving for one reason or another before returning to the city. I have just finished a portrait of the farmer's two boys which I seem to like but have not done any fall work. Am worked out and am trying to get the expenses on the farm reduced and something accomplished. I bounced the head man and have been running the farm myself up to the present, making a check system so as to stop unnecessary expense. Our apartment I fear will swamp us, so much more expensive than I had any idea of.[40]

77

Figure 40   Childe Hassam, "Road to the Land of Nod," oil on canvas, 1910 (Wadsworth Athenaeum, Hartford.   The Ella Gallup Sumner and Mary Catlin Sumner Collection Fund).

'igure 41   J. Alden Weir, "The Return of the Fishing Party," oil on canvas, 1906 (High
                    Museum of Art, Atlanta, Georgia, gift of Miss Mary E. Haverty, 61.65).

It is difficult to know how to interpret this letter, especially since Weir was writing from Windham. It would seem logical that the Weirs would have stayed at Branchville rather than Windham through Thanksgiving, although there seem to have been farm problems at Windham as well. Weir writes about "bouncing" the head man, which at Branchville would surely have been Paul if Paul were still there. However, the last mention of Paul or any of his family by name is in the 1904 letter from John F. Weir, quoted above. In any case, neither of Paul's sons, Willie and Carl, seems to have taken over after their father's retirement as John F. Weir had anticipated. The painting of the farmer's two boys that Weir referred to in this letter is a portrait called "The Adams Children."[41] The Adamses could either have been a farm family in Branchville who are not mentioned elsewhere, or they could have been the farmers at Windham.

In spite of these difficulties, Weir produced several fine paintings and pastels of the farm in the period ca. 1907–1910. Among them is "Autumn" (figure 42), which shows the stone walls, bridge, etc., on the approach to the pond. An undated pastel called "The Ice House" (figure 43) shows this structure before its transformation into a chicken house under the Young ownership.[42] Another work is "Afternoon by The Pond" (figure 44), painted around 1908–1909, an impressionistic view of the pond but one in which specific features can be positively identified. The tree with three trunks at the left of the painting may still be seen today.[43] In the beautiful pastel entitled "Branchville Pond" (figure 45), which is undated, the trunks of two trees, the outline of a rowboat, and a hint of the surrounding topography are visible. "The Tulip Tree, Branchville," also undated, is illustrated in figure 46 and may depict the tulip tree still surviving in the meadow on the east side of Nod Hill Road.

To conclude this section, a photograph showing Weir's house, studio, barn, and various outbuildings from the rear is included (figure 47). Although this photograph can be dated only ca. 1901–1932 (i.e., after the Platt additions to the house and before the construction of the Mahonri Young studio), it vividly illustrates the openness of the land, as well as the picturesque massing of the main and subsidiary buildings with their varied roof lines. Taken from the southwestern part of the core area, this photograph is also one of the few that shows an overall view of the site. It also illustrates some outbuildings and features of the landscape that are not well documented elsewhere. For example, a large tree, which does not appear in any other photograph, may be seen near the northwest corner of the Weir house. The small building, usually referred to as the "bindery," which was later moved and became Mahonri Young's etching room, is clearly seen in its original location, but its window appears to be boarded up.[44] Further to the north and west is a distant view of another outbuilding, which, to judge from its door and window openings, pitch of roof, and general dimensions, is almost certainly the chicken house in J. Alden Weir's pastel, "Feeding the Chickens, Branchville," illustrated in the previous chapter (figure 22).

80

J. Alden Weir, "Autumn," oil on canvas, ca. 1907 (In the Collection of the Corcoran Gallery of Art, Museum Purchase, Gallery Fund).

Figure 43   J. Alden Weir, "The Ice House," pencil and pastel on paper, n.d. (Private
                   Collection).

igure 44   J. Alden Weir, "Afternoon by the Pond," oil on canvas, ca. 1908–1909 (The
                    Phillips Collection, Washington, DC).

83

Figure 45   J. Alden Weir, "Branchville Pond," pencil and pastel on paper, n.d. (Private
                   Collection).

Figure 46   J. Alden Weir, "The Tulip Tree, Branchville," pencil, watercolor and pastel on paper, n.d. (Private Collection).

85

Figure 47   Weir house, studio, etc., from the rear. Photograph, ca. 1900–1934 (WFNHS-HP
                   No. 8).

911–1919

1911–1912 was a period of remarkable professional success for Weir, in which several exhibitions f his work were held and received high critical praise. In January 1911, an exhibition was held at the t. Botolph Club at Boston and then moved on to the Century Association in New York. Another large xhibition was held at the Carnegie Institute in Pittsburgh in the spring, and a small group of pastels was ent to Wood in Portland, Oregon. In the fall, a group of his paintings was shown in Buffalo, and in the pring of 1912, nineteen of his works were shown in Cincinnati. As a result of these exhibitions, several f Weir's works were sold, including the entire group of pastels, which, thanks to Wood, were purchased ɔ decorate the breakfast room of a club in Portland. Unfortunately, in March 1911 Weir was diagnosed ith valvular disease of the heart, and he was also in considerable pain from a longstanding lame leg.[45]

The exhibitions and subsequent sales of work seem to have given Weir the confidence to enlarge d improve the farmhouse yet another time. In 1911 he decided to have the prestigious New York chitectural firm of McKim, Mead and White extend his dining room to the north. (The reason why Weir anted this change is not recorded, but it was perhaps intended to accommodate larger family gatherings in anticipation of the arrival of grandchildren.) Blueprints for the project exist. The architect in charge of the dining room enlargement was F. J. Adams.[46] (Two of the original partners in the McKim, Mead and White firm were deceased.) The enlarged dining room was relatively simple in concept but proved to be frustrating in execution, as Weir wrote to Wood:

> I, flushed with success, decided to enlarge the dining room and put in a bathroom, adjoining the bed room on the ground floor at Branchville. What worry and trouble I have had. It has almost busted the pleasure of the early spring, and not half done, everyone disappointing us is the case in such matters.[47]

And again:

> I have only now got to work, as we put in a bathroom and added to the dining room, and the work has dragged on and most unsatisfactory, especially the d—n plumber's bill that is out of all proportion and all this is dry season. However, I must grin and bear it, but I could not do much work now. I have a number of canvasses underway and am beginning to feel more cheerful. . . We did not get up here this year until the middle of June and then moved in with the workmen. No more improvements for me until I have an unlimited account and lose my head.[48]

Adding to Weir's frustration was the fact that his chestnut trees had begun to die of blight:

> I went to Branchville yesterday and had a fine time and yet a sad one as all our fine chestnut trees
> have died with some disease so that I have sold them, as the wood is yet good. But to see these
> fine trees lying all about, it was pitiable.[49]

This was the beginning of the American chestnut blight, which virtually eliminated this American
forest tree after about 1920. However, today at least two American chestnuts on the former
Webb/Burlingham property have regenerated and reached a medium height, although they are now in poor
condition.[50]

In 1912 Weir wrote to Wood mentioning cherry trees on the property.[51] However, during the
summer of 1912 the Weirs did not stay in Branchville but instead travelled in England, where Weir fished
in the River Dove and in Scotland.[52] Before leaving, he visited the farm and commented on his new
farmers:

> Yesterday I went up to Branchville for the day. It was balmy and the birds were singing and the
> odor of the earth was a most exhilarating perfume. The men were burning brush and everything
> looked lovely. I have a man who has not princely qualities, but who is a very good fellow. The
> two men are advanced in age and remind me of two old nutcrackers.[53]

Upon his return he again wrote to Wood about "getting a number of artists together for a spree."[54] In
December he wrote about having the pump at the reservoir dismantled.[55]

In 1911 the Association of American Painters and Sculptors was organized, and, in February 1913,
it sponsored the International Exhibition of Modern Art, or the Armory Show. Although best known for
its displays of European avant-garde art, such as Marcel Duchamp's painting, "Nude Descending a
Staircase," American painters, including Whistler, Ryder, Twachtman, and Hassam, were well represented.
Weir exhibited twenty-five works, including "The Orchid" (1899). Younger American artists, primarily
of the realist school, such as George Bellows, John Sloan, and Weir's future son-in-law, Mahonri Young,
also displayed work.[56]

Back in Connecticut, Weir noted in May 1913 that the strawberry bed looked fine.[57] In July of
this year, the Weirs were again in England and also visited Scotland.[58] By October they were back in
Branchville, as Weir wrote:

> Mama and I came down here yesterday for the first time to see how things were. . . . We found
> the old house very comfortable and everything looking very well, the flowers still blooming in the

88

garden and a large bowl of roses on the dining table. The fires are burning and the odor of smoke pervades the house. . . . I have had a walk over the farm to see the improvements . . .[59]

In March of 1915, Mr. and Mrs. Boughten (possibly one of the two new farmer families) moved to the old Webb house, leaving the farmhouse "for an Italian who can drive oxen."[60] One photograph rom this period (figure 48) is a view of the fence along Nod Hill Road and the Weir barn looking north (WFNHS-HP No. 161). This photograph also shows an enormous tree looming over the fence. The large oak tree seems to be the same one that appears in one of the 1889 cyanotypes (figure 12, WFNHS-HP No. 231, 1889) and in an early undated view of the first fence (figure 15, WFNHS-HP no. 90). Two other ca. 1915 photographs show the pond. In figure 49 (WFNHS-HP No. 171), two people are in a rowboat. In figure 50 (WFNHS-HP No. 167), Clara Boardman, a friend of the family, is sitting on the stump of a tree with the pond, a little boat landing, and two rowboats directly behind her. In the distance, part of the boathouse may be seen. From the same period is Weir's "The Fishing Party" (figure 51), which shows the bridge and the way to the pond.

In May 1915, Weir wrote to Dorothy from San Francisco, where he was a member of the international jury for the Panama-Pacific Exposition: "Cora got some pines and juniper trees (small) and sent them to Caro yesterday by Ex."[61] Weir also exhibited at the Panama-Pacific Exposition and won a medal.[62] He finally visited Wood in Oregon and fished with him in the Mackenzie River.[63] Back in Branchville, Weir wrote:

> I am staying out here trying to get through with a couple of canvasses. The days of October have changed the aspect of things and it begins to look like fall, always to me a sad suggestion of the bleak autumn when the glory of nature wanes.[64]

Still in Branchville in December, Weir reported that the snow was so deep that the man had to get to the barn by walking on the stone wall and that the snow drifted ten or twelve feet deep.[65]

Secret Garden, ca. 1915

In chapter I, it was noted that Anna Weir planted a flower garden, possibly the first at Weir Farm, in 1886. Her garden, which at least in its first year was not a success, may have consisted mostly of annuals.[66] The letter in which this early flower garden was mentioned gives no clue as to where it was located. Although there are some references in later correspondence to a garden, the context generally suggests a vegetable garden. In 1905 Weir did a series of four paintings or sketches of a flower garden that was located to the north of his studio (figure 37). If Weir's depiction in this and the other related

Figure 48   Fence and barn looking north. Photograph, 1915 (WFNHS-HP No. 161).

Figure 49   The pond. Photograph, ca. 1915 (WFNHS-HP No. 171).

Figure 50   Clara Boardman by the pond. Photograph, ca. 1915 (WFNHS-HP No. 167).

Figure 51   J. Alden Weir, "The Fishing Party," oil on canvas, ca. 1915 (The Phillips
                   Collection, Washington, DC).

paintings can be considered accurate, the 1905 garden was a relatively simple affair: a comparatively small space, fenced with posts and possibly chicken wire, and with one plain wooden gate on the southern side and what may have been either a gazebo or another, roofed gate at the western end. (The enclosure was presumably made to keep out animals.) No sundials or other garden ornaments can be made out, and while there are obviously flowers growing in the garden, they cannot be identified. The 1905 paintings are moonlit scenes, making it even more difficult to extract information from them. The letter from Joseph Pearson (Weir's student at Branchville in the late 1890s) quoted at the end of chapter I suggests that the early flower garden and its structures may have been the work of Paul Remy:

> The things made by the faithful Paul found a place in his pictures: sapling fences, rustic arbors and bridges as well as hen runs, and informal gardens . . .[67]

By about 1915, the date of a series of photographs, the garden had apparently been enlarged, fitted with a fountain, sundial, and two rather elaborate rustic gates, and planted intensively with perennials, vines, and encircling hedges. No designer's name is associated with the replanning of the garden at this time, and, surprisingly, it is not even mentioned in any of the correspondence. It is possible that the changes could have been incremental, but this is unlikely, since in the ca. 1915 photographs all the structures look new and the plants seem recently installed. Which member of the family initiated these changes can only be a matter of speculation. There is no evidence that Weir was ever personally involved in planning the flower garden at any stage, although his studio had the best view of it. Ella seems to have been an experienced gardener as early as 1886.[68] Dorothy may also have been interested in flower gardening at this stage in her life, and her sister Cora was an enthusiastic and skilled gardener.[69]

As will be described in chapter III, the enclosed garden became progressively more overgrown during the ownerships of Dorothy Weir Young and Mahonri Young (1931–1957). It seems to have been during these years that it became known as the "secret" garden, perhaps in acknowledgment of Frances Hodgson Burnett's children's story or perhaps simply because overgrowth had given it a hidden and mysterious quality.[70]

Figure 52 is a recent plan documenting the remaining historic features, missing historic features, and existing features that may be of later origin, as well as the boundaries and general distribution of spaces in the garden. In plan, the garden seems crowded, almost cluttered.[71] It is unclear, for example, why two gates were needed for such a small space. The patte d'oie arrangement of paths in the northeast corner of the garden is also puzzling, especially since none of the three paths leads to a gate or any particular terminus.

94

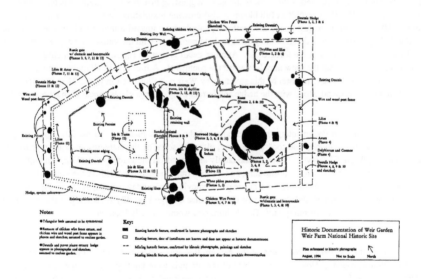

Figure 52   Plan showing documentation of Weir Garden. Olmsted Center for Landscape
                   Preservation, August 1994 (Olmsted Center).

In the ca. 1915 photographs, however, the luxuriant planting and numerous structures of this little garden have great charm. For example, figure 53 shows a woman at the garden's southeast gate, which is covered with clematis and honeysuckle. To the woman's right is perennial phlox *(Phlox paniculata)* and behind her is the fountain. In figure 54 a phlox planting appears in the foreground. In figure 55 a woman is seen again, this time near the fountain. Behind her is part of the box hedge and a bed of lilies. Figure 56 is a close-up view of the fountain. In figure 57 another woman is consulting the sundial. This photograph also gives a good general view of the garden and its plantings. Another photograph with considerable information is figure 58, which was taken from just outside the northwest gate looking toward the sundial, the southeast gate, and Weir's studio. Plants visible in this view include iris foliage among the rocks just inside the northwest gate and daylilies and phlox on the south side of the garden. In this photograph a large tree can also be seen just behind the southeast garden gate. This may be the large oak, still extant, which presses up against the front of the Weir studio, although the tree in the photograph does not seem close enough to the building. In figure 58 both gates are visible and neither has webbed mesh over it. In figure 59, which shows Dorothy and Caro Weir at one of the gates, some kind of mesh, possibly chicken wire painted white, covers the gate, suggesting that this photograph was taken slightly later than ca. 1915. Honeysuckle in full bloom is also growing luxuriantly over the entire gate structure. Figure 60 was taken from just inside the northwest gate looking toward a mown path that leads to the orchard. Figure 61 shows a detail of the garden looking northwest, with the vine-covered gate to the right and lilies and iris foliage in the foreground. Another detail is seen in figure 62. The orientation is not absolutely clear here, but the view may be toward the southwest. A roof of a small outbuilding, probably the original chicken house (a pastel of this structure by Weir was illustrated in figure 22 in chapter I), is visible in the background, along with the hedge and border lilies. Yucca plants appear in the foreground.[72]

In addition to documenting the appearance of the garden, many of the ca. 1915 photographs vividly portray the activities that took place there, although some of the activities are a bit mystifying. For example, figure 63 shows members of the family and friends in the garden, with Weir standing at the sundial, another man standing opposite him, and various other people sprawled on the ground absorbed in reading. It is unclear whether this is a house party enjoying the Sunday newspaper or a group studying a script for amateur theatricals! In figure 64 Caro's fiancé George Page Ely is standing at the sundial in a posture that is difficult to interpret.[73] Beside him, two women quietly look on.

With the ca. 1915 photographs of the garden, this area suddenly becomes the best documented part of Weir's property. However, other parts of the grounds were photographed at the same time and demonstrate that flower planting was not confined to the enclosed garden. In figure 65, a little white dog lies in front of a small round flower bed in the middle of the lawn to the west of the house. In the bed are lilies in full bloom with iris foliage in the foreground. The point of view is toward the southwest, since the well and Pelham Lane are both visible. Although the photograph in figure 66 is poorly focussed, the view is a valuable one because it shows hollyhocks growing luxuriantly on the south side of the Weir tack house.

Figure 53   Woman at southeast gate to the garden. Photograph, ca. 1915 (WFNHS-HP
                             No. 3).

Figure 54   Weir garden with phlox. Photograph, ca. 1915 (WFNHS-HP No. 163).

Figure 55   Woman near the fountain in the garden. Photograph, ca. 1915 (WFNHS-HP
                             No. 4).

Figure 56   Fountain in Weir garden. Photograph, ca. 1915 (WFNHS-HP No. 165).

Figure 57   Woman in Weir garden. Photograph, ca. 1915 (WFNHS-HP No. 179).

Figure 58   View of garden and Weir's studio from northwest gate. Photograph, ca. 1915
                  (WFNHS-HP No.162).

Figure 59   Dorothy and Caro at the garden gate. Photograph, ca. 1916 (WFNHS-HP No.
                             178).

Figure 60   View through the northwest gate looking toward mown path leading to orchard.
                   Photograph, ca. 1915 (WFNHS-HP No. 164).

Figure 61　　　　　Detail of Weir garden, showing lilies. Photograph, ca. 1915 (WFNHS-HP No. 174).

Figure 62   Detail of Weir garden, showing lilies and yuccas. Photograph, ca. 1915(?)
                     (WFNHS-HP No. 176).

Figure 63   Group in Weir garden. Photograph, ca. 1915 (WFNHS-HP No. 168).

Figure 64   George Page Ely and two women in Weir garden. Photograph, ca. 1915
                   (WFNHS-HP No. 182).

108

Figure 65   Flower bed and white dog, west lawn, Weir house Photograph, ca. 1915
                   (WFNHS-HP No. 166).

Figure 66   Tack house and hollyhocks, Weir grounds. Photograph, ca. 1915 (WFNHS-HP
                   No. 177).

After 1915, there are relatively few references in the correspondence to gardening, farming, or other landscape activities at Weir Farm. In 1916, Weir talked about filling up the ice house.[74] In March 1917, Albert Pinkham Ryder ("Pinky"), so often a visitor to Connecticut, died.[75] In October, Weir noted that Dorothy had gone to Storrs College to study gardening for a week.[76] In 1917 the family gathered for the christening of baby Anna Weir Ely, an event for which another series of photographs was taken.

A feature in the Weir Farm landscape for which there is no documentation in correspondence is the birdbath carved into the large outcropping of ledge between the Weir studio and the barn. This is a natural depression, but it was enlarged, probably by a drill. However, it is certain that the birdbath dates from the Weir ownership, since it existed when Dorothy Weir and Mahonri M. Young were married.[77]

AGRICULTURAL ACTIVITIES AT WEIR FARM, 1882–1919

J. Alden Weir's letters and those of his brother and friends are filled with references to farming. Similarly, his paintings are replete with stone walls, farm animals, outbuildings, farm machinery, and other agricultural accoutrements. Nevertheless, specific crops and their exact locations cannot be determined from the paintings. When the correspondence is examined closely, there is surprisingly little concrete information about farm activities. Details about crop schedules, marketing, and manpower are entirely missing. In general, this kind of information is almost impossible to reconstruct unless farm diaries or account books have survived.[78] As far as farm animals are concerned, we know that Weir kept horses, cattle, oxen, pigs, and poultry. A donkey was kept for a time (see figure 35) but was probably more of a children's pet than a farm animal. Sheep are not mentioned in any of the correspondence but were also kept for a time since they appear in a watercolor, "Sheep in Pen, Branchville."[79] Bees were also kept for honey.

This section reprises all of the data currently available about farming during Weir's ownership. Except for the period from 1915 on, it does not introduce any new material, and specific references may be found in the appropriate sections of chapters I and II.

Before the purchase of the 32-acre, $25.00 lot, all of the farming must have taken place on the east side of Nod Hill Road. There would have been no space in the vicinity of the house and barn, and the low-lying wetland to the west would have been unsuitable. The first reference to anything agricultural is in a letter of October 1882, when Weir writes about bringing in Alderney cattle. In the summer of 1883, his brother, John, stayed at the farm and wrote to Weir that the crops—hay, potatoes and corn— were doing well. Oats were also being grown this year. Holsten was Weir's first tenant farmer. In 1885 Weir's farmer let 500 heads of celery freeze. In the summer of 1888, there was another good harvest of

111

vegetables, grass, and grain (not specified). By this time, Weir had a new tenant farmer, whom he does not refer to by name; the farmer and his wife were both Scots. They stayed only a year since, by 1889 or 1890 at the latest, Paul Remy had become Weir's farmer. By the late 1880s and probably earlier, Weir used red oxen on the farm.

In the summer and fall of 1891, John again stayed on the farm. Paul plowed the "big field." Rocks were still being removed from the ground. John described cherry trees on the far side of Nod Hill Road and distant bushy chestnuts with a "pretty field of millet" in the middle ground. In 1892 John stayed again at the farm, and Paul cleared a field for sowing. Paul also plowed the rough field beyond the rye using oxen. In 1895 lima beans, tomatoes, and sweet peas were grown, probably in the vegetable garden rather than as crops. By the late 1890s, asparagus was grown in beds. By 1898, at the latest, buckwheat was grown on the farm. In 1899 corn overheated in the barn and had to be thrown out. During Paul's tenure, there are frequent references to cider making and sauerkraut beans.

In 1900 Weir bought the $25.00 lot, and his brother, John, and Paul Remy removed rocks from it. In 1904 there is a reference to the hay harvest. This is also the last specific reference to Paul. In 1907 Weir purchased the 50-acre Webb Farm and may have needed two farmers for the two properties. In 1912 there is a reference to cherry trees, and Weir noted that he has two elderly farmers: "two old nutcrackers." In 1913 Mr. Boughten (one of the elderly farmers?) kept the family supplied with strawberries from "good beds."[80] In 1915 Mr. and Mrs. Boughten moved into the Webb House, leaving the farmhouse for an Italian (unnamed) who could drive oxen. In 1916 there are references to Neil McGonigle, perhaps a new farmer, although obviously not Italian.[81] Later the same year he wrote that he had a very good man at Branchville, and in spring 1917 he referred to two good men at Branchville.[82] In 1918 strawberries and raspberries were set out.[83] In the same year there are references to a "lazy man" who didn't cut enough wood and a one-legged man with a good instinct for hoeing.[84]

In 1920 records are available concerning the local property taxes due on Weir's estate in both Ridgefield and Wilton. In Ridgefield, the buildings and land assessed were the house, two barns, and a studio, as well as the total acreage of the property and a five-acre house lot.[85] Smaller outbuildings were apparently not taxed, since another document naming the executrix of the estate lists, in addition, a woodshed, tank house, bindery, another shed (probably the wagon shed), ice house, pump house, corncrib, etc.[86] On the Ridgefield tax list, livestock, consisting of three horses, two oxen, three cows, and two yearlings, was also itemized.[87] (Poultry was probably not taxed.) In Wilton, Weir's taxable property included two dwelling houses (Webb Farmhouse and the caretaker's house), two outbuildings (probably the barn and woodshed), the acreage of the farm, two house lots, and two "neat cattle."[88]

112

WEIR'S DEATH

To conclude this chapter, a few beautiful photographs that date from the last year of Weir's life are illustrated. Figure 67 shows the south elevation of Weir's house as it appeared in 1919; Pelham Lane is visible in this photograph, but only as a very narrow dirt road. Two of the loveliest photographs of the pond also date from 1919: Figure 68 (printed backward), which shows the pond and a distant view of the summer house, and figure 69, which shows the island and summer house at closer range. Both photographs show the island and part of the surrounding shore planted with birches. Toward the end of the summer of 1919, Weir became ill at Windham. As he began recuperating in October, he was carried downstairs and laid in the swing on the lawn, where he rested and contemplated the autumn landscape, saying: "What a beautiful world it is!"[89]

His recovery, however, was only temporary. J. Alden Weir became progressively weaker and died on December 8, 1919, in New York City.[90]

SUMMARY

Between 1901 and his death, Weir continued to develop the landscape of his Connecticut property. In 1899 he gave up his winter teaching in New York City, allowing him to extend his summer stays at Branchville from May to December. In 1900 he enlarged the house, using the services of Charles Adams Platt, and in 1911 he engaged another prestigious New York architectural firm, McKim, Mead and White, to extend his dining room. Farming continued to be a very important activity, although after the departure of Paul Remy, ca. 1904, finding suitable farmers was a chronic problem for Weir. In 1907 Weir purchased the adjacent 50-acre Webb Farm, possibly to protect his land from encroachment. One of the most important landscape activities in this period of Weir's life was his development of the garden, later known as the Secret Garden, near his studio. A garden in this location had existed since at least 1905, but around 1915 it was enlarged, extensively replanted, and ornamented with a fountain, sundial, and rustic fence, and gates. No landscape architect is associated with this garden design, and it is documented only in photographs.

As in the first decades of his ownership of the farm, family activities were very important to Weir. He also continued to enjoy frequent visits from numerous artists and other friends, including the lawyer and art patron, C. E. S. Wood. As in earlier years, the farm continued to inspire his art.

113

Figure 67   Weir house, south elevation. Photograph, 1919 (WFNHS-HP No. 206).

Figure 68   Pond, Weir farm. Photograph, 1919 (WFNHS-HP No. 205).

Figure 69   Island and summerhouse in pond. Photograph, 1919 (WFNHS-HP No. 207).

LANDSCAPE FEATURES AND CONDITIONS, CA. 1919

Methodology

In the absence of historic maps, property surveys, or illustrative plans, the major landscape developments up to 1919 were determined through close scrutiny of over thirty-five historic photographs, aerial photographs, twenty-six paintings, written correspondence, and several interviews. Manmade objects such as buildings, wells, fences, steps, walls, paths, and gardens were mapped using photographs and paintings as primary sources, while aerials of later dates (1939, 1941, and 1949) were referenced to confirm the location of features known to have existed in 1919.

Certain areas of the site, such as Weir's house and studio area, the fishing bridge area, the Burlingham barn area, and pond area, were more thoroughly documented than other areas. Where such graphic evidence existed, features were located in plan using triangulation (a process of placing a feature in plan using a photograph that shows the feature along with another feature whose location is already determined in plan). Stone walls seen on the 1949 aerial and located outside the core area were assumed to be in existence in 1919 because of Weir's reference to extensive wall construction and the subsequent lack of field maintenance between Weir's death and 1949.

Trees were located using a variety of techniques depending on availability of sources. Individual trees in the core area were located using historical photographs and paintings. This information was cross-referenced using the 1949, aerial which clearly shows individual trees of significant maturity. Areas on the 1949 aerial showing younger successional growth were assumed to be open fields maintained for farming and grazing while mature stands of trees were assumed to be in existence in 1919. These mature stands defined field boundaries, wetlands, hedgerows, and steep slopes as described and referenced in Weir's paintings. Historical photographs giving hints of distant horizon lines and open vistas were also used to cross-reference open versus wooded areas.

In addition, Professor William Niering of Connecticut College was consulted for his knowledge of plant succession to establish which areas were most likely open, cultivated, grazed, or forested in 1919. It is not entirely clear if the area west of the Weir Farm core area was in an open or forested condition in 1919, therefore it has been shown as open on exhibits 3 and 18. A list of sources and references used to prepare the ca. 1919 plans (exhibits 3 and 4) has been included in exhibit 5.

117

Landscape Character

The landscape character of Weir Farm in 1919 (238 acres), at the time of J. Alden Weir's death, was one of open, rocky fields, stone walls and hedgerows, intimate views, distant vistas, and glaciated topography (see exhibits 3 and 18). The property had been maintained as a working farm by tenant farmers during Weir's tenure. The cultivation of crops and the upkeep of livestock altered the natural landscape and created a civilized, productive atmosphere in which Weir, his family, and friends lived and painted.

Major Landscape Developments

As shown in exhibits 3 and 4, the most important landscape developments at the Branchville Farm during Weir's tenure from 1882 to 1919 included: the building of Weir's studio in 1885 as part of the complex of farm buildings that were actively used, such as the main house, barn, ice house, tack house, wagon shed, corncrib, caretaker's house, and two wells;[91] the construction of the dam and creation of the 3.6-acre pond (1896-1902) and its various related amenities, such as the boathouse, wooden bridge to the pond, stone steps at the pond, and summerhouse; the creation of the Secret Garden complete with sundial, fountain, garden fencing. and gates (see figure 58); and the alteration of the landscape for farming practices, such as the cultivation of various crops (rye, corn and hay), fruit trees, and the vegetable garden west of the house. Other, smaller developments in the landscape included the stonework improvements adjacent to the house such as the walks, steps, stone picnic table, and carved birdbath.

Features No Longer Extant

Of the important landscape features that existed in 1919, several are no longer in existence today. Missing farm structures include the old chicken house, the fences and gates north and south of the barn, and the wood structure over the well shown in figure 29. The old bindery/washhouse was moved from its 1919 location to its later location attached to Young's studio for use as an etching room. Also missing are the pond-related facilities such as the summerhouse, the boathouse, and the wooden fishing bridge and dock. Missing features in the Secret Garden include the wood gates and fences and the majority of the perennial plant materials. All of the fields and meadows used for crops and grazing have become overgrown through natural succession. Only remnants of the original orchard can be found today and the vegetable garden is no longer in existence, except for remnant asparagus and onion beds.

118

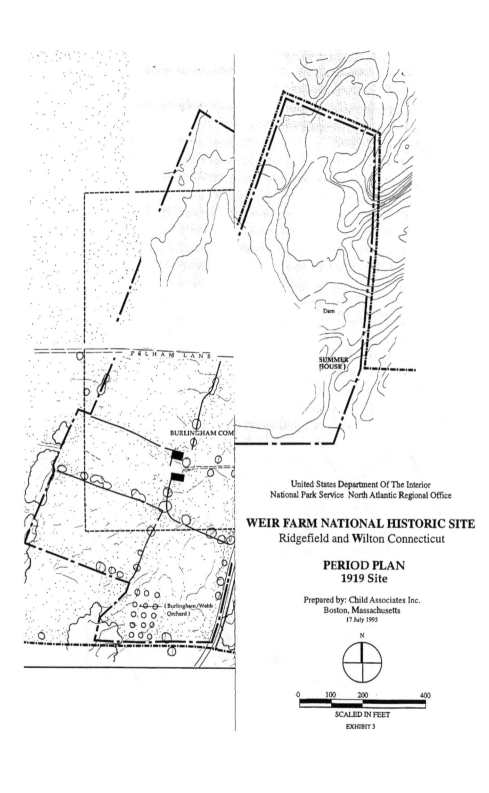

PELHAM LANE

Dam

SUMMER
HOUSE)

BURLINGHAM COM

(Burlingham/Webb
Orchard)

United States Department Of The Interior
National Park Service North Atlantic Regional Office

WEIR FARM NATIONAL HISTORIC SITE
Ridgefield and Wilton Connecticut

PERIOD PLAN
1919 Site

Prepared by: Child Associates Inc.
Boston, Massachusetts
17 July 1995

N

0   100   200   400

SCALED IN FEET

EXHIBIT 3

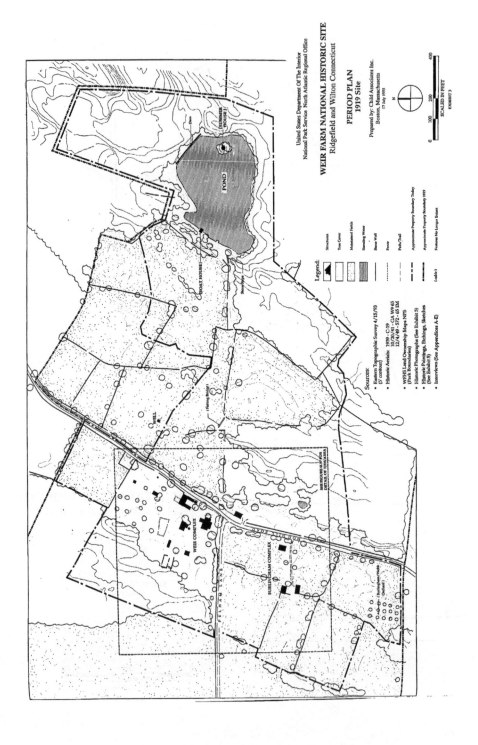

United States Department Of The Interior
National Park Service North Atlantic Regional Office

WEIR FARM NATIONAL HISTORIC SITE
Ridgefield and Wilton Connecticut

PERIOD PLAN
1919 Site

Prepared by: Child Associates Inc.
Boston, Massachusetts
17 July 1995

Legend:
- Structures
- Tree Cover
- Maintained Fields
- Standing Water
- Stone Wall
- Fence
- Path/Trail
- Approximate Property Boundary Today
- Approximate Property Boundary 1919
- Features No Longer Extant (table)

Sources:
- Eastern Topographic Survey 4/15/93 (5' contour)
- Historic Aerials: 1939 - C39
  10/20/41 - GA W9 65
  12/4/49 - 572 - 65 1M
- WFHS Land Ownership Maps NPS (Park Boundaries)
- Historic Photographs (See Exhibit 5)
- Historic Paintings, Etchings, Sketches (See Exhibit 5)
- Interviews (See Appendices A-E)

SCALED IN FEET
0 100 200 400

EXHIBIT 3

	Standing Water
	Stone Wall
············	Fence
— — —	Path/Trail
▬ ▬ ▬	Approximate Property Boundary Today
▬·▬·▬·▬	Approximate Property Boundary 1919
` ´	Features No Longer Extant
	Garden
▶◀	Gate/Barway

Sources:

- Eastern Topographic Survey 4/15/93 (5' contour)
- Historic Aerials: 1939 - C-19
  10/20/41 - GA W9 65
  12/4/49 - 572 - 65 1M
- WFHS Land Ownership Maps NPS (Park Boundaries)
- Historic Photographs (See Exhibit 5)
- Historic Paintings, Etchings, Sketches (See Exhibit 5)
- Interviews (See Appendices A-E)

United States Department Of The Interior
National Park Service North Atlantic Regional Office

WEIR FARM NATIONAL HISTORIC SITE
Ridgefield and Wilton Connecticut

PERIOD PLAN
1919 Core Area

Prepared by: Child Associates Inc.
Boston, Massachusetts
17 July 1995

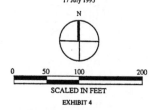

0   50   100   200

SCALED IN FEET

EXHIBIT 4

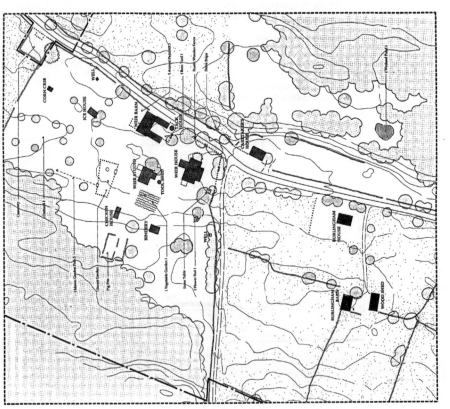

United States Department Of The Interior
National Park Service North Atlantic Regional Office

WEIR FARM NATIONAL HISTORIC SITE
Ridgefield and Wilton Connecticut

PERIOD PLAN
1919 Core Area

Prepared by: Child Associates Inc.
Boston, Massachusetts
17 July 1995

Legend:

- Structures
- Tree Cover
- Maintained Fields
- Standing Water
- Stone Wall
- Fence
- Path/Trail
- Approximate Property Boundary Today
- Approximate Property Boundary 1919
- Features No Longer Extant
- Garden
- Gate/Raceway

Sources:

- Eastern Topographic Survey 4/15/93 (5' contour)
- Historic Aerials: 1939 - C-19
  10/20/41 - GA W9 65
  12/4/49 - 572 - 65 1M
- WFHS Land Ownership Maps NPS (Park Boundaries)
- Historic Photographs (See Exhibit 5)
- Historic Paintings, Etchings, Sketches (See Exhibit 5)
- Interviews (See Appendices A-E)

N

SCALED IN FEET

0 50 100 200

EXHIBIT 4

United States Department Of The Interior
National Park Service North Atlantic Regional Office

WEIR FARM NATIONAL HISTORIC SITE
Ridgefield and Wilton Connecticut

SOURCES FOR 1919 PERIOD PLAN

Prepared by: Child Associates Inc.
Boston, Massachusetts
17 July 1995

EXHIBIT 5

United States
National Park Servi[ce]

WEIR FARM NA[TIONAL]
Ridgefield a[nd]

SOURCES F[OR]

Prepared[...]
B[...]

PAINTINGS, ETCHINGS, AND SKETCHES

Figure 4 Albert Pinkham Ryder, "Weir's Orchard," oil on canvas, ca. 1885-1890 (Wadsworth Atheneum).

Figure 9 J. Alden Weir, "Autumn Landscape," oil on canvas, 1889-1890 (Private Collection).

Figure 10 J. Alden Weir, "Early Spring at Branchville," oil on canvas, 1880-1890 (Private Collection).

Figure 17 J. Alden Weir, "Paul Remy," n.d. (ca. late 1890s) (Private Collection).

Figure 18 J. Alden Weir, "The Palace Car," n.d. (ca. 1892) (Museum of Art, Brigham Young University, Provo, Utah).

Figure 19 J. Alden Weir, "Road to the Farm," oil on canvas, 1890 (Private Collection).

Figure 20 J. Alden Weir, "Farm Scene at Branchville," oil on canvas, ca. 1890.

Figure 21 J. Alden Weir, "Midday," oil on canvas. (Private Collection).

Figure 22 J. Alden Weir, "Ploughing the Outlands; Branchville," pastel on paper mounted on canvas, early 1890s (Private Collection).

Figure 23 J. Alden Weir, "The Gray Trellis," oil on canvas, 1891 (Private Collection).

Figure 24 J. Alden Weir, "Building and Stone Wall," ink wash on paper, ca. 1894 (Private Collection).

Figure 25 J. Alden Weir, "A Look Across the Fields," ink and brush on paper, ca. 1894. (Brigham Young University, Provo, Utah).

Figure 26 J. Alden Weir, "The Laundry, Branchville," oil on canvas, ca. 1894 (Weir Farm Heritage Trust).

Figure 30 J. Alden Weir, "The Farm in Winter," oil on canvas, 1895 (Private Collection).

Figure 31 J. Alden Weir, "The Old Rock," oil on canvas, 1895 (Private Collection).

Figure 36 J. Alden Weir, "New England Barn," oil on canvas, ca. 1904 (Phillips Collection, Washington, DC).

Figure 37 J. Alden Weir, "The Shadow of My Studio," oil on canvas, 1905 (Private Collection).

Figure 39 Childe Hassam, "Weir's Garden," watercolor, 1903 [from the Collection of Art, Dartmouth College, Hanover, New Hampshire].

Figure 40 Childe Hassam, "Road to the Land of Nod," oil on canvas, 1910 (Wadsworth Atheneum, Hartford, Connecticut).

Figure 41 J. Alden Weir, "The Return of the Fishing Party," oil on canvas, 1906 (High Museum of Art, Atlanta, Georgia).

Figure 42 J. Alden Weir, "Autumn," oil on canvas, ca. 1907 (Corcoran Gallery of Art, Washington, DC).

Figure 43 J. Alden Weir, "The Ice House," pencil and pastel on paper, n.d. (Private Collection).

Figure 44 J. Alden Weir, "Afternoon by the Pond," oil on canvas, ca. 1908-1909 (Phillips Collection, Washington, DC).

Figure 45 J. Alden Weir, "Branchville Pond," pencil and pastel on paper, n.d. (Private Collection).

Figure 51 J. Alden Weir, "The Fishing Party," oil on canvas, ca. 1915. (The Phillips Collection, Washington, DC).

Figure 106 J. Alden Weir, "The Farm Lot," n.d. Etching and drypoint on paper. (Museum of Art, Brigham Young University, Provo, Utah).

Figure 107 J. Alden Weir, "Webb Farm," n.d. Etching and drypoint on paper (Collections of the Library of Congress).

Figure 108 J. Alden Weir, "Webb Farm," n.d. Etching (Private Collection).

Figure 110 J. Alden Weir, "Webb's Apple Orchard, Spring," Ca. 1910-1919 oil on canvas (Private Collection).

PHOTOGRAPHS

Figure 6 Weir Home. Photograph, ca. 1885-1887 (WFNHS-HP No. 5).

Figure 8 Aunt with baby by the Weir barn. Photograph, ca. summer 1885 (WFNHS-HP No. 70).

Figure 11 Group of people near front steps of Weir home. Cyanotype, 1889 (WFNHS-HP No. 233, 1899).

Figure 12 People sitting on grass near south side of Weir Home. Cyanotype, 1889 (WFNHS-HP No. 230, 1889).

Figure 13 Group of people under awning. Weir home. Cyanotype, 1889. (WFNHS-HP No. 231, 1889).

Figure 14 Group of people in field opposite south side of Weir home. Cyanotype, 1889 (WFNHS-HP No. 232, 1889).

Figure 15 Fence along Nod Hill Road in front of Weir's home. Photograph, before ca. 1915 (WFNHS-HP No. 90).

Figure 16 Open cart with a pail of hay on Nod Hill Road (WFNHS-HP No. 175).

Figure 27 Weir home from the rear. Photograph, ca. 1888-1890 (WFNHS-HP No. 235).

Figure 28 Weir home from the rear. Photograph, ca. 1888-1890 (WFNHS-HP No. 234).

Figure 29 Wall before the Weir home. Photograph, after 1893 (WFNHS-HP No. 16).

Figure 32 J. Alden Weir fishing from boat on the pond. Photograph, after 1896 (WFNHS-HP No. 32).

Figure 33 Woman crossing bridge. Photograph, after 1896 (WFNHS-HP No. 3).

Figure 34 J. Alden Weir with palette near house. Photograph, ca. 1900. (WFNHS-HP No. 37).

Figure 48 Fence and barn looking north. Photograph, 1915 (WFNHS-HP No. 162).

Figure 49 The pond. Photograph, ca. 1915 (WFNHS-HP No. 172).

Figure 53 Woman at southeast gate to the garden. Photograph, ca. 1915 (WFNHS-HP No. 3).

Figure 54 Weir garden with phlox. Photograph, ca. 1915 (WFNHS-HP No. 163).

Figure 55 Woman near the fountain in the garden. Photograph, ca. 1915 (WFNHS-HP No. 163).

Figure 56 Fountain in Weir garden. Photograph, ca. 1915 (WFNHS-HP No. 163).

Figure 57 Woman in Weir garden. Photograph, ca. 1915 (WFNHS-HP No. 179).

Figure 58 View of garden and Weir's studio from northwest gate. Photograph, ca. 1915 (WFNHS-HP No. 162).

Figure 59 Dorothy and Cora at the garden gate. Photograph, ca. 1916 (WFNHS-HP No. 173).

Figure 60 View through the northwest gate looking toward brown path leading to orchard. Photograph, ca. 1915 (WFNHS-HP No. 164).

Figure 62 Detail of Weir garden, showing lilies and peonies. Photograph, ca. 1915(?) (WFNHS-HP No. 179).

Figure 63 Group in Weir garden. Photograph, ca. 1915 (WFNHS-HP No. 168).

Figure 65 Flower bed and white dog, west lawn, Weir home. Photograph, ca. 1915 (WFNHS-HP No. 165).

Figure 66 Tack house and hollyhocks, Weir grounds. Photograph, ca. 1915 (WFNHS-HP No. 177).

Figure 67 Weir house, south elevation. Photograph, 1919 (WFNHS-HP No. 206).

Figure 68 Pond, Weir farm. Photograph, 1919 (WFNHS-HP No. 205).

Figure 69 Island and manure bunker in pond. Photograph, 1919 (WFNHS-HP No. 207).

Not Shown Child, dog and man outside Weir studio. Photograph, after 1885 (Ca. 1887-1893) (WFNHS-HP No. 33).

Not Shown Group of children and adults on grass outside Weir's studio. Photograph, after 1885 (WFNHS-HP No. 14).

Outstanding Research Questions

Based on the sources listed above, most of the important landscape features that existed in 1919 can be documented. However, the existence or exact location of several landscape features mentioned in Weir's correspondence remains in question. For example, where were the tennis courts located? What did the caretaker's yard consist of? What was the extent of the stone walls and fencing in 1919? Did the stone terraces west of the house exist in 1919 and when were they built? And finally, what was the extent in 1919 (see exhibit 18) of the open or cultivated land west of the current National Park Service property boundary?

With ongoing research, awareness, and study, we hope these questions can one day be answered.

ENDNOTES TO CHAPTER II

1.   Dorothy Weir Young, *The Life and Letters of J. Alden Weir* (New York: Kennedy Graphics, Inc., Da Capo Press, 1971), 200–201.

2.   David F. Ransom, Consultant, "National Register of Historic Places Inventory-Nomination Form for the J. Alden Weir Farm in Ridgefield, Connecticut," edited by John Herzan, National Register Coordinator, January 16, 1983. Copy at Weir Farm National Historic Site; Blueprints, Mr. and Mrs. Sperry Andrews; Keith N. Morgan, *Charles A. Platt: The Artist as Architect* (Cambridge, MA.: M.I.T. Press), 242 (Entry in list of works only, no discussion); Weir Farm National Historic Site, Historic Structure Report (in progress). Marie Carden, Coordinator of Historic Structure Report, "Summary Chronology of Weir House, Weir Farm National Historic Site," rev. August 5, 1994, Weir Farm National Historic Site. These issues will be discussed in Volume I of the "Weir Farm Historic Structure Report," which is forthcoming.

There is surprisingly little correspondence in the Weir manuscript collections about these major architectural changes. There are no additional architectural drawings for the Weir remodellings in the Platt collection at the Avery Architectural Library, Columbia University, and this collection contains no correspondence for any project. In general, Platt correspondence survives only when descendants of his clients have kept it.

3.   Morgan, *Platt*, 5–23. Interestingly, a Charles C. Burlingham wrote unpublished reminiscences of Platt, but this Burlingham knew Platt as early as the late 1880s.

4.   Ibid., 24–52.

5.   Ibid., 242–245.

6.   About 1910–1911, Platt wrote Weir thanking him for "your [nice?] cheque. The whiskey bill is in N.Y. I'll return your balance when I get back next week. I haven't got your letter No. 1 here. . . . I'm sorry I cannot come over to Windham." (Charles A. Platt to Weir, August 30, (1910?), AAA, Reel 125.) It is tempting to interpret any letter from Platt as relating to an architectural commission (in this case possibly the 1911 dining room addition), but it appears from the.context that Weir had simply sent Platt a check reimbursing him for whiskey that Platt had purchased.

7.   Weir to Ella, September 5, 1900, AAA, Reel 125.

8.   C. E. S. Wood to Weir, January 2, 1901, AAA, Reel 125.

9.   John F. Weir to daughter Edith, March 17, 1901, AAA, Reel 529.

10.   The terraces were definitely there when Doris and Sperry Andrews purchased the property in 1959. The Andrews believe the terraces were put in by Mahonri and Dorothy Young, but thus far documentation is lacking.

11.   Weir, Ella, and the three daughters travelled to London primarily to authenticate a painting by Luini that Percy Alden (the son of Weir's patroness) wanted to sell. There, the family visited John Singer Sargent and Whistler. They then went to France, visiting Mont-Saint-Michel, Chartres, and Paris, and then Weir went alone to Berlin (Young, *Life and Letters*, 201–204).

12.   Ibid., 205.

13.   Weir to C. E. S. Wood, November 30, 1902. Quoted in Young, *Life and Letters*, 217.

14.   Ibid., 206–209.

15.   Wilfred Von Glehn to J. Alden Weir, August 3, 1903, BYU. Also quoted in Young, *Life and Letters*, 206.

16.   Young, *Life and Letters*, 210–218. The originals of letters to and from Wood are at the Huntington Library in San Marino, California. This collection is almost certain to include Weir/Wood letters not on microfilm at AAA, since the Wood Collection is very large and has also been added to recently.

17.   Weir to C. E. S. Wood, June 29, 1903, AAA, Reel 125. By mid-August, Weir had finished haying. See Wood to C. E. S. Wood, August 15, 1903, AAA, Reel 125.

18.   C. E. S. Wood to Weir, July 21 or 24, 1903, AAA, Reel 125.

19.   Weir to C. E. S. Wood, August 15, 1903, AAA, Reel 125.

20.   Ryder to Weir, August 8, 1903, AAA, Reel 125.

21.   Young, *Life and Letters*, 220–221.

22.   These daylilies may be *Hemerocallis fulva*, a type of daylily that blooms in July and that, although native to Europe and Asia, frequently naturalizes itself along New England roadsides. See Liberty Hyde Bailey, *The Standard Cyclopedia of Horticulture* (New York: MacMillan, 1928 edition), 1457. We would like to thank Phyllis Andersen of the Arnold Arboretum for her assistance in locating this information.

23.   Ryder to Weir, June 30, 1904, AAA, Reel 125.

24.   John F. Weir to Weir, July 26, 1904, AAA, 125.

25.   John F. Weir to Weir, August 11, 1904, AAA, Reels 125 and 529.

26.   Ryder to Weir, September 22, 1904, AAA. Also quoted in Young, *Life and Letters*, 223.

27.   Weir Farm National Historic Site, Scrapbook - Blue - Vol. 4 - Pages, 300.

28.   Quoted in Susan G. Larkin, "A Curious Aggregation: J. Alden Weir and His Circle," in *J. Alden Weir: A Place of His Own* (Storrs, Connecticut: The William Benton Museum of Art and the University of Connecticut, Storrs, 1991), 75–76.

29.   Larkin, "A Curious Aggregation," 74–75.

30.   Weir's "The Shadow of My Studio" and Hassam's "Weir's Garden" were painted about the same time. It is remotely possible that the gate/fence construction in Hassam's watercolor is part of the enclosed garden, although in Weir's painting the only visible gate is much simpler in style.

31.   Hassam to Weir, July 7, 1906, BYU and AAA, Reel 125.

32.   Celia Thaxter, *An Island Garden*, illustrated by Childe Hassam (Ithaca, New York: Bullbrier Press, 1985, reprint of 1894 edition). The book was written in 1893, and Thaxter died in 1894.

    See also David Park Curry, *Childe Hassam: An Island Garden Revisited* (Denver: Denver Art Museum in association with W. W. Norton & Company, New York and London, 1990).

33.   Childe Hassam to Weir from Appledore House, August 14, 1906, BYU.

34.   Postcard from Hassam to Weir, August 23, 1909, BYU. In 1913, Weir wrote to Wood about Hassam: "He now goes to the Isles of Shoals where it seems to fascinate him and where there is no well to fall into. He is a great lover of swimming and although the weather is as cold as the Arctic he revels in it." (Weir to Wood, nd [1913], quoted in Young, *Life and Letters*, 243.)

35.   See Ellen Paul, "History and Documentation of Weir Farm" (1990), 6–7, 12. Weir paid off his 1886 mortgage on the Weir Farm in 1907, which may have been another factor in his decision to purchase the Webb Farm at this time.

    See also Memo from Maureen Phillips to Gay Vietzke, May 9, 1994, Weir Farm National Historic Site.

36.   It is also discussed fully in the Historic Structures Report for the Burlingham property.

37.   Young, *Life and Letters*, 224–228.

38.   Weir to Wood, May 24, 1907, AAA.

39.   Weir to Wood, September 12, 1910, AAA. Also quoted in Young, *Life and Letters*, 227.

40.   Weir to Wood from Windham, November 13, 1910. Also quoted in Young, *Life and Letters*, 227–228.

41.   Portrait: "The Adams Children: The Farmer's Two Boys," n.d. (1910?). Scrapbook 5/472; AAA, Reel 126, Frame 1110.

42.   The ice house/chicken house is discussed in chapter III of this report.

43.   "Weir Farm Historic Painting Sites Trail" (Ridgefield and Wilton, CT: Weir Farm Heritage Trust and National Park Service, 1994), Site 10.

44.   The bindery/etching room is discussed in chapter III of this report.

45.   Young, *Life and Letters*, 228–235.

46.   National Register of Historic Places, Inventory-Nomination Form, J. Alden Weir Farm. See Marie L. Carden and Richard C. Crisson, "Weir Farm Historic Structures Report, Weir Farm National Historic Site." Volume I: "The Site and Weir Complex" (Lowell, Massachusetts: Building Conservation Branch, Cultural Resources Center, Northeast Region, National Park Service, U. S. Department of the Interior, 1995), 97-104.

47.   Weir to Wood, May 21, 1911, AAA, Reel 125.

48.   Weir to Wood, August 5, 1911, AAA, Reel 125.

49.   Weir to Wood, January 23, 1911, AAA, Reel 125; also Weir to Wood, December 1, 1912, AAA, Reel 125.

50.   Information on the present condition of the chestnut trees is from Bob Fox, Weir Farm National Historic Site.

51.   Weir to Wood, July 2, 1912, AAA.

52.   Young, *Life and Letters*, 243.

53.   Weir to Wood, March 31, 1912, AAA, Reel 125.

54.   Weir to Wood, November 15, 1912, AAA, Reel 125.

55.   Weir to Wood, December 1, 1912, AAA, Reel 125.

56.   Young, *Life and Letters*, 237-240; Doreen Bolger Burke, *J. Alden Weir: An American Impressionist* (Newark: University of Delaware Press, 1983), 299.

57.   Weir to Ella, May 1913, AAA.

58.   Young, *Life and Letters*, 242-243.

59.   Weir to Dorothy and Cora, October 19, 1913, AAA, Reel 125.

60.   Weir to Dorothy, March 25, 1915, and Weir to Ella, April 23, 1915, AAA.

61.   Weir to Dorothy, May 20, 1915, AAA.

62.   Weir to John F. Weir, June 2, 1915, AAA.

63.   Young, *Life and Letters*, 250-251.

64.   Weir to Wood, October 23, 1915, AAA.

65.   Weir to Wood, December 29, 1915, AAA.

66.   Weir to Ella Baker, July 14, 1886, AAA, Reel 125.

Nothing in the flower garden had bloomed by midsummer. Weir attributed this to the fact that they had not sown seeds at the right time, which suggests annuals.

67.   Letter from Joseph Pearson to Dorothy Weir Young, quoted in Young, *Life and Letters,* 193–194.

Remy is first mentioned in the Weir correspondence in 1889. The last mention of him by name is in 1904. However, he may have stayed until 1907, when Weir was again looking for a farmer. It is quite likely that Remy was responsible for the lattice and gate construction visible in the Hassam 1903 watercolor of Weir's garden.

68.   Ibid. Weir wrote to Ella about the early flower garden and says that he wished they had her advice.

69.   Mahonri Sharp (Bill) Young, interview with Cynthia Zaitzevsky, May 15, 1994, Anna Weir Ely Smith, informal telephone interview with Cynthia Zaitzevsky, August 12, 1994.

70.   Mahonri Sharp (Bill) Young, interview with Cynthia Zaitzevsky, May 15, 1994.

71.   Olmsted Center for Landscape Preservation, *Historic Landscape Assessment of Weir Garden, Weir Farm National Historic Site*, prepared for the Weir Farm National Historic Site in collaboration with the Ridgefield Garden Club, April 1994.

72.   According to the Olmsted Center Report (23), this photograph may be somewhat later than the other ca. 1915 photographs in Scrapbook No. 22. All plant identifications given in this paragraph were made by Dr. Peter Del Tredici of the Arnold Arboretum and are in the Olmsted Center Report (16–23).

73.   Caro and George Page Ely were not married until June 7, 1916, although they could have been engaged or dating in 1915 (Weir to John, April 8, 1916, AAA, Reel 126, Frame 0126).

Their daughter, Anna Weir Ely Smith, has suggested that the group was playing charades, which was popular with the family and their friends. Anna Weir Ely Smith, informal telephone interview with Cynthia Zaitzevsky, August 12, 1994.

74.   Weir to Wood, January 14, 1916, AAA.

75.   Young, *Life and Letters,* 256.

76.   Weir to John F. Weir, October 19, 1917, AAA.

77.   Anna Weir Ely Smith, informal telephone interview with Cynthia Zaitzevsky, August 12, 1994. Follow-up telephone interview with Mahonri Sharp (Bill) Young, by Cynthia Zaitzevsky, August 10, 1994, There is a photograph of the birdbath at Brigham Young University. (Information from Weir Farm National Historic Site).

78.   See Peter Benes, ed., *The Farm: Proceedings of the 1986 Dublin Seminar for New England Folklife* (Boston: Boston University, 1988). The articles in this publication focus on New England farms of the late 18th and early 19th centuries. Extensive bibliographies are given of agricultural titles, farm studies publications, and farm diaries and account books.

79.   Scrapbook 2:11 AS-LE, 45-b.

80.   Weir to Ella, May 9, 1913, AAA, Reel 125, Frame 1321.

81.   Weir to Ella, June 21, 1916, AAA, Reel 126, Frame 0127;   Weir to Ella, July 22, 1916, AAA, Reel 126, Frame 0151.

82.   Weir to John F. Weir, December 9, 1916, AAA, Reel 126, 0167;   Weir to John F. Weir, Spring 1917, AAA, Reel 126, Frame 00194.

83.   Weir to Wood, November 4, 1918, AAA.

84.   Weir to Wood, June 1918, AAA, Reel 126, Frame 0248;   Weir to Wood, December 2, 1918, AAA, Reel 126, Frame 0302.

85.   Records at the Ridgefield Town Hall, File #2100, J. Alden Weir, dated 1920, Folder #1. Notes on these records and those cited in notes 81 through the end of this chapter were gathered by Gay Vietzke in December 1992 and are at Weir Farm National Historic Site.

86.   Records at the Ridgefield Town Hall, File #2100, J. Alden Weir, dated 1920, Folder #2. This appears to be the first mention of the "bindery." The "other shed" may well refer to the wagon shed, probably built between 1900 and 1915. See Maureen K. Phillips and Marie L. Carden, "Weir Farm Historic Structures Report, Weir Farm National Historic Site, Wilton, Connecticut." Volume II-A: "Weir Farm Outbuildings" (Lowell, Massachusetts: Building Conservation Branch, Northeast Cultural Resources Center, National Park Service, U.S. Department of the Interior, 1995), 239.

87.   Ibid., Folder #1.

88.   Town of Wilton, Town Clerk's Office, Tax Records, Grand Lists, 1920, under "Estate of J. Alden Weir."

89.   Young, Life and Letters, 258–260.

90.   Ibid., 260.

91.   Maureen K. Phillips and Marie L. Carden, "Weir Farm Historic Structures Report, Weir Farm National Historic Site, Wilton, Connecticut." Volume II-A: "Weir Farm Outbuildings" (Lowell, Massachusetts: Building Conservation Branch, Northeast Cultural Resources Center, National Park Service, U.S. Department of the Interior, 1995), 107-130, 149-189, 203-212, 221-244.

CHAPTER III: THE ELLA WEIR/DOROTHY WEIR; MAHONRI YOUNG/DOROTHY WEIR YOUNG; AND MAHONRI YOUNG OWNERSHIPS, 1920 – 1957

The years 1920 through 1957 constitute one period in the history of Weir Farm, but this thirty-seven-year span falls naturally into three distinct phases. The years 1920 through 1930 cover the time when Dorothy Weir lived at the farm during the summer with her stepmother Ella, who died in 1930. Dorothy Weir's marriage to sculptor Mahonri M. Young spanned the years 1931 through 1947, when the Youngs spent their summers at the farm but also spent considerable time there in the off-season as well. Between Dorothy's death in 1947 and his own in November 1957, Young continued to use the farm but probably less frequently than before. Because of the Mahonri Young correspondence and drawings, the years from 1931 through 1957 are much better documented than the first (1920–1930) period.

ELLA WEIR/DOROTHY WEIR, 1920–1930

After Weir's death in 1919 his widow, Ella Baker Weir, and his three daughters Caro, Dorothy, and Cora inherited his estate. In 1922 Caro and Cora transferred their rights in Weir's Branchville property to Ella and Dorothy. In return, they received rights in the Baker family farm in Windham, Connecticut.[1]

Evidence concerning the use of Weir Farm in the years immediately following Weir's death is very fragmentary. In the early 1920s, Ella seems to have spent the early part of each summer in Branchville and Augusts in Windham. After Weir's death, Ella supervised the running of the farm in Branchville.[2] As a young woman, she was interested in and apparently skilled at flower gardening, as evidenced by a letter from Weir to his then sister-in-law in 1886.[3] This was an interest that she seems to have sustained in later life since, during the 1920s, she and Dorothy both gardened in the Secret Garden and elsewhere on the property. Their farmer also worked in the flower and vegetable gardens as well as being responsible for the farm crops.[4] However, although Ella was not well in the last few years of her life, the state of her health during the decade as a whole is unknown. No photographs of Weir Farm have been located that can be dated to the 1920s.

Among the few pieces of information that have emerged thus far concerning Weir Farm during the 1920s is the date of the ash tree formerly located just outside the northeast corner of the flower garden, which was removed in spring 1994 because of disease. This ash, on ring count, proved to be 73 years old, meaning that it would have been planted in 1921.[5] However, the possibility also exists that the ash was self-sown. This is quite likely since it would not have been logical to plant a shade tree so close to the flower garden.

During the 1920s, Dorothy Weir is, of course, the other individual who played a part with respect to farming, gardening, and other landscape activities. By the late 1920s, Dorothy had met Mahonri Young and invited him from time to him to visit her in Branchville. Among the few records of events on the farm during these years are two drawings by Young, illustrated in figures 71 and 72, which will be discussed later in this chapter.

At this point, it is useful to summarize Dorothy's life and background. Dorothy was born in 1890, the second daughter and third child of J. Alden Weir and Anna Baker Weir. Of the three daughters, Dorothy was the only one who actually studied under Weir. Her best work was in oils and watercolors, and she was particularly interested in still life. She also did some woodblock printing, mostly between about 1910 and 1930. After her marriage to Mahonri M. Young in 1931, she was probably less active as an artist.[6] The Museum of Art at Brigham Young University in Provo, Utah, has a sizeable collection of Dorothy's works.[7] Although her still-life paintings may depict flowers from the garden at Weir Farm, none of Dorothy's paintings or drawings at Brigham Young shows the Weir Farm landscape. Dorothy devoted much of her mature life to collecting her father's letters and writing his biography, which was published in 1960 after Dorothy's death.[8] She also undertook to catalog all of his works of art, a huge project which her sister Cora took over after her death and which has never been completed or published.[9]

Dorothy's husband has left a delightful account of Dorothy's life as an artist. Written to accompany a posthumous exhibition of her work, it reads in part:

> Dorothy Weir was an artist all her life. But how could she have escaped? Her artistic inheritance was not confined to her father, the renowned painter, J. Alden Weir. Her grandfather, Robert Walter Weir, was for over forty years Professor of Drawing at West Point. . . . Dorothy's uncle, John Ferguson Weir, was a painter of international reputation, a sculptor and the founder of the Art School at Yale. . . . On her mother's side her uncle Rufus Baker, who lived most of his life in Europe was a painter. . . .

> Dorothy began, while still a child, making drawings and watercolors; sometimes along side her father. A graduate of The Brearley, she worked at the Art Students League, and studied drawing with Mrs. Kenyon Cox.

> She won several prizes with her oils and exquisite woodblock prints, in the Japanese method, not in the Japanese manner.

134

When I first knew her she showed me her pictures in oil, and her woodblock prints, but no water colors. On a trip we took through the South and the Southwest (stopping at Tucson for ten days) we visited St. Xavier del Bac and were charmed with its setting, its beautiful and interesting interiors and the exterior views of the Cathedral, with the vast and very characteristic landscape.

Dorothy fell in love with the interior; so much so that she got out her watercolors and went every day, from Tucson, out to St. Xavier, where she—having been given permission by the Fathers—installed herself and commenced the interior of St. Xavier del Bac. This was not done in one sitting, but was the result of many days of concentrated work. The result you may see in the exhibition. It is her first successful watercolor. . . .

In Santa Barbara she became fascinated with the fruit growing on the trees. The result was the not quite completed study of lemons. . . . Then in Salt Lake she became interested in the native flora and made of herself quite a botanist. She did several studies of native plants and flowers in oil and the two small studies of roses in watercolor, one belonging Mrs. Burlingham and the other which she gave to my mother.

It was at Salt Lake that she achieved her first landscape—"Over the Valley From Capitol Hill," which I have always considered a remarkable accomplishment. . . .

Back at Branchville, Connecticut, she took up her flower studies again, this time in watercolor. One of the first came near to becoming a catastrophe. We had at that time, an amaryllis plant which lived in the cellar in the winter, and out-of-doors in the spring and summer. One late winter it decided to bloom and put forth a resplendent flower, brilliant red in color. Dorothy decided to do a water color of it. Taking a piece of mounted paper she started it, about life size.

As the view from our upstairs windows was very lovely in new and still falling snow, I decided to try a water color myself. The snow stopped falling so I took what I'd done and went down stairs to find out how Dorothy was making out. I found her in a terrible state. She had laid out her study and was fighting the amaryllis. Now you don't fight watercolor — that is, if you're wise. . . .

As spring came on she became interested in the flowers out-of-doors and tried one of a spread of dandelions growing by a stream. But it wasn't a go. Then she did the rest of the pictures you see. There was no more losing the temper; but a quiet self-contained confidence; no technical problems seemed to thwart her; she calmly surmounted them.[10]

The painting of dandelions by the stream is not among the works of art by Dorothy Weir Young at Brigham Young University, although the BYU collection includes at least two of her still lifes done at Weir Farm. These were probably of flowers that were grown in the garden: a watercolor, "Irises in Glass, Branchville," not dated, and another watercolor, "Two Poppies, Branchville," also not dated.[11] Around 1915, irises grew in both the Secret Garden and the small round flower bed in the lawn to the west of the house. See figures 58, 61, and 65 in chapter II, in all of which iris foliage appears. Poppies could have been grown as well, although by midsummer when all of the Secret Garden photographs seem to have been taken, poppy foliage has died down and is no longer visible.

DOROTHY WEIR YOUNG/MAHONRI M. YOUNG, 1931–1947

Introduction

As an artist, Mahonri M. Young is of considerable interest in his own right. In addition, his occupancy of the Weir House for nearly twenty-seven years is a significant period in the history of Weir Farm. Young was born in Salt Lake City on August 9, 1877, the first child of Agnes Mackintosh and Mahonri Moriancumer Young and the grandson of Mormon pioneer Brigham Young. As a new baby, he was taken to the Beehive House, Brigham Young's Salt Lake City residence, to be blessed by his grandfather, who died on August 29, 1877. Brigham Young always encouraged the fine arts, including theater and architecture, and was himself a skilled craftsman in carpentry and painting, influences that were passed along to the young Mahonri by his father. (Young's father died in 1884 but nonetheless left an indelible impression on his young son.) The boy's first home was the Deseret Wooden Mill near Salt Lake City, where he first developed an interest in observing men at work, a theme that became a constant in his sculpture and drawings.[12]

Young completed grade school in Salt Lake City but dropped out of high school after only one day. Eventually he and his good friend Jack Sears obtained jobs as artists with the *Salt Lake Tribune*. By fall 1899, he had saved enough money to undertake serious study of art in New York City. Between 1899 and 1901, his studies were focused primarily on drawing and illustration at the Art Students League, where he took classes with Kenyon Cox and others. Young wanted to study sculpture (and later stated that he would have if Augustus Saint-Gaudens had been teaching), but sculpture classes were more expensive, and in any case, illustration seemed a more reliable source of future income. In 1901 he travelled to Paris for a two-year course of study at the Académies Julien, Colarossi, and Delecluse. After a brief visit home in 1903, he went back to Paris for a further two years of "post-graduate" study, primarily on his own, and travel through Italy. He also began etching. At some point in his return trip to Europe, Young met Gertrude and Leo Stein.[13] On his return to the United States, he taught sculpture in New York City for one year before returning to Salt Lake City, where he began to establish himself as a sculptor. In 1907 he married Cecilia Sharp, with whom he had two children, Cecilia Agnes Young (Lay), born in 1908, and Mahonri Sharp (Bill) Young, born in 1911.[14] Cecilia Sharp Young died in 1917.

Although he was never an observant Mormon, the Mormon Church was a source of major commissions for Young, beginning with sculptures of church founder Joseph Smith and his brother Hyrum Smith in 1907.[15] In the same year, Young began sketches for the Sea Gull Monument, but money was not forthcoming for some time. This monument commemorates an event in Mormon history that took place in 1848, when the Mormon pioneers' crops were threatened by an infestation of crickets. However, masses of sea gulls, who live in Utah because of Great Salt Lake, came and destroyed the crickets. In

136

1913, the Sea Gull Monument was dedicated; it stands in Temple Square, Salt Lake City, not far from the sculptures of Joseph and Hyrum Smith.[16] Figure 70 is a photograph of Mahonri Young standing beside the base of the Sea Gull Monument in 1936. The picture was taken on the trip described by Young, when Dorothy painted the interior of San Xavier del Bac, Tucson, Arizona; "Over the Valley from Capitol Hill," Salt Lake City; lemons in Santa Barbara, etc.[17] Young's masterpiece, the This-Is-the-Place Monument, which was largely created in his Branchville studio for a spectacular site in Emigration Canyon, Salt Lake City, belongs to a later phase of his career and will be discussed in that context.

Young apparently first met J. Alden Weir sometime around 1910. His contacts with Weir are best described in his own words:

> The first time I saw J. Alden Weir was in Durand Ruel's Galleries in East 36 St. They had moved from their galleries on Fifth Avenue, temporarily, and had taken a brownstone on the north side of 36 St. There they held exhibitions and it was in one of these exhibitions of Renoir's work that I first saw him with Childe Hassam. There was no mistaking either of them. My memory of them and of the rooms, fitted up as galleries, is visual; I can still see them; I can see their gray overcoats, their slow movements as they looked at the pictures. They were not looking at them with any great interest or enthusiasm. In fact, I felt at the time that they didn't approve; and yet they were the outstanding American impressionist painters, now that Theodore Robinson and Twachtman were dead. It was rather surprising that they showed so little interest, as, in that show were most of Renoir's greatest and loveliest masterpieces. Most of the great pictures from the Durand Ruel House were there. If I should make a list of the ones there exposed it would contain most of his outstanding works which unfortunately have since been scattered to the ends of the earth.

> When I entered the galleries, Weir and Hassam were already there. At the time, they were standing in a sort of cross hall between the entrance and the exhibition rooms. Hassam was standing up very straight expressing silent disapproval. Weir was leaning on a cane and that was the first intimation I had that he was lame. He walked with a very decided limp. He was, also, much older in appearance than I had expected from the portraits I had seen of him and from the descriptions I had heard. His face was seamed and drawn and impressed me as one who had bad health or had, otherwise, suffered.

> The next time I saw Weir, and I have no recollection of seeing him in between was at my first one-man show in New York at the Berlin Photograph Gallery on Madison Avenue in 1912. The gallery had only recently moved from their old quarters on 14th St., "up town" . . .

> Weir came to my show and looked at everything there. As he was leaving he stopped and spoke to me but the only thing I remember his saying was, after looking at some drawings of animals and birds, done in the zoo: "Do you know John Swan's drawings? I used to know him in Paris years ago." I distinctly remember his going out—again the memory is visual. I can still see the limp in his gait. He also said that he used to do animals himself.

> During the years after that first meeting I saw Mr. Weir often, at the Academy, the New Society, the Century and elsewhere. He was always kindness itself. He was always quite willing to talk;

137

Figure 70   Mahonri M. Young beside the base of the Sea Gull Monument, Salt Lake City.
                             Photograph, 1936 (Jack Sears Papers, Special Collections, Lee Library, Brigham
                             Young University, Provo, Utah).

138

but he was no monologist. None of the talks were so interesting or so memorable as that last one recorded in another place a quarter of a century ago.

I remember him at the National Academy opening one year when I had my group of Alkema on view. He was standing in line welcoming the visitors. When I introduced him to my wife (Cecilia Sharp Young) he was graciousness itself and asked me what I had exposed. As Alkema was only a few feet from where we stood he walked over to give it the once over. I tell this little incident as I am sure most of the younger painters and sculptors have had similar experiences. His friends ran the whole gamut of the art world. . . .

He worked to forward the understanding and appreciating of Theodore Robinson.

He was always interested in and ready to join any movement which seemed to him to promise the advancement of art. . . .

My one other meeting with him which stand[s] out like those early ones was when I had a show at Mrs. C. C. Rumsey's Gallery in 1919. Mrs. Rumsey had given me the use of the gallery and Mrs. Force had organized the show, which was very much in the nature of a retrospective. Weir came and looked over everything and picked out something he wanted; but here comes one of my greatest disappointment[s]. When he looked over his funds he felt he couldn't go through with the purchase. . . . But whatever the cause the disappointment I felt very keenly. Had he bought the thing he had picked out I should have felt I had received equal approval with my friends Maurice Stern and Paul Manship.

No matter how friendly Weir always was to us then younger artists he never introduced us to any of his three charming daughters. We never met any of them until after he died.

But it was because I enjoyed the most beautiful, the finest, the most talented of them, Dorothy, in 1931. . . .

Emil Carlsen said to me one day . . . that Twachtman was the more perfect artist but Weir was the greater man. . . . [18]

Young also left an account of how he met Dorothy Weir and how their relationship developed, which is quoted here in part:

Duncan Phillips was organizing the Phillips Memorial Gallery; he had invited a number of friends and associates to a dinner at the Coffee House. They were to constitute a board of directors. It was at this dinner that I first met Dorothy Weir. . . . I can see her now as she came up the stairs into the room. She was wearing a dress with a long and rather full skirt. She was holding the skirt up as she stepped up the last step. . . . I immediately recognized her as Alden Weir's daughter. Her nervous laugh as she came into the room, I can still hear. . . . I . . . remember that I was not introduced, but introduced myself. This, in after years, was one of our little jokes. I always insisted I "picked her up." We had only a short talk together when the cocktails arrived and the conversation became general. . . .

It might be just as well before going further to say that the next day after that dinner at the Coffee House I told my children that I had met Mr. Weir's daughter and in answer to Agnes' inquiry as to how she looked I said she was very like her father but not quite so handsome. I also told them that she was the only woman I knew I would think of marrying. This I also told Gifford Beal. But, what was the use! I was the father of two young children to provide for and no income. And she was a wealthy lady living on Park Ave. with a stepmother to whom she was devoted. She was also the only daughter still at home. The other two had married.[19]

According to the records of the Phillips Collection, this dinner must have been the first full meeting of the Committee on Scope and Plan for the Phillips Memorial Gallery, which took place at the Coffee House Club in New York City on December 12, 1921. Dorothy Weir and Mahonri Young were both members of this committee, which seems to have met only a few times before Duncan Phillips decided he didn't need it.[20]

Young had several other brief meetings with Dorothy in New York:

Then I went to Paris with Aggie and Bill and stayed two and a half years. She came over with Mamma and Tina Fisher. Mrs. Weir took us to a small, but very good restaurant on the right bank. I was impressed with her familiarity with French ways and the French language. She spoke it like a Parisian. At that time I did not know that she had spent many years as a girl and a young woman in France and in Europe.

One day I met Dorothy in the Louvre by appointment and had a most delightful time with the pictures. I told her that I would take her to the Dome but I never did and she went back home soon afterwards. She never forgave me for that. When I came back to N. Y. I saw her several times and then went to Hollywood to work on the Fox Lot. . . .

After returning to America I saw much more of her. . . .

One night, going home in the taxi, I put my arm around Dorothy and kissed her. She was startled and protested but assured me I must see her again.

There were trips to Branchville with friends, with the Freddy Cunninghams, the McCallisters, the [?] Palmers and others. Delightful house parties where we all took a hand at cooking. . . .

There were picnics down to the ponds, where we cooked our supper and rides in the boat on the pond. Sometimes we fished but not often.[21]

Unfortunately, there is no indication of precisely where by the pond they cooked their suppers.

Young seems to have resumed his friendship/courtship with Dorothy in the mid-1920s. However, the first dated example of the many drawings and prints that Young ultimately made in Branchville is illustrated in figure 71: "Trench and Excavation for Well House, April 12, 1927." It has not been determined which well house this might have been; thus the location of the drawing is unclear. In figure 72, we see another early drawing: "Made from Weir's House at Branchville, Conn., May 30, 1928." This drawing shows a meadow with low trees and a stream, but its exact orientation cannot be determined. Another drawing made by Young during a visit to the farm in March 1930 is illustrated in figure 73. In this drawing, preparations are being made for spring vegetable planting in the field to the south of the caretaker's house. Visible in the background is the south facade of the caretaker's house. Only one letter survives from the Youngs' courtship, written by Dorothy in 1929:

> Dear Mahonri,
>
> > It was awfully nice to hear from you. How wonderful you are to get so much work accomplished. You must feel cheered. Heavens, 17 pieces in 13 weeks seems like a miracle to me. How do you do it? What *are* they? . . .[22]

Apparently, Mrs. Weir was not enthusiastic about the prospect of Young and Dorothy marrying, and her health also deteriorated in the late 1920s, requiring attention from Dorothy. For these reasons, the marriage did not take place until after Ella's death, which occurred on December 27, 1930.[23] George Page Ely and Mahonri Young had become acquainted as members of the Century Club, and at Christmas time 1930, the Elys gave a party to introduce him to the rest of the family.[24] On January 25, the Elys announced the engagement of Dorothy and Mahonri, only two days after Young announced the engagement of his daughter to Oliver Ingraham Lay.[25] Dorothy and Mahonri were married on February 17, 1931, in the Elys' apartment at 1120 Fifth Avenue, New York City, with the Rev. Dr. Donald Aldrich of the Church of the Ascension performing the ceremony.[26] (Weir and Anna had been married at the Church of the Ascension.) At the time of the marriage, Young was fifty-four and Dorothy forty-one. An undated photograph of Mahonri and Dorothy Weir Young standing in front of the Weir House is illustrated in figure 74. The Youngs spent their honeymoon in Europe but seem to have begun serious work on the Branchville property as soon as they returned home.

In the early years of their marriage, the Youngs continued to spend winters in the apartment at 1192 Park Avenue, New York City, which had been Ella's and Dorothy's winter home. (Eventually they relocated to an apartment at 24 Gramercy Park where Young lived until his death.) Beginning in 1934, Young was an instructor at the Art Students League. Dorothy and Mahonri intended, however, to spend much of the spring and fall and also occasional periods in the winter on the Branchville farm, which Dorothy had inherited as sole owner. (The Webb Farm now belonged to Cora as sole owner and was no longer part of Weir Farm.) In the summer of 1931, Dorothy had both heat and electricity installed in the Weir house, and the first Christmas of their marriage was spent at the farm. Young's most pressing need, however, was for a studio of a size that could accommodate large-scale sculpture. In 1932 he had a studio for himself constructed from designs by his son-in-law, Oliver Lay, adjacent to Weir's studio. Lay was

141

Figure 71   Mahonri M. Young, "Trench and Excavation for Well House, Branchville, April
                   12, 1927," graphite drawing (Museum of Art, Brigham Young University, Provo,
                   Utah, No. 832080240).

Made from Weir's house

Figure 72   Mahonri M. Young, "Made From Weir's House, Branchville, Conn., May 30, 1928," ink drawing (Museum of Art, Brigham Young University, Provo, Utah, No. 832071066).

Figure 73   Mahonri M. Young, "Branchville, March 29, 1930," ink drawing (Museum of
                   Art, Brigham Young University, Provo, Utah, No. 832070235).

Figure 74   Mahonri M. Young and Dorothy Weir Young in front of Weir house.
                   Photograph, n.d. (ca. 1940) (Mahonri M. Young Papers, Special Collections, Lee
                   Library, Brigham Young University, Provo, Utah).

145

a recent graduate of the Columbia University School of Architecture and son of the noted landscape architect Charles Downing Lay. Oliver Lay was also a landscape architect. During the Depression, he worked for the New York City Parks Department. He was later a site planner for York and Sawyer, a New York architectural firm specializing in hospitals, especially Veterans' Hospitals.[27] The contractor was Charles Meyer of Charles Meyer, Builders, Wilton, Connecticut.[28]

In 1932 Young made a pen and ink drawing that was later exhibited under the title "Excavation for Mr. Young's Studio," but which now appears to be lost.[29] For the next twenty-five years, the studio was not only Young's workspace but also his retreat and the place where he felt most at home on the farm. This was especially true of the upstairs balcony, where Young kept his library and wrote and sketched.[30] According to his son, Young "spent most of his life in a studio. When he wasn't working, he would think in it (in a creative way)."[31]

At the same time that Young's studio was being constructed, the east entrance hall of the Weir house was converted into a library with built-in cabinets and bookcases.[32] The new library was Dorothy's workspace, where she worked on her biography of her father.[33]

Undoubtedly the most valuable written source for the development of Weir Farm under Young's ownership is Young's correspondence with his boyhood friend Jack Sears, who was then on the faculty of the University of Utah. These letters, now in the Jack Sears Papers in the Lee Library at Brigham Young University, range in date from 1932 through 1956. Additionally, many of Young's letters include, below the signature, either sketches of the farm or a sketch self-portrait in profile. Sears' wife Florence was an art dealer, apparently specializing in prints, who handled Young's etchings, etc., and there are also a few letters from Dorothy Weir Young to Florence in the Sears papers. Sears' letters to Mahonri were returned to Sears by Young's heirs after his death; their present whereabouts is unknown.[34] On August 8, 1932, the day before his birthday, Young wrote to Sears:

> Tomorrow is the fateful day. 55 and not well started yet. But at last I've got a studio large enough to do anything I want to do in paint or clay. Dorothy has her Father's place here in Conn. about 50 miles from N.Y.C. It's a farm with horses and cows in it with a pond big enough for a boat and a lot of poor fields and a great deal of timber. We can stay here from early spring until late in the fall. Dorothy has put in electricity and heat so it's fine even in midwinter. If I ever have a big thing to do again, I will do it here even if I have to stay all winter. The Studio is finished, but there have been a lot of things to do before I can get to work. So far I have made a sketch or two and played on a large canvas with a subject I saw last fall in Danbury Fair. I can't finish it until I see the fair again. . . .
>
> Agnes and her husband are staying with us and Bill and his girl were here until recently but week before last they got married and are now in Paris where they expect to stay for a year or maybe

two. Bill got through Dartmouth with highest honors in three years but he has to wait for his degree until the four years are up. The Powers that be allowed him to spend the fourth year in Paris where he is expected to attend the Sorbonne.

We may go over and see them next year for a short time. . . .

I was pleased to get the award at Los Angeles; and frankly I like being written up on the Sports Page. . . .[35]

About four years later, Young had "a big thing to do again." The commission for the This-Is-The-Place Monument, which had been under discussion since at least 1920, finally began to move forward in 1936, when the Youngs were visiting Salt Lake City. However, money was to come from both the Mormon Church and the Utah State Legislature, both of which continued to move very slowly. Young's preliminary work was all done under provisional contract, including the large-scale model, which he completed in Connecticut. The final work in granite and bronze was also done in his studio at the farm.[36] For This-Is-The-Place, Young had an assistant, Spiro Anagonos, who lived on Nod Hill Road.[37] While this monumental piece was in progress, the Youngs spent much of the winter in Connecticut although they always maintained their New York City residence. Probably as relaxation from this very demanding sculptural work, Young produced many drawings of the farm during the fall and winter months.

After Weir's death and throughout the Young ownership, his studio was left as it was and continued to house many of his paintings.[38] Figure 75 is a photograph of Weir Farm dating from about 1942. Taken probably in late fall or early winter from the second story of the chicken house, it provides an almost panoramic view of the grounds immediately to the north of the house. From left to right, we can see the barn, the north elevation of the house, Weir's studio, and the Mahonri Young studio with a supply of firewood piled beside it. In the foreground on the righthand side are a large haystack, Mahonri Young (who looks almost diminutive in this context), and a bit of the eastern end of the Secret Garden. This panorama is one of the very few extant photographs of Weir Farm during the Young ownership.

Fortunately, as observed above, Young produced an abundance of drawings, prints, and paintings of the site, although not all of these are dated, and in many, especially the farming scenes, the exact orientation is difficult to determine. Several drawings by Young, primarily of agricultural subjects, are illustrated in this chapter, even though the exact locations cannot now be identified. They are included because they give an excellent sense of the agricultural ambience and actual farming activities at Weir Farm and (in some cases) at neighboring properties. Furthermore, Weir Farm National Historic Site is a recent National Park Service acquisition, and new photographs and other documentation are continually coming to light. It is possible that at some point in the future the locations of these drawings can be identified precisely.

147

Figure 75   View from chicken house, Weir Farm, showing the barn, north elevation of
                   house, Weir studio, Young studio, Mahonri M. Young, and a corner of the Secret
                   Garden. Photograph, ca. 1942 (WFNHS-HP No. 150).

Figure 76 is an undated painting of the Weir Studio by Young, that shows it looking very much as it does today except that the great northern red oak *(Quercus rubra)* at the front is slightly smaller than it is now.[39] Another drawing dating from about 1937, which shows the Young studio, a corner of Weir's studio, the toolshed, and the Youngs' setter, Hank, is illustrated in figure 77.[40] In the foreground is a small vegetable garden with a grape trellis at its northern edge.[41] Figure 78 is a Young watercolor done ca. 1938 that shows a close-up view of the tool shed with its door open and gardening implements visible. Part of the lattice can also be seen, with plants, possibly a grapevine, growing on it. Figure 79, an undated drawing of the well near Pelham Lane, shows that the well's wooden superstructure or canopy, which also appears in figures 29 and 63, lasted into the Young ownership.[42]

From the beginning of his time at Weir Farm, Young took great delight in the beauty not only of his and Dorothy's own acres but of the whole surrounding countryside. This is vividly demonstrated in a letter he wrote to Jack Sears in August 1937, which can almost certainly be related to a specific drawing:

> . . . . Our weather here has been marvelous for the last few days. Today is so beautiful it is hard to realize that it is the second of Aug. I walked down the road a little ways, this morning, just to enjoy it, with Hank the setter and, of course, a sketch book and the fountain pen (the red one). I made a little drawing of a stone wall, with a bar-way, and in the next field, an upstanding crop of fodder corn; beyond the corn some apple and other trees. I believe the drawing is the most successful one I have yet made of the growing corn. . . . [43]

The drawing that Young was so pleased with must be the one illustrated in figure 80. The details all fit, and the date is clearly 1937. The first part of the date is hard to read but seems to be August 2.

The Farm, Vegetable Garden, and Orchard

According to Mahonri Young's son, Bill Young, farming operations during his father's and Dorothy's occupancy were of the "Marie Antoinette" or gentleman-farmer type.[44] (Strictly speaking, this would undoubtedly be true of the farm during Weir's lifetime as well, but he and his brother John, with Paul Remy's help, at least tried valiantly to make it break even.) By the 1930s, little was sold from the farm except perhaps excess milk. Dorothy had apparently picked up her father's enthusiasm for agriculture and, after Ella's death, personally ran the farm, supervising the farmers. Dorothy also supervised the making of cream and cheeses, an activity she enjoyed, although she had a maid. The first of the farmers during the Youngs' ownership was a man called Bass, followed by the Gullys, who stayed on after Dorothy's death.[45] Extra men were undoubtedly hired as needed, especially during the harvest. (Several men appear in many of Young's farming scenes.)

149

Figure 76   Mahonri M. Young, Weir's studio, n.d. Oil on canvas board (Museum
                          of Art, Brigham Young University, Provo, Utah, No. 824000028).

150

Figure 77   Mahonri M. Young, Young and Weir studios, toolshed, vegetable garden, and
                             setter, Hank, n.d. (ca. 1937). Ink drawing (Museum of Art, Brigham Young
                             University, Provo, Utah, No. 832070201).

Figure 78   Mahonri M. Young, Toolshed, vegetable garden, and studios, n.d. (ca.
                   1938). Watercolor (Museum of Art, Brigham Young University, Provo, Utah,
                   No. 832010209).

152

Figure 79   Mahonri M. Young, The Wellhouse, Branchville, n.d. Ink drawing.
                   (Museum of Art, Brigham Young University, Provo, Utah, No. 832071108).

153

Figure 80   Mahonri M. Young, Corn field, Branchville (August 2?), 1937. Ink drawing
                   (Museum of Art, Brigham Young University, Provo, Utah, No. 832070176).

154

Into the early 1940s, the Youngs still used the pond for ice cutting, and chunks of the dark yellow ice were stored in the original Weir ice house (figure 43) in sawdust. Although the main house had been electrified in 1931, they continued to use a large icebox. However, during World War II the Youngs came to the farm more frequently, and the oldfashioned, spartan life lost some of its appeal. About 1941, they converted the old ice house into a chicken house and stopped cutting ice.[46] Most of the farm crops—primarily hay—were grown to feed the horses and cows. The hay was grown mostly in the area north of the house near the cemetery and in a triangular field on the east side of Nod Hill Road.[47] In addition to these, there was a vegetable garden for the use of the family. Parsnips were grown as a crop for at least one year. Between 1931 and 1947, pigs and poultry were kept on the farm as well as horses and cows.[48] During World War II, when meat was rationed, the pigs and other livestock were a welcome source of a scarce commodity. Mahonri's letters to Jack Sears describe some of the farming activities, which are also the subject of a great many of his drawings.

Two early drawings of the farm are shown in figures 81 and 82. Figure 81 shows scything on the farm in 1931; the location and orientation cannot be determined. In figure 82, two men are shingling the corncrib on July 26, 1932. There are numerous Young drawings of haying, but the locations of the fields are again hard to determine; see figure 83, for example, showing hay being harvested in June 1938. Another crop was corn, as seen in figure 84, dating from August 1939. Plowing at Weir Farm in 1939 is illustrated in figure 85, but again the location cannot be determined. Dorothy's active role in the running of the farm is further documented in a letter from Young to Sears in December 1939, when he wrote: "I hear Dorothy's voice coming in from a walk in the woods. She took the farmer and his son along to clean out one of the fields. I stayed to write to you."[49]

In 1940 the Addison Gallery of American Art at Phillips Academy, Andover, Massachusetts, held a major retrospective exhibition of Young's sculpture, paintings, watercolors, drawings, and prints.[50] Young was pleased with the Addison's permanent collection, which he described as "absolutely first class."[51] This exhibition, part of which travelled to the Kraushar Gallery in New York City, was a critical success and a very happy experience for Young.[52]

In the early 1940s, there are several more Young drawings showing agricultural activities. Figure 86 shows the Youngs' farmer Bass digging parsnips in November 1942. On January 6, 1943, Young wrote to Sears:

Figure 81   Mahonri M. Young, Scythe Cutters at Branchville, 1931. Ink drawing (Museum
                   of Art, Brigham Young University, Provo, Utah, No. 832070622).

156

Figure 82   Mahonri M. Young, "Shingling the corncrib, July 26, 1932," ink drawing
                   (Museum of Art, Brigham Young University, Provo, Utah, No. 832070224).

Figure 83   Mahonri M. Young, Haying at Branchville, June 1938. Ink drawing (Museum
                   of Art, Brigham Young University, Provo, Utah, No. 832070259).

158

Figure 84   Mahonri M. Young, Corn field, Branchville, August 1939. Ink drawing.
                   (Museum of Art, Brigham Young University, Provo, Utah, No. 832070263).

Figure 85   Mahonri M. Young, Plowing at Branchville, May 11, 1939. Crayon drawing
                       (Museum of Art, Brigham Young University, Provo, Utah, No. 832190201).

Figure 86   Mahonri M. Young, "Bass Digging Parsnips, Nov. 1942." Graphite Drawing
                       (Museum of Art, Brigham Young University, Provo, Utah, No. 832080134).

Our Christmas was wonderful. . . .

Now we are alone and it is very quiet here. Dorothy is going over her sketchbook, Hank is asleep in front of the open fire and Molly's in the kitchen and I'm writing to you. Outside it is all white and, most of the time, the wind is howling when it is not whistling or moaning. We are staying here all winter, as I believe I told you, and from now on we expect to get a lot of work done— Dorothy on her life of her father and me on "This is the Place." I have put some good licks on it since the first of the year and it is getting on to the finish as far as I finish it in the plaster... [53]

In April 1943, Young again wrote to Sears:

Again, it is spring. Bass the farmer and his son are out spreading manure on the gardens. Aggie's son, Charles Mahonri Lay, age 4, is riding on the high seat of the spreader as proud as a peacock.[54]

Figure 87 shows horses grazing at Branchville in May 1943. In neither this drawing nor figure 86 can the location be determined.[55] A drawing done in 1941 shows the chicken yard at Branchville (figure 88), while an undated drawing shows the area immediately to the west and north of the barn (figure 89).[56]

In 1943 and 1944 Young described to Jack and Florence Sears their efforts to provide their own meat by slaughtering pigs and calves. In December 1943, he wrote to Florence: "We have just killed our pig. At this moment, he is lying on the floor in my etching room cut up and frozen stiff. Dorothy and Molly are making a pork cake."[57] This etching room was formerly Caro Weir Ely's book bindery; after her marriage, she no longer used the bindery in Branchville but instead had studios in New York and Old Lyme. The bindery was listed in the Ridgefield tax records at the time of Weir's death.[58] Either at the time of the construction of the Young studio or at an undocumented later date, the bindery was moved a short distance and attached to the studio for an etching room.[59] Bill Young also remembers slaughtering chickens himself.[60]

In March 1944, Young described to Sears the beauty of a late winter icestorm, also noting that they now had a bull calf:

. . . . last night it snowed again slightly and then froze with rain. This morning the world was a fairyland; every tree, every limb and twig and every blade of grass was covered with ice. It is now approaching one o'clock and everything is still encased in ice. I walked down into the woods to cut a stick to repair the corral fence where the bull calf was getting out. It was unbelievably beautiful.[61]

Figure 87   Mahonri M. Young, Horses grazing at Branchville, May 1943. Graphite
                     drawing (Museum of Art, Brigham Young University, Provo, Utah, No.
                     832080402).

163

Figure 88   Mahonri M. Young, Chicken yard at Branchville, 1941. Colored pencil
                     (Museum of Art, Brigham Young University, Provo, Utah, No. 832090090).

Figure 89   Mahonri M. Young, near the barn, Branchville, n.d. Ink drawing (Museum of
                   Art, Brigham Young University, Provo, Utah, No. 832070227).

165

In the fall and winter of 1944, Young wrote again to Sears about the bull calf—his origins, rambunctious habits, and ultimate fate:

> We have a young bull we are raising for beef. He was born on Washington's birthday and is one of the new kinds of birth in which his mother was impregnated by a vet with a syringe. If our wonderful cook Molly wasn't a Catholic and if George hadn't been born on the 22 of February we would surely have been tempted to call him Immaculate Conception but . . . we wouldn't hurt Molly's feelings for anything in the world. And so he's George Washington or just George for short.
>
> Now George has a bad habit of socking his mother; though he is a great big boy. For three months, last summer, he, with a young heifer about his age, were over in the Burlingham lots, across from our place, where they couldn't see our cows at all and yet, when the water ran dry and they had to be moved over to our fields, his mother called him and encouraged him to nurse her. He was nothing loath. Bass put a spiked contraption on his nose but he and she managed to circumvent that . . . they managed to defraud us of her milk.[62]

George was kept in line by some fairly extreme measures:

> He is now staked out, at the end of a chain to which is attached a long hickory pole, to which, a little past the middle, is attached a large block of wood, through the lower end of which passes the long pole, attached by a bolt. At the far end is placed, or hung rather, a curled up piece of lead pipe to weight down that end and keep George's end elevated in the air. The block of wood has a hole drilled in the bottom side into which is inserted the end of a crowbar, the other end of which is driven deep into the ground. Even with this machine George manages to get loose, pulls over the crowbar or twists the chain so that a jerk snaps it.
>
> I sometimes move George to new pasture, and, sometimes there is quite a circus. Me with the pole over my shoulder, a sledge hammer and the crowbar in my hand, leading, or trying to lead George, like a very unruly and very large fish, with feet planted firmly in the ground . . . we make at times fine Frost subject matter.[63]

And finally:

> Well that's all past and gone now and George is baby bull in the quick freeze.[64]

In the 1930s and probably into the 1940s, the field to the south of the Caretaker's House was kept open and may have been used for crops. Figure 90 is an undated drawing by Young showing a worker sawing a fallen tree. Beyond is the field and the south side of the Caretaker's house with its one-story porch and lean-to-kitchen on the east side of the structure. Also visible is an outbuilding, variously called

166

Figure 90   Mahonri M. Young, Cutting tree, Branchville, n.d. Drawing, mixed media
                   (Museum of Art, Brigham Young University, Provo, Utah, No. 832120116).

167

a barn, shed or carriage house, which is no longer extant, although its foundations still remain. The present Caretaker's Garage (built between the 1920s and 1947) may have been constructed by the time Young made this drawing, but, if so, it would have been hidden behind the earlier outbuildings.[65]

The fruit crop was also important to Dorothy and Mahonri, and the orchard appears in several Young drawings, including figure 91, which shows several people picking apples in October 1936. There are also at least two drawings and one watercolor of the orchard, all of them undated and all of them featuring the same tree. Figure 92 illustrates Young's orchard watercolor.[66] An ice storm in 1940 damaged their fruit trees, especially the peaches, and severe weather in the winter of 1942–1943 destroyed their fruit harvest.[67] In March 1944, he and Dorothy spent an hour trimming the peach tree, even though there were four inches of snow on the ground.[68] On September 17, 1944, two elm trees went down in a hurricane, and a branch was lost off a maple tree near Young's window (presumably in his studio).[69]

As observed earlier, Young enjoyed the countryside around his house as well as his own property, and when he went for a walk, he always took his sketchbook with him. It is possible that many of the drawings labelled simply "Branchville" may be of other people's woods and fields, but this is very difficult to determine except in unusual cases like that of the 1937 drawing illustrated in figure 81, where a written record by Young has survived. To conclude this section on farming, an undated drawing by Young of a field that may or may not have been on his property is shown in figure 93. This drawing illustrates how eloquently Young could convey a very simple subject, in this case, an open field, triangular in shape, with an (elm?) tree in the foreground, surrounded by a stone wall with a wooden gate. Figure 93 is one of two drawings that Young made of this field.[70]

The Secret Garden

Although flower gardening was not an area of intense interest for Dorothy, the only written references to the flower garden during the Young ownership are in two letters from Dorothy to the Searses. In October 1936, she wrote to them:

> Florence, I'm sending you some rue seeds, which I gathered in my garden yesterday. Rue, I think, is one of the prettiest of the herbs, and it makes a pretty green to put with other flowers. I thought you might be amused to have some from a Connecticut garden. We had our first frost last night, and it was a killing one for the flowers—which look black and dead today.[71]

Two years later, she wrote from 24 Gramercy Park about the Great Hurricane of 1938:

Figure 91   Mahonri M. Young, "Apple Picking at Branchville, October 1936." Ink drawing.
                   (Museum of Art, Brigham Young University, Provo, Utah, No. 832070210).

Figure 92   Mahonri M. Young, The Orchard, n.d. Watercolor (Museum of Art,
                   Brigham Young University, Provo, Utah, No. 832010066).

Figure 93   Mahonri M. Young, Field, Branchville, n.d. Mixed media drawing.
                     (Museum of Art, Brigham Young University, Provo, Utah, No. 832120067).

Tell Florence I don't expect to find much left of my garden, when we go back to the country again —that terrific storm hit us hard—though we cannot complain when the tales pour in of the really fearful damage that was done elsewhere in Connecticut.[72]

However, additional documentation of the Secret Garden can be gleaned from several drawings by Mahonri Young. Young drew approximately ten sketches of the garden, all of which, as described in the previous chapter, show it in a much more overgrown state than in the ca. 1915 photographs. Only three of the Young garden drawings are dated, but all seem to show it in more or less the same condition. In the foreground of figure 94, which is dated March 1942, are two men working in a coldframe just outside the southeast gate to the garden. With them is a dog, probably Hank, and there is also a wheelbarrow between Hank and one of the men. Besides the gate and the hedge, which even under March conditions seems very voluminous, nothing can really be seen of the garden itself. In the background are a fruit tree and the branches of a conifer, probably a spruce, both of which appear in some of the other drawings. By contrast, the undated drawing in figure 95 shows the inside of the garden with the sundial and a woman, whose figure and hairdo seem unlike Dorothy's, tending flowers. One of the rustic gates, which must be the northwest gate, although the sundial seems too close, also appears. Flowers can be seen but not closely enough to be identified. The very full, bushy hedge visible in most of the other drawings does not appear here. Instead, there is a plain rail fence, which like the gate seems slightly askew.[73]

In figure 96, dated 1936, the same gate and fruit trees appear as in figure 94. The two spruce trees, one of which is still standing, are particularly prominent in this drawing, as is the ice house (later the chicken house), which seems closer to the garden than it actually is. What may be the eastern end of the original Weir chicken house can also be seen at the far left of the drawing.[74] Figure 97 shows the garden under snow but is best described in Young's own words:

Jan. 1 1943. It began to snow early in the morning and by noon the ground was all white and snow was clinging to the branches of the trees. It brought back memories of early snows in Salt Lake especially walking home from work on the Tribune or Herald, passing the Eldridge place on 1st South. I don't know why but I seem to remember the fresh snow in their place more clearly than any other out home. After dinner, when we had goose, which everybody liked, and after the people had scattered and Aggie and Oliver had left for Stratford in the snow, I looked out of almost all of the windows of the house—all were beautiful. I felt I should make an oil or a watercolor out of one of them but I didn't seem to have the gumption to get out the paint boxes. Instead I went down to the studio and sat at my desk in the balcony and looked out of the window. It too was very lovely. This piece of wrapping paper was lying on the desk. I read over what I had scribbled on it, months ago, and picked up a fountain pen—the one I'm now using and copied onto a white sheet what I'd written. Then without any thought at all I started a sketch of the ash tree in the left center of the above drawing and still without thinking extended the drawing until I had covered the piece of paper. At no time was there any thought of a picture or a composition until the very last. I have never worked that way before. After supper I brought the drawing up:

Figure 94   Mahonri M. Young, "The Cold Frame. Branchville, March 1942." Ink drawing
                   (Museum of Art, Brigham Young University, Provo, Utah, No. 832070225).

Figure 95   Mahonri M. Young, Garden, Branchville, n.d. Ink drawing (Museum of
                   Art, Brigham Young University, Provo, Utah, No. 832071124).

Figure 96   Mahonri M. Young, Garden, Branchville, 1936. Ink drawing (Museum of Art, Brigham Young University, Provo, Utah, No. 832070155).

Figure 97   Mahonri M. Young, "The First Snow of the New Year, January 1, 1943."
                   Drawing, mixed media. (Museum of Art, Brigham Young University, Provo,
                   Utah, No. 832120076).

176

from the studio and worked on it a bit, clarifying it and insisting more on the structure. . . . This drawing should be called "The First Snow of the New Year." M.M.Y.[75]

Lovely as they are, Young's drawings and paintings of the Secret Garden provide almost no information about what was growing in it. However, Anna Weir Ely Smith remembers many specific plants that grew in the garden from the 1920s into the 1940s. These included raspberry-colored moss roses, white and pale pink phlox, hollyhocks, pink and white lilies, and single white and red peonies.[76] Young's drawings of the Secret Garden demonstrate that many of the structural elements present in the ca. 1915 photographs—fence, gates, sundial, etc.—survived into the 1930s and 1940s, and that a coldframe was in use in the early 1940s. The ash tree in figure 97 may be the one that was recently taken down, but it looks rather large for a tree only twenty-two years old.[77]

There is one extant undocumented feature in the immediate vicinity of the Weir/Young house and garden that may date from the Young ownership: the terraces to the rear (west) of the house. The terraces are not mentioned in correspondence and do not appear in drawings or photographs. The only thing that is known about them is that they were on the grounds when the Andrews took ownership in 1958 and probably predate the Andrews' friendship with Young in the early 1950s.

The Pond

The pond is not well documented in the Young years. As noted near the beginning of this chapter, during Dorothy and Mahonri's courtship, there were frequent house parties involving picnics at the pond, boating and fishing.[78] However, Young was not the committed fisherman that Weir had been, and as an artist he does not seem to have been as fascinated by the pond as he was by farming activities. Nevertheless, in July 1935 Young drew a pair of charming ink sketches of Weir's pond (as he always referred to it): one of a frog "from life" and another of a swimmer sitting on the bank (figure 98). Swimming was a popular activity during the ownership of Dorothy and Mahonri Young.[79] Young also painted a beautiful watercolor, undated, showing one end of the pond with a boat (figure 99). In the 1920s the little summerhouse that Weir had erected on the island in the pond was still extant, but during the 1930s it seems to have been reduced to remnants or have disappeared altogether.[80] At one point, the Youngs planned to build a round classical temple in its place. Although they had stone blocks transported down to the pond, the temple was never built. At this time, the path to the pond was still well defined, and the little bridge, which Bill Young helped to keep in repair, was extant into the 1930s and 1940s.[81] During the Youngs' marriage, artists from the Century Club or the Art Students League came to visit almost every weekend and frequently painted the pond and the landscape. Young's grandchildren also enjoyed swimming in the pond.[82] At this time, the boathouse was still intact and may have survived into the early 1960s.[83]

177

Figure 98   Mahonri M. Young. Pair of sketches of "Weir's Pond, July 18, 1935." Ink
                   drawings (Museum of Art, Brigham Young University, Provo, Utah, No.
                   832070350).

Figure 99   Mahonri M. Young, Pond at Branchville, n.d. Watercolor (Museum of
                   Art, Brigham Young University, Provo, Utah, No. 832010070).

Dorothy's Death

About 1940 Dorothy was first diagnosed with cancer, which was initially treated, successfully, with radiation and surgery.[84] In May 1947, however, Mahonri Young wrote to Sears:

> What I'm writing you is definitely bad news. A week ago Dorothy went to the hospital for a check up. She had been feeling poorly for over two months and when she didn't get any better her Drs. had her go to the hospital. There they made all the tests but could find nothing definite. Last Thursday she underwent an exploratory operation of the abdominal region with most disastrous revelations. The conditions couldn't have been much worse. We can only hope that she will not suffer too much.[85]

Two months later Dorothy died, fortunately without too much pain.[86] Young wrote to Sears:

> It has been a real consolation to me, to hear from friends of hers that she was very happy with me. To have been a source of happiness to a lovely woman like Dorothy is a help and a comfort in her loss. But I shall miss her for a long, long time.[87]

The town records of Ridgefield and Wilton include an affidavit dated July 8, 1947, concerning the payment of property taxes on Dorothy Weir Young's estate. In Ridgefield, her buildings, land, livestock, etc., were itemized as follows: one dwelling house, one barn, two studios, four garages, one poultry house, one house lot (five acres), 76-1/2 acres of land, one station wagon, two old horses, three grade cows, household furnishings assessed at $18,133.00. In Wilton (the caretaker's house parcel), the following were listed: one dwelling house, two private garages, one lot, 76 acres of land, one swine.[88] (Since Cora Weir Burlingham had taken possession of the Webb Farm in 1931, this property was not included.)

MAHONRI M. YOUNG, 1948–1957

Dorothy Young's death coincided with a decline in Mahonri's health, but despite physical infirmities he retained his mental alertness and his sense of humor for the rest of his life. Not long after Dorothy's death, Mahonri posed for a photograph with his grandson and namesake, Mahonri M. Young, 2nd, aged about one year (figure 100). This photograph shows in the background the tool shed, vegetable garden, and lattice at Weir Farm. While it is not dated, the slightly overblown appearance of the vegetation in this photograph suggests late summer or early fall, probably 1948.[89] As a young child, Charles Mahonri Lay, another of Young's grandsons, posed for one of the panels in the This-Is-the-Place

180

Figure 100   Mahonri M. Young and his grandson Mahonri M. Young, 2nd, at Weir Farm, n.d.
                      (ca. 1948). Photograph (Young Papers, Special Collections, Lee Library, Brigham
                      Young University, Provo, Utah).

Monument. Young taught both grandsons to shoot a .22 rifle out of the studio double doors.[90]

On July 24, 1947, only two months after Dorothy's death, the This-Is-the-Place Monument was dedicated in Pioneer State Park in Salt Lake City.[91] Two years later, Sears took several photographs of Mahonri at a special event celebrating the monument (figure 101). Young's final major work of art, which was completed in 1949, was a commission from the state of Utah for a marble statue of Brigham Young to be placed in Statuary Hall (the Old House of Representatives) in the United States Capitol.[92] Beginning in the 1950s, he suffered from a series of ailments, including problems with his veins (what he described as "Venus trouble" but not the "Venus trouble I know and which all of us suffer from, more or less"), ulcers, and phlebitis.[93]

It appears that until at least 1955 Young went to Connecticut quite frequently and continued to draw and etch there, even though big sculptural commissions were a thing of the past. He remained a registered voter in Branchville, and in spite of his "Venus trouble," he went up to the farm in 1952 to vote for Adlai Stevenson.[94] In 1954 the house needed repainting and the pump went on the blink, causing him unexpected expenses on top of hospital bills.[95] After Dorothy's death, farming activities were gradually phased out, although the Gullys remained in the caretaker's house, where they had a kitchen garden. The Gullys also kept cows and chickens in the Weir/Young barn and grew hay in the field to the north. As the affidavit discussed above indicates, they probably also kept a pig somewhere on the grounds of the caretaker's house, possibly near the caretaker's house. During the Gullys' tenancy, the caretaker's house was in poor condition.[96]

Understandably, Young's artistic output slowed after he began suffering health problems, but there are a still a few very interesting Branchville drawings from the 1950s. In 1952 he did a series of drawings of a "Blasted Elm," one of which is illustrated in figure 102. A large limb from this tree, which may have suffered from Dutch elm disease or simply have been old, fell and damaged a picket fence. In August 1955, Young did what is probably his last Branchville drawing, illustrated in figure 103, which shows a small field surrounded by trees and a wooden fence. In neither figure 102 nor figure 103 can the exact locations be determined.

In the last two years of his life, in between visits to the hospital, Young spent most of his time at 24 Gramercy Park. In January 1956, his granddaughter Darcy Lay stayed in the apartment with him while working at Rockefeller Center:

> I'll have company and a delightful companion which I haven't had since Dorothy died. She is going to Bennington a progressive school which don't approve of me but when the weather gets cold they close the school and tell the pupils to get out and hunt a job while the school can turn

182

Figure 101   Jack Sears (partially visible), Mahonri M. Young and unidentified woman at the
                  This-Is-the-Place Monument, Salt Lake City, November 24, 1949. Photograph
                  (Sears Papers, Special Collections, Lee Library, Brigham Young University,
                  Provo, Utah).

Figure 102   Mahonri M. Young. Blasted Elm, Branchville, August 18, 1952. Ink drawing
                    (Museum of Art, Brigham Young University, Provo, Utah, No. 832070645).

Figure 103   Mahonri M. Young. Field, Branchville, August 26, 1955. Ink drawing (Museum
                    of Art, Brigham Young University, Provo, Utah, No. 832071060).

the heat off and save oil.[97]

In March 1956, he was back in "durance vile" (the hospital) with phlebitis. While still there, he received a telephone call from the plumber in Connecticut, saying that the furnace door had blown off and further:

> Then my brother-in-law, Charles Burlingham, sent me a note saying he had tried to call and very important . . . my neighbor was having his place surveyed and . . . I might as well have mine done at the same time as it would avoid a duplication. And: the squatter on my property was on my land and had built two houses and sold some acreage.[98]

However, the survey would cost between $2000 and $3000, an expense Young didn't feel he could handle on top of doctor and hospital bills.[99] In September and October of 1956, the Oral History Research Office of Columbia University conducted a series of interviews with Young, which were interrupted by his final illness. Although a substantial amount of information was gathered, the emphasis was on the early part of the artist's life and career, and the transcript was never edited.[100]

In January 1957, Young suffered a stroke and was diagnosed with advanced heart disease. On October 5, 1957, he fell ill with an acute ulcer attack from which he never recovered. On November 2, 1957, he died at the age of eighty from a bleeding ulcer complicated by pneumonia.[101]

HISTORIC AERIAL PHOTOGRAPHS

During the Weir/Young ownership, aerial photographs were taken of the Ridgefield/Wilton area in 1939, October 1941, May 1949, and September 1951. All were shot from a great height, and the site was only a tiny part of the total area photographed. Even under magnification, little detail can be made out. The early aerials are slightly more helpful for the Burlingham portion of the property, which was more open, than for the Weir/Young portion. In fact, the chief value of the aerials taken in 1941, 1949, and 1951 is that they vividly demonstrate how much more open the entire site was than it is today. The area between Nod Hill Road and the pond became progressively more overgrown between 1941 (figure 104) and 1951 (figure 105), but by comparison with the aerials taken for this Cultural Landscape Report in December 1992 it was still fairly open even in 1951.[102] On the 1951 aerial, which is the clearest in this series, the Weir/Young House and the larger outbuildings can be seen, but landscape details are difficult to make out.

186

Figure 104   Aerial photograph of Ridgefield/Wilton (detail), October 20, 1941 (SCS, GS W9
                      66).

Figure 105   Aerial photograph of Ridgefield/Wilton (detail), September 24, 1951 (SCS, DPD-9H-72).

188

SUMMARY

Between 1920 and 1957, Ella Weir, Dorothy Weir Young, and Mahonri Young maintained and enjoyed the property that J. Alden Weir had established in 1882. The period when Weir Farm was most intensively used during this span of almost four decades was that of the Youngs' marriage. Between 1931 and 1947, Dorothy and Mahonri Young lived at Weir Farm on a more consistent and regular basis than even Weir ever had. It was the Youngs' country residence, their primary workplace, and a constant source of relaxation and refreshment. During these years, the only major interventions in the landscape were the construction of the Young studio in 1932 and the conversion of the ice house into a chicken house in the early 1940s. Both of the Youngs were sensitive and enthusiastic lovers of nature and the country scene, but their creative energies went into sculpture, painting, and writing. Unlike Weir himself, Twachtman, and Augustus Saint-Gaudens, their artistic impulses didn't carry over into reshaping their personal landscape.[103] However, there were gradual and incremental changes in the landscape of Weir Farm between 1920 and 1957 that were not intentional or designed but that came about as the result of the encroachment of trees, less intensive farming, and less rigorous maintenance of the grounds, especially in the later years. In general, however, the Youngs were stewards of the Weir landscape rather than reworkers or manipulators of it.

LANDSCAPE FEATURES AND CONDITIONS, CA. 1947

Methodology

Similar to the documentation of the previous time period, five historic photographs, eleven paintings, written correspondence and interviews were used to determine the existing conditions in 1947. However, the 1949 aerial photograph is the primary source for the location of buildings and the study of field succession and vegetation and reduction of open space in this period. Other sources referenced are listed in Exhibit 8. Only those features whose location could be documented using the above sources appear on the period plan. Other features whose existence, but not location, could be documented using other sources and features that were developed after 1919 and were no longer extant in 1947 are discussed in the text but do not appear on the period plan.

Landscape Character

The landscape character of Weir Farm in 1947, at the time of Dorothy Weir Young's death, was less open with fewer cultivated fields than the landscape of 1919 (see exhibits 6 and 18). Dorothy and Mahonri Young were stewards of a gentleman's farm but did not attempt to maintain it as a profitable

189

economic enterprise. The only fields remaining in cultivation were the fields northeast of the Weir Farm and those around the Webb/Burlingham property. Most crops were grown to feed the horses and cows, the vegetables were grown for family consumption, and the other fields previously cultivated or grazed were in the early stages of succession. The Secret Garden was beginning to become overgrown without the rigorous attention needed to maintain its splendor of ca. 1919. The rugged, rural qualities of the site, with increased forestation, became the dominant character of the site.

Major Landscape Developments

Along with the appearance of several additional farm buildings such as the animal shelter and caretaker's garage as shown in exhibits 6 and 7, the most important landscape development was the building of Mahonri Young's studio in 1932 (including the relocation and attachment of the old bindery building to the new sculpture studio).

Perhaps the primary landscape development of this period was the transition, or succession, of the site from its more cultivated state to a more natural condition. Included in this transition was the decline of the Secret Garden as a showplace and location of many social activities. In addition, the previously cultivated fields were beginning to become overgrown, the forested lands expanded, and landscape structures such as the summerhouse were falling into a state of disrepair. However, the path to the pond was still well defined in 1947 and the other pond-related amenities such as the stonewall and gate to the pond and the boathouse were in existence until the 1960s.

Features No Longer Extant

Landscape features that existed ca. 1947 but that no longer exist today include the four structures east of Nod Hill Road and the Burlingham complex, the caretaker's garden, the Weir/Young vegetable garden above the terraced stone walls west of the house, the paddock north of the barn, the wooden fishing bridge, the orchard, the cornfield, the boathouse, and finally, the Secret Garden (though remnants of the garden and orchard do exist today).

Outstanding Research Questions

The outstanding questions that remain to be answered regarding changes to the landscape during this period include: What were the four buildings east of Nod Hill Road and the Burlingham complex and when did they disappear? When were the stone terraced walls west of the Weir house built? When were the circular pools on the west side of the pond built, why, and by whom?

190

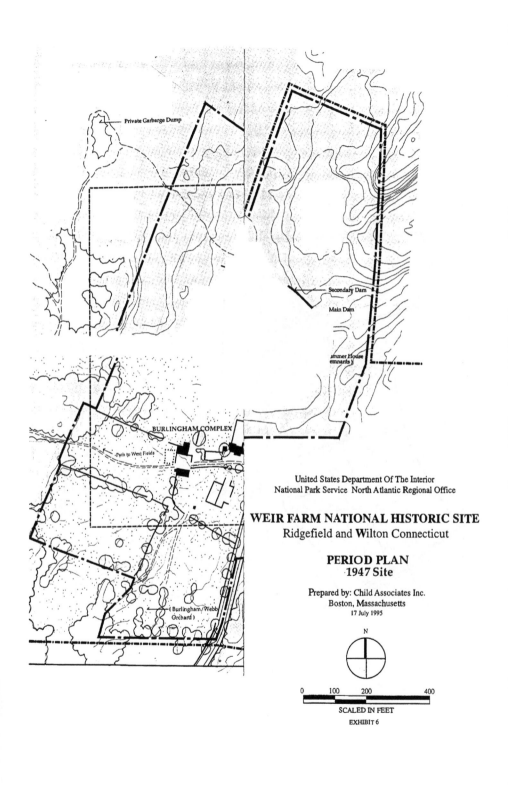

United States Department Of The Interior
National Park Service North Atlantic Regional Office

WEIR FARM NATIONAL HISTORIC SITE
Ridgefield and Wilton Connecticut

PERIOD PLAN
1947 Site

Prepared by: Child Associates Inc.
Boston, Massachusetts
17 July 1995

0   100   200   400

SCALED IN FEET

EXHIBIT 6

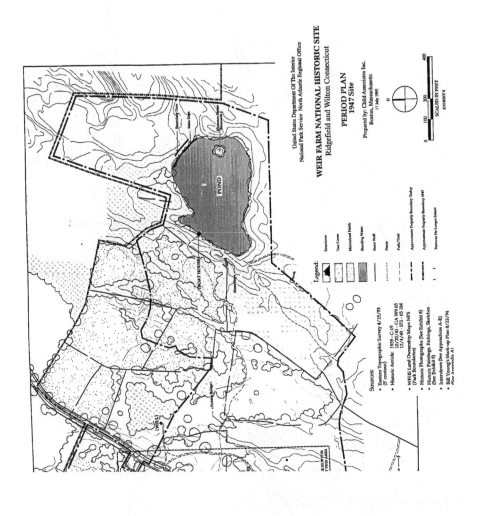

United States Department Of The Interior
National Park Service North Atlantic Regional Office

WEIR FARM NATIONAL HISTORIC SITE
Ridgefield and Wilton Connecticut

PERIOD PLAN
1947 Site

Prepared by: Child Associates Inc.
Boston, Massachusetts
17 July 1995

N

SCALED IN FEET
0   100   200   300   400

EXHIBIT 6

Legend:

	Structures
	Tree Cover
	Maintained Fields
	Standing Water
	Stone Wall
	Fence
	Path/Trail
	Approximate Property Boundary Today
	Approximate Property Boundary 1947
	Features No Longer Extant

Sources:
- Eastern Topographic Survey 4/15/93 (5' contour)
- Historic Aerials: 1939 - C-19
  10/20/41 - CA W9 65
  12/4/49 - 572 - 65 IM
- WFHS Land Ownership Maps NPS (Park Boundary)
- Historic Photographs (See Exhibit 8)
- Historic Paintings, Etchings, Sketches (See Exhibit 8)
- Interviews (See Appendices A-E)
- Bill Young's Mark-up Plan 8/23/94 (See Appendix A)

POND

BOAT HOUSE

[WELL]

BURNER FEED AREA

Main Drive

Standing Water

Stone Wall

Fence

Path/Trail

Approximate Property Boundary Today

Approximate Property Boundary 1947

Features No Longer Extant

Garden

Gate/Barway

Sources:

- Eastern Topographic Survey 4/15/93 (5' contour)
- Historic Aerials: 1939 - C-19
  10/20/41 - GA W9 65
  12/4/49 - 572 - 65 1M
- WFHS Land Ownership Maps NPS (Park Boundaries)
- Historic Photographs (See Exhibit 8)
- Historic Paintings, Etchings, Sketches (See Exhibit 8)
- Interviews (See Appendices A-E)
- Bill Young's Mark-up Plan 8/23/94 (See Appendix A)

United States Department Of The Interior
National Park Service North Atlantic Regional Office

WEIR FARM NATIONAL HISTORIC SITE
Ridgefield and Wilton Connecticut

PERIOD PLAN
1947 Core Area

Prepared by: Child Associates Inc.
Boston, Massachusetts
17 July 1995

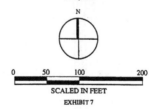

0   50   100   200

SCALED IN FEET

EXHIBIT 7

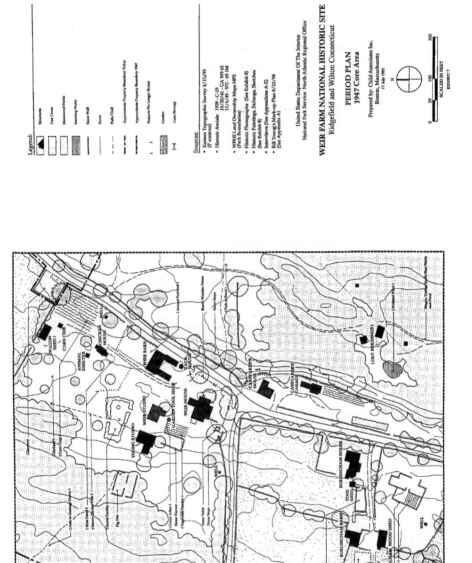

Legend:

Structures
Tree Cover
Maintained Fields
Standing Water
Stone Wall
Fence
Path/Trail
Approximate Property Boundary Today
Approximate Property Boundary 1947
Features No Longer Extant
Garden
Gate/Bars(p)

Sources:

- Eastern Topographic Survey 4/15/93 (5' contour)
- Historic Aerials: 1939 – C.19
  10/20/41 – CA W65
  12/4/49 – 572 – 65 BM
- WFHS Land Ownership Maps NPS (Park Boundaries)
- Historic Photographs (See Exhibit 8)
- Historic Paintings, Etchings, Sketches (See Exhibit 8)
- Interviews (See Appendices A-E)
- Bill Young's Mark-up Plan 8/23/94 (See Appendix A)

United States Department Of The Interior
National Park Service North Atlantic Regional Office

WEIR FARM NATIONAL HISTORIC SITE
Ridgefield and Wilton Connecticut

PERIOD PLAN
1947 Core Area

Prepared by: Child Associates Inc.
Boston, Massachusetts
17 July 1995

N

SCALED IN FEET
0   50   100   200

EXHIBIT 7

United States Department Of The Interior
National Park Service North Atlantic Regional Office

WEIR FARM NATIONAL HISTORIC SITE
Ridgefield and Wilton Connecticut

SOURCES FOR 1947 PERIOD PLAN

Prepared by: Child Associates Inc.
Boston, Massachusetts
17 July 1995

EXHIBIT 8

United States I
National Park Servic
WEIR FARM NA
Ridgefield an
SOURCES FO

Prepared

PAINTINGS, ETCHINGS, AND SKETCHES

Figure 73 Mahonri M. Young, "Brandsville, March 29, 1936," Ink drawing, (Museum of Art, Brigham Young University, Provo, Utah, No. E330T0350).

Figure 76 Mahonri M. Young, Weir's studio, n.d. Oil on canvas board (Museum of Art, Brigham Young University, Provo, Utah, No. E34000025).

Figure 77 Mahonri M. Young, Young and Weir studios, undated, Ink drawing and notes, blank, n.d. (Ca. 1937), Ink drawing, (Museum of Art, Brigham Young University, Provo, Utah, No. E320T0001).

Figure 82 Mahonri M. Young, Sleeping cat or sketch, July 24, 1932, Ink drawing, (Museum of Art, Brigham Young University, Provo, Utah, No. E330T0224).

Figure 88 Mahonri M. Young, Chicken yard at Brandsville, 1941, Colored pencil (Museum of Art, Brigham Young University, Provo, Utah, No. E330S0005).

Figure 89 Mahonri M. Young, Near the barn, Brandsville, Undated, Ink drawing, (Museum of Art, Brigham Young University, Provo, Utah, No. E330T0227).

Figure 94 Mahonri M. Young, "The Cold Frame, Brandsville, March 1942," Ink drawing, (Museum of Art, Brigham Young University, Provo, Utah, No. E330T0223).

Figure 95 Mahonri M. Young, Garden, Brandsville, n.d. Ink drawing, (Museum of Art, Brigham Young University, Provo, Utah, No. E330T1241).

Figure 96 Mahonri M. Young, Garden, Brandsville, 1936, Ink drawing, (Museum of Art, Brigham Young University, Provo, Utah, No. E330T0153).

Figure 97 Mahonri M. Young, "The Fast Snow of the New Year, January 1, 1945," Drawing, mixed media (Museum of Art, Brigham Young University, Provo, Utah, No. E3212O076).

Figure 99 Mahonri M. Young, Pond at Brandsville, n.d. Watercolor (Museum of Art, Brigham Young University, Provo, Utah, No. E330J0070).

Figure 102 Mahonri M. Young, Blasted Elm, Brandsville, August 18, 1933, Ink drawing (Museum of Art, Brigham Young University, Provo, Utah, No. E3320S0045).

Figure 117 Mahonri M. Young, "Jen Knocke Builds a New Stone Wall," n.d. (ca. 1940s) Etching (Museum of Art, Brigham Young University, Provo, Utah, No. E330G0211).

Figure 119 Mahonri M. Young, Plowed field, Crayon drawing, 1939 (Museum of Art, Brigham Young University, Provo, Utah, No. E3219O039).

PHOTOGRAPHS

Figure 25 View from chicken house, Weir farm, showing the barn, south elevation of house, Weir studio, Young studio, Mahonri M. Young, and a corner of the Secret Garden. Photograph, ca. 1943 (WFNHS-HP No. 150).

Figure 100 Mahonri M. Young and his studio (Mahonri M. Young, 2nd, n.d. Etc. (ca. 1940). Photograph (Young Papers, Special Collections, Lee Library, Brigham Young University, Provo, Utah).

Figure 104 Aerial photograph of Ridgefield/Wilton (detail), October 20, 1941 (SCS, Gd W9 60).

Figure 105 Aerial photograph of Ridgefield/Wilton (detail), September 24, 1951 (SCS, DPD-9K7-72).

Figure 112 Weir/Burlingham house from the east. Photograph, ca. 1940s (WFNHS-HP No. 87).

Figure 113 Burlingham modern garden. Photograph, ca. 1930s (WFNHS-HP No. 138).

Figure 114 Burlingham modern garden. Sunken garden by Cornelia Schuster, ca. 1955 (from Fletcher Steele, Treasury of American Gardens, 1946).

Figure 120 Bill Caulke on a pony he peddled by Burlingham woodshed. Photograph, ca. mid-1930s (WFNHS-HP No. 143).

Figure 121 Burlingham and Young families in dog pen at rear of Burlingham house. Photograph, before 1940 (WFNHS-HP No. 123).

ENDNOTES TO CHAPTER III

1.   Records, Weir Farm National Historic Site. Weir is said to have died intestate, which would probably mean that his widow inherited half his estate and his three daughters equal shares in the other half.

2.   Anna Weir Ely Smith, informal telephone interview with Cynthia Zaitzevsky, August 12, 1994.

3.   Weir to Ella Baker, July 14, 1886, AAA, Reel 125.

4.   Anna Weir Ely Smith, informal telephone interview with Cynthia Zaitzevsky, August 12, 1994. Mrs. Smith was unable to remember the name of the farmer in the 1920s. Bass was apparently the farmer by the 1930s, when Dorothy married Mahonri Young.

5.   Olmsted Center for Landscape Preservation, *Historic Landscape Assessment of Weir Garden, Weir Farm National Historic Site,* prepared in cooperation with the Ridgefield Garden Club for the Weir Farm National Historic Site, (Brookline, MA.: National Park Service, April 1994), 11.

6.   Charles Burlingham, telephone interview with Sarah Olson, April 24, 1992, Weir Farm National Historic Site.

7.   Brigham Young University, Provo, Utah, Museum of Fine Arts Collection, computer printout of works by Dorothy Weir in their collection. (Brigham Young University, copy at Weir Farm National Historic Site.) Most of Dorothy's works owned by BYU are linoleum cuts, but there are a few pastels, monotypes, and watercolors.

8.   Dorothy Weir Young, *The Life and Letters of J. Alden Weir* (New York: Kennedy Graphics, Inc., Da Capo Press, reprint ed., 1971).

9.   Records, Weir Farm National Historic Site.

10.   Mahonri M. Young, "Dorothy Weir Young," introduction to *Dorothy Weir Young, 1890–1947* (The Cosmopolitan Club, n.d.). Copy in the Mahonri M. Young Papers, Special Collections, Lee Library, Brigham Young University, Provo, Utah, cited hereafter as Young Papers. The incident of Dorothy's watercolor of the amaryllis and Mahonri's of the new falling snow occurred in early spring 1944 and is also the subject of a lovely description in the following letter: Mahonri M. Young to Jack Sears, April 6, 1944, continuation of letter of March 30, Jack Sears Papers, Special Collections, Lee Library, Brigham Young University Provo, Utah, cited hereafter as Sears Papers.

11.   Computer printout of works of art by Dorothy Weir Young, "Irises in Glass, Branchville" (No. 824001418) and "Two Poppies, Branchville" (No. 824001419).

12.   Mahonri M. Young, "Notes at the Beginning: Being Excerpts from the Early Pages of a Projected Autobiography," *Mahonri M. Young: Retrospective Exhibition* (Andover, Massachusetts: Addison Gallery of American Art, Phillips Academy, 1940), 47; Wayne K. Hinton, *A Biographical History of Mahonri M. Young, A Western American Artist,* a dissertation presented to the Department of History, Brigham Young University in partial fulfillment of the requirements for the degree Doctor of Philosophy, April 1974, 24–32. (Lee Library, Brigham

Young University, Provo, Utah); Mahonri M. Young, "The Reminiscences of Mahonri M. Young," typescript, Oral History Research Office, Columbia University, 1958, 1–10, copy at Weir Farm National Historic Site.

13.   Young, "Notes at the Beginning," 48–56.

14.   "A Biographical History," 35, 49–51; "The Reminiscences of Mahonri M. Young," 10–74, 89, 109–117.

15.   "The Reminiscences of Mahonri M. Young," 74–75.

       See Wayne K. Hinton, "Mahonri Young and the Church: A View of Mormonism and Art," *Dialogue*, 35–43. Young was always very proud of his Mormon heritage, but he did not serve the two-year missionary period recommended for devout young men, didn't tithe or attend church, and did not observe the Word of Wisdom, which forbids the use of alcohol, tobacco, and caffeine.

16.   "The Reminiscences of Mahonri M. Young," 89–90; "In Grateful Remembrance for Winged Deliverance," *Deseret News* (Salt Lake City), Christmas edition, 1924, 16.

17.   The Youngs went to Tucson for the unveiling of Young's monument to Father Kino, an early Catholic missionary in the Southwest. The trip was Dorothy's first to the western part of the country and Young's first visit to Salt Lake City in some time. See "Famous Artist Predicts End of Modernism: Mahonri Young Arrives to Visit Salt Lake, His Birthplace," *Salt Lake Tribune*, May 3, 1936.

       The Mahonri Young Papers at Brigham Young University include sketches and a beautiful watercolor by Young of the exterior of San Xavier del Bac, dated March 26, 1936 (Young Papers, box 4, folder 1). For San Xavier del Bac, see William H. Pierson, Jr., *American Buildings and Their Architects: The Colonial and Neoclassical Styles* (Garden City, New York: Doubleday & Company, 1970), 185–196.

18.   Mahonri M. Young, "Julian Alden Weir," part of a projected autobiography, Young Papers.

       In quoting these unpublished letters and fragments, I have corrected Young's spelling, which was sometimes erratic.

19.   Mahonri M. Young, "D. Weir," part of a projected autobiography, Young Papers.

20.   Information from a chronology in the working files of Erika Passantino, Research Curator, Phillips Collection, Washington, DC. A "Chronology" of the Phillips Collection by Erika Passantino and Sarah Martin in *Duncan Phillips: Centennial Exhibition, June 14 to August 31, 1986* (Washington, DC: The Phillips Collection, 1986), 26–46, is also helpful but does not mention the Committee on Scope and Plan.

21.   Young, "D. Weir," part of a projected autobiography, Young Papers.

22.   Dorothy Weir to Mahonri M. Young from Windham, September 20, 1929, Young Papers.

23.   "Mrs. J. Alden Weir" (Death Notice), *New York Times*, Monday, December 29, 1930, page 21, column 5.

24.   Anna Weir Ely Smith, informal telephone interview with Cynthia Zaitzevsky, August 12, 1994. Mahonri Sharp (Bill) Young, interview with Cynthia Zaitzevsky, May 15, 1994.

25.   "Dorothy Weir to Wed Mahonri Young," *New York Times*, Sunday, January 25, 1931, Part II, page 6, column 8.

26.   "Young-Weir," *New York Times*, Wednesday, February 18, 1931, page 12, column 4.

Dorothy and Mahonri were not married at Weir Farm, as is sometimes reported. In February 1931, the house had not yet been winterized. A story about a cow falling down a well on their wedding day actually refers to an incident, probably in the summer of 1932, when Dorothy was entertaining her cousin, the Presiding Episcopal Bishop of New York, Bishop Peary, at the farm, and *then* a cow fell down the well. Follow-up telephone interview with Mahonri Sharp (Bill) Young, by Cynthia Zaitzevsky, August 10, 1994. The well in this incident may have been the well covered by a wellhouse now on J. Whipkey's property on Nod Hill Road, which was once part of Weir Farm. This wellhouse is the only original Weir Farm structure remaining that is not on National Park Service land (Information from Weir Farm National Historic Site).

27.   Mahonri Sharp (Bill) Young, interview with Cynthia Zaitzevsky, May 15, 1994.

Oliver's father was Charles Downing Lay (1877–1956), son of a painter. In addition to being an important landscape architect and a cofounder in 1910 of the magazine *Landscape Architecture*, Lay was an architect, planner, etcher, and painter, who apparently studied art as a young man with Mahonri Young. He had a property called "Wellsmere" in Stratford, Connecticut, which he designed himself and which is still extant. See Robert Wheelwright, "Charles Downing Lay, September 3, 1877–February 15, 1956. A Biographical Minute," *Landscape Architecture*, Vol. XLVI, no. 3 (April 1956), 162–164. There is no evidence that Charles Downing Lay ever did any landscape design work on the Weir/Young grounds.

28.   Information on Charles Meyer is courtesy of Marie Carden, National Park Service, North Atlantic Regional Office, Cultural Resources Center, Lowell, Massachusetts, July 6, 1994. Carden interviewed Ray Meyer, Charles' son.

29.   *Mahonri M. Young: Retrospective Exhibition*, 30. This drawing is not one of those illustrated in the Addison catalogue. It also does not appear to be among the Young drawings at the Museum of Art, Brigham Young University. Their computer listing includes three drawings entitled "Excavating," but the media and measurements of none of them match "Excavating for Mr. Young's Studio."

30.   Interview by the Weir Farm Heritage Trust with Mahonri Sharp (Bill) Young, Charles Mahonri Lay, Mahonri M. Young II, and George Lay, August 7, 1989.

31.   Follow-up telephone interview with Mahonri Sharp (Bill) Young, by Cynthia Zaitzevsky, August 10, 1994.

32.   Marie Carden, Coordinator, Historic Structure Report, "Summary Chronology of Weir House, Weir Farm National Historic Site," revised August 5, 1994, 2. Bathrooms were added to the second floor and basement by the Youngs, possibly at the same time.

33.   Follow-up telephone interview with Anna Weir Ely Smith by Cynthia Zaitzevsky, August 21, 1994.

David H. Wallace in the "Historic Furnishings Report, Weir Farm, Weir Farm National Historic Site, Wilton, Connecticut," Draft Report (Harpers Ferry: Division of Historic Furnishings, Harpers Ferry Center, National Park Service, 1994), 54-58, does not suggest such a use for the library. He also suggests that a victrola, which was not listed in the estate inventories until after Mahonri Young's death but which was then listed in the dining room, may have belonged in the library. However, many writers and also serious readers find music while working a distraction. After Dorothy's death, when he presumably ate alone much of the time, Young may have enjoyed listening to music during his meals. Young's son might be asked about this.

34.   Note in Box 1, Folder 14, Sears Papers. The letters from Sears to Young do not seem to be in the Sears Papers. However, this collection, which is in four boxes, has only been roughly catalogued and has no finding aid, so this cannot be stated definitively. Sears, who lived until 1968, intended to write a biography of Young, but this was never completed.

35.   Young to Sears, August 8, 1932, Sears Papers.

36.   Hinton, "Mahonri Young and the Church," 40–42.

37.   Interview by Weir Farm Heritage Trust with Mahonri Sharp (Bill) Young et al. In 1989, Spiro Anaganos was living in San Francisco.

38.   Follow-up interview with Mahonri Sharp (Bill) Young, by Cynthia Zaitzevsky, August 10, 1994.

39.   This oak has been identified by Charlie Pepper of the Olmsted Center for Landscape Preservation, Brookline, Massachusetts, as a northern red oak *(Quercus rubra)*, and he estimates that, conservatively, it is 100 to 120 years old. It therefore is quite possible that the oak pre-existed Weir's ownership but might have been quite small when he came, thus explaining why today it is so close to the studio.

The works of art listed in the 1940 Addison Gallery exhibition include a watercolor entitled "Alden Weir's Studio" and dated 1929, which does not appear to be at Brigham Young University. See *Mahonri M. Young: Retrospective Exhibition,* 26. It is also not illustrated in the catalogue.

40.   The Youngs had Hank from at least 1937 through 1943. See the letters from Young to Jack Sears, August 2, 1937, and January 6, 1943, quoted below. Young also drew numerous undated sketches of Hank, which are at BYU.

41.   Information from Mahonri Sharp (Bill) Young and Mahonri M. Young II, August 31, 1994. We are very grateful for the information about the grape trellis and other valuable information about the site during the Young years.

42.   Brigham Young University has this drawing of the well titled "Branchville Out House."

43.   Young to Sears, August 2, 1937, Sears Papers.

44.   Mahonri Sharp (Bill) Young, interview with Cynthia Zaitzevsky, May 15, 1994.

45.   Ibid., 8–9; Anna Weir Ely Smith. Informal telephone interview with Cynthia Zaitzevsky, August 12, 1994.

46.   Mahonri Sharp (Bill) Young, second follow-up telephone interview with Cynthia Zaitzevsky, August 21, 1994. For the date and nature of the conversion, see Maureen K. Phillips and Marie L. Carden, "Weir Farm Historic Structures Report, Weir Farm National Historic Site, Wilton, Connecticut. Volume II-A: "Weir Farm Outbuildings" (Lowell, Massachusetts: Building Conservation Branch, Northeast Cultural Resources Center, National Park Service, U. S. Department of the Interior, 1995), 164-166. .

47.   Information from Mahonri Sharp (Bill) Young and Mahonri M. Young II, August 31, 1994.

48.   Mahonri Sharp (Bill) Young, interview with Cynthia Zaitzevsky, May 15, 1994.

49.   Young to Sears, December 13, 1939, Sears Papers.

50.   *Mahonri M. Young: Retrospective Exhibition,* introduction by Frank Jewett Mather, Jr. The catalog also includes excerpts from Young's projected autobiography, 47–56. Correspondence, lists of works, and other files relating to this exhibition, which was held from September 21 through November 5, 1940, are at the Addison Gallery and have kindly been made available by Susan Faxon, Curator. This was the first exhibition at the Addison that was seen to completion by Bartlett H. Hayes, Jr., who was Acting Director and then Director until 1970. Hayes went both to Young's New York apartment and to Ridgefield to cull works of the art for the show (Bartlett H. Hayes, Jr. to Frank Jewett Mather, Jr., July 18, 1940, Archives of the Addison Gallery of American Art).

51.   Young to Sears, May 16, 1940, Sears Papers.

52.   Young to Sears, October 21, 1940, Sears Papers. For one of the reviews, see "Mormon Artist," Newsweek, Vol. XVI, no. 13, (September 23, 1940), 58. A slightly later article in another national news magazine, which does not mention the Addison Gallery exhibition, illustrates the growing interest in Young as the work on the "This is the Place" monument progressed. See "Mahonri Young's Sculpture Preserves His Mormon Past," Life, Vol. 10, no. 7 (February 17, 1941), 76, 79.

53.   Young to Sears, January 6, 1943, Sears Papers.

54.   Young to Sears, April 12-13, 1943, Sears Papers.

55.   Two 1943 drawings of haying in Branchville are not illustrated here because they are somewhat repetitive of figure 81. They are a drawing showing a farmer on a haystack, dated March 15, 1943 (BYU No. 832080194), and another showing hay being gathered in the fields, dated June 1943 (BYU No. 832080180).

56.   In figure 88, too little is shown of the chicken house to tell for sure whether it is the original or converted chicken house, although the small square window that today appears over each long rectangular window in the converted chicken house does not seem to be present. The line of the eaves also does not seem to correspond.

    Mahonri Sharp (Bill) Young and Mahonri M. Young II report that there was a chicken enclosure attached to the south of the chicken house (Communication, August 31, 1994).

57.   Young to Florence Sears, December 17, 1943, Sears Papers.

    Mahonri Sharp (Bill) Young and Mahonri M. Young II also report that there was a pigpen in the back of the caretaker's house (Communication, August 31, 1994).

58.   Follow-up telephone interview with Anna Weir Ely Smith by Cynthia Zaitzevsky, August 21, 1994. Records at the Ridgefield Town Hall, File #2100, J. Alden Weir, dated 1920, Folder #2.

59.   Mahonri Sharp (Bill) Young, Interview with Cynthia Zaitzevsky, May 15, 1994.

60.   Ibid., 7.

61.   Young to Sears, March 30, 1944, Sears Papers.

62.   Young to Sears, October 19, 1944, Sears Papers.

63.   Ibid.

64.   Ibid., December 21, 1944, continuation of letter of October 19, 1944.

65.   Maureen K. Phillips, "Weir Farm Historic Structure Report, Weir Farm National Historic Site, Wilton, Connecticut. Volume II-B: "Weir Farm Outbuildings: Caretaker's House. Caretaker's Garage," (Lowell, Massachusetts: Building Conservation Branch, Northeast Cultural Resource Center, National Park Service, U. S. Department of the Interior, 1995), 85-93. Elements from a disused shed/barn/carriage house may have been used to enlarge the garage (93).

66.   The two drawings are "Mowing in the Orchard" (BYU, No. 832070262), and an untitled orchard drawing (BYU, No. 832080777).
         Another undated drawing not illustrated here is called "The Old Cherry Tree, Branchville" and shows a very large, almost dead cherry tree, which was probably not grown for fruit (BYU, No. 832070211). The fencing visible in this drawing makes it doubtful whether this is even the Young property. There was a cherry tree near the Burlingham house that Charles Burlingham remembers (Information from Weir Farm National Historic Site).

67.   Young to Sears, March 30, 1944, Sears Papers.

68.   Young to Jack Sears, March 20–21, 1944, Sears Papers. Peach and apple trees are also mentioned in a letter to Young dated April 27, 1944.

         Anna Weir Ely Smith, Caro's daughter, also remembers the orchard, especially the peach trees. See Olmsted Center, *Historic Landscape Assessment of Weir Garden*, 8.

69.   Young to Sears, September 17, 1944, Sears Papers. The Youngs had also just visited the famous *New Yorker* cartoonist Helen Hokinson, who had a house down the road in Branchville.

70.   The other is also an undated and untitled drawing (BYU No. 832071129).

         This was probably a field owned by the Youngs on the east side of Nod Hill Road (Communication, Mahonri Sharp (Bill) Young and Mahonri M. Young II, August 31, 1994).

71.   Dorothy Weir Young to Jack and Florence Sears, October 1936, Sears Papers.

72.   Dorothy Weir Young to Jack Sears, September 1938, Sears Papers.

73.   Another undated drawing that is very similar to figure 93 is a sketch at BYU (832080794), not illustrated here,, which was drawn from the same point of view and also shows the sundial, fence, and gate. There is no woman in this drawing, however, and much less detail.

74.   This drawing raises some problems about the 1940s date of the ice house/chicken house conversion, since the original Weir ice house, as seen in figure 43, does not seem to have a gambrel roof. However, there are some Weir drawings of an ice house that show a gambrel roof (Information from Weir Farm National Historic Site).

75.   Mahonri M. Young, Text written on the cardboard mount of "The First Snow of the New Year," Museum of Art, Brigham Young University, Provo, Utah.

This drawing seems to show both the original Weir chicken house and the ice house to the left.

76.   See Olmsted Center, *Historic Landscape Assessment of Weir Garden,* 8.

77.   Other Young drawings of the garden not illustrated or cited here are an undated view (BYU No. 832071115); a charcoal drawing titled by BYU "Woodland Scene with House," also undated (BYU No. 832100297); another undated drawing titled by BYU "Golden Gate at Branchville," probably a misprint for "Garden Gate" (BYU No. 832070175); an undated watercolor, "Carnival, Mid-day" (BYU No. 832010062); and an undated drawing, which has several dog studies at the top and a sketch of the garden with a gate and woman at the bottom (BYU No. 832070454). There may well be additional Young drawings of the garden and other parts of the site, since the BYU collection of approximately 7000 works of art has been only partially catalogued by subject.

78.   Young, "D. Weir," Young Papers.

79.   Mahonri Sharp (Bill) Young, interview with Cynthia Zaitzevsky, May 15, 1994.

80.   Ibid.; For the summerhouse in the 1920s, Anna Weir Ely Smith interview with Cynthia Zaitzevsky, August 12, 1994.

81.   Mahonri Sharp (Bill) Young, interview with Cynthia Zaitzevsky, May 15, 1994; follow-up interview with Mahonri Sharp (Bill) Young, by Cynthia Zaitzevsky, August 10, 1994.

82.   Weir Farm Heritage Trust, interview with Mahonri Sharp (Bill) Young et al., August 7, 1989.

83.   Jim Brown, interview with Sarah Olson and Gay Vietzke, June 14, 1994. Mr. Brown was born in 1942 or 1943, lived on Old Branchville Road from age one until 1964 and came back for a year around 1967–1968. Most of his memories must postdate Dorothy's death, although he played at the pond as a young child.

He remembers the boathouse being locked or only accessible from the water in a boat. He approached the pond from Old Branchville Road, and "99% of the time you didn't see another soul back at the pond." It was Brown's secret place, although he didn't either swim or skate there. He didn't even realize the pond was part of the Weir/Young property until the Gully kids told him. The pond was known locally as "Weir Pond." There was no gazebo or any kind of structure on the island during Brown's childhood.

84.   Young to Sears, July 4, 1940, and April 29, 1943, Sears Papers.

85.   Young to Sears, May 20, 1947, Sears Papers.

Dorothy apparently responded well to her earlier treatment and was healthy for several years. When the cancer recurred, her final illness was brief. Follow-up telephone interview with Mahonri Sharp (Bill) Young, by Cynthia Zaitzevsky, August 10, 1994.

86.   Young to Sears, July 23, 1947, Sears Papers.

87.   Young to Sears, July 23, 1947, Sears Papers.

88.   Ridgefield Probate Court Records, File #G2889, Dorothy Weir Young, affidavit concerning the payment of taxes on choses in action and other property, dated July 8, 1947 (notes at Weir Farm National Historic Site).

89.   Mahonri Sharp (Bill) Young, follow-up telephone interview with Cynthia Zaitzevsky, August 10, 1994.

90.   Weir Farm Heritage Trust, interview with Mahonri Sharp "Bill" Young, Charles Mahonri Lay, Mahonri M. Young, 2nd, and George Lay, August 7, 1989.

91.   Hinton, "Mahonri Young and the Church, " 41–42; Engraved invitation, Sears Papers.

92.   Hinton, *A Biographical History of Mahonri M. Young,* Chapter VIII, "The Twilight Years," 222–244.

        Although Hinton gives the date of completion of the United States Capitol Brigham Young as 1949, the base of the sculpture itself is signed "Mahonri. 1947" (Cynthia Zaitzevsky, site visit, Statuary Hall, United States Capitol, July 16, 1994). It may have been that the sculpture was not installed in Statuary Hall until 1949.

93.   Ibid., 236–239. Quotation from Young to Sears, November 3, 1952, Sears Papers.

94. .   Young to Sears, November 3, 1952, Sears Papers. Young was a lifelong Democrat and an ardent supporter of both Woodrow Wilson and Franklin D. Roosevelt. See Hinton, *A Biographical History of Mahonri M. Young,* 240–242.

95.   Young to Sears, November 1, 1954, Sears Papers.

96.   Mahonri Sharp (Bill) Young, interview with Cynthia Zaitzevsky, May 15, 1995. Jim Brown, interview with Sarah Olson and Gay Vietzke, June 14, 1994.

97.   Young to Sears, January 13, 1956, Sears Papers. See also Young to Sears, March 19, 1956, Sears Papers.

98.   Young to Sears, March 19, 1956, Sears Papers.

99.   Ibid. It is difficult to see how a squatter could sell Young's land without having clear title to it himself. In the same letter, Young mentions that landscape architect Charles Downing Lay, Oliver's father, had died suddenly.

100.   Young, "The Reminiscences of Mahonri Young."

101.   Hinton, *A Biographical History of Mahonri M. Young,* 244.

102.   Jim Brown, whose memories of the pond date from around 1951, remembers the area around it being wooded with few trails. Jim Brown interview with Sarah Olson and Gay Vietzke, June 14, 1994.

103.   For Twachtman and the landscape of his country home in Cos Cob, Connecticut, see Alfred Henry Goodwin, "An Artist's Unspoiled Country Home," *Country Life in America,* vol. 8, no. 6 (October 1905), 625–630, photographs by Henry Troth. For Augustus Saint-Gaudens and the landscape of Aspet in Cornish, New Hampshire, see Marion Pressley, A.S.L.A., Pressley Associates, Inc., and Cynthia Zaitzevsky, Ph.D., Cynthia Zaitzevsky Associates, *Cultural Landscape Report for Saint-Gaudens National Historic Site, Volume I: Site History and Existing Conditions,* Cultural Landscape Publication No. 3 (Boston, MA: National Park Service, North Atlantic Region, Division of Cultural Resources Management, Cultural Landscape Program, 1993), Chapters I and II.

CHAPTER IV: THE BURLINGHAM PROPERTY. THE WILLIAM WEBB; J. ALDEN WEIR; ELLA WEIR; AND CORA WEIR BURLINGHAM OWNERSHIPS: 1882–1986

What is known about the pre-1882 history of this property, which includes nothing specifically about the landscape, has been summarized in the prologue. The Webb family continued to own this farm after J. Alden Weir's purchase of the adjoining Beers Farm; in 1907 Weir purchased it from the estate of William Webb.[1] After Weir died intestate in 1919, his entire estate, including the 50-acre parcel of the former Webb Farm, was inherited by his wife Ella Baker Weir and his three daughters. In 1922 Caro and Cora transferred their rights in the Branchville property to Dorothy. After Ella's death in 1930, her share was inherited by Dorothy, who in 1931 gave the Webb Farm to her sister, Weir's youngest daughter, Cora Weir Burlingham.[2] Cora lived at the Webb Farm on weekends and early in the summer until the death of Charles Burlingham, Sr., in 1979, when she rented it out. Cora died in 1986. The only one of these four ownership periods that is at all well documented is the last.

WILLIAM WEBB, (1882)–1907

As discussed in the prologue, the original 1748 grant for Webb Farm consisted of two parcels of land (41 acres and 9 acres) out of 2200 acres of common land in Ridgefield known as Rockhouse Woods. In 1882 when Weir purchased the adjacent Beers Farm, it had been in the possession of the Webb family for 50 years.[3]

What we know about the landscape of the Webb Farm from 1882–1907 comes primarily from the etchings, watercolors, and pastels that Weir did while the farm was still in the ownership of the Webbs. The earliest of these may be the watercolor illustrated in figure 3, "Spring Landscape: Branchville," painted in 1882 just before Weir's purchase of the Beers Farm. As noted in chapter I, this painting cannot be absolutely identified as the Webb Farm; however, today it more closely resembles the fields belonging to what is now the Burlingham property than any other on or near Weir Farm proper.

The etchings by Weir of the Webb Farm all depict its rear outbuildings and rear and side fields. The Webb/Burlingham house does not appear in any of these works of art. Whether this was because Weir found the fields and outbuildings more interesting aesthetically or because he was reluctant to trespass near the house while Webb still owned it cannot be determined. One such view is Weir's undated etching "The Barn Lot," illustrated in figure 106. Although few of Weir's etchings are dated, he was

207

Figure 106   J. Alden Weir, "The Barn Lot," n.d. Etching and drypoint on paper (Museum of
                    Art, Brigham Young University, Provo, Utah).

active as an etcher only between about 1887 and 1893. During the summer of 1888, Twachtman rented a house in Branchville, and the two artists painted and etched together and used Weir's new etching press.[4]

An etching showing the same general area as "The Barn Lot" is "Webb Farm," undated (figure 107). This shows the western end of the Webb barn and the gate and enclosure immediately adjacent to it. Another state of the same etching, which takes in only about the western two-thirds of figure 107, is also called "Webb Farm" (not illustrated).[5] Figure 108 shows a third etching entitled "Webb Farm." The orientation is very difficult to determine in this view, since the outbuilding at the right is not the Webb barn and there is also a large barn in the distance that does not resemble either the Webb or the Weir barn.

Weir also did at least one pastel of the Webb Farm, "The Edge of Webb Farm," undated (figure 109). Unfortunately, it is very difficult to tell which edge of the Webb Farm this might be. The topography does not fit the field across from Weir's house.

The only photograph from this period that shows even the edge of the Webb Farm is the 1889 cyanotype illustrated in figure 14, which shows people in the field opposite Weir's house and the northern border of the field. As it appears in this cyanotype, there is nothing especially distinctive about the field, except, of course, that the photograph was taken before the construction of the present stone wall along Pelham Lane, which was put up by Cora Weir Burlingham in the 1940s. What appears to a clump of sumac may also be seen in the lower left-hand corner of the view.

J. ALDEN WEIR, 1907–1919

Surprisingly little is known about this period in the history of the property. In the fall of 1906, William Webb died, and in November 1906 his son William Foster Webb was appointed executor of his estate. In March 1907 Weir purchased the 50-acre parcel of the Webb Farm from the estate.[6] It is probable that he did this primarily to protect his original purchase from encroachment, since during his and his widow's lifetimes the family does not seem to have used the property. Instead, between 1907 and 1932 it appears to have been always occupied by a farmer (whether for rent or in partial payment for services is not known). It is possible that during this period Weir and then Ella may have had two farmers: the farmer who lived in the Webb house being responsible for the upkeep of the Webb property while the farmer occupying the caretaker's house remained in charge of the original Weir property. It has been suggested that Weir used the Webb Farm primarily for haying.[7]

There are almost no references to the Webb Farm in Weir's correspondence during this period.

Figure 107   J. Alden Weir, "Webb Farm," n.d. Etching and drypoint on paper (Collections
                    of the Library of Congress).

Figure 108   J. Alden Weir, "Webb Farm," n.d. Etching (Private Collection).

211

Figure 109   J. Alden Weir, "The Edge of Webb Farm," n.d. Pencil and pastel on paper.
                    (Private Collection).

However, in March 1915 he wrote to his daughter that Mr. and Mrs. Boughten, a farmer and his wife who had been with Weir since at least 1913, had moved into the old Webb house.[8] By this time, Weir had ceased etching actively, and the only work of art showing the Webb Farm that can be tentatively dated to this period is the oil painting "Webb's Apple Orchard, Spring," ca. 1910–1919 (figure 110). The topography that appears in this work suggests that it was painted from a point of view near the well on the Webb grounds looking due south. Apparently, even after his purchase Weir continued to refer to this property as the Webb Farm, so his title of "Webb's Apple Orchard" does not necessarily mean that the work was painted before 1907. One photograph from this period that may be of the Webb property is figure 111, which shows Weir, with a bundle of straw under his arm, walking into a space between the house and an outbuilding.

ELLA WEIR, 1920–1930

About this ownership we know virtually nothing except that the property, which was still referred to as the Webb Farm, appears to have been occupied or leased to a farmer during the entire decade.[9]

CORA WEIR BURLINGHAM, 1931–1979 (1986)

Introduction

As noted above, at some point after her marriage to Mahonri Young in February 1931, Dorothy gave the Webb Farm to her sister Cora to whom she was very close, possibly in exchange for Cora's rights at Windham.[10]

Cora Weir was born in 1892, the youngest child of J. Alden Weir and Anna Baker Weir. Although Cora did not attend college, she was professionally trained in interior design and practiced with a firm in New York City in the late 1920s.[11] Cora also painted watercolors and had a great interest in gardening. After World War I she was a volunteer Red Cross nurse in France, where she met her first husband William Edward Carlin (Ed), who was 24 years her senior. Shortly after the birth of their son, Bill, in 1927, Ed Carlin died. In 1929 Cora married Charles Burlingham, and the following year their son, Charles Jr. (Charlie), was born. Cora was an energetic person, taking a three-and-a-half mile walk every day in her seventies and working at the New York Botanical Garden in the Bronx well into her eighties.[12]

213

Figure 110   J. Alden Weir, "Webb's Apple Orchard, Spring," ca. 1910–1919. Oil on canvas
                    (Private Collection).

Figure 111   J. Alden Weir at the Webb Farm. Photograph, ca. 1915 (Weir Family Papers, Special Collections, Lee Library, Brigham Young University, Provo, Utah).

The Burlingham's principal residence was in New York City. However, they faithfully spent weekends in Wilton and also stayed there in the late spring from about May 10 through June 20, after which they went to Black Point in Niantic, Connecticut, on Long Island Sound for the summer months. During the six weeks in Wilton, Cora would work furiously in the flower and vegetable gardens, assisted by a paid gardener.[13] In 1932, the first year she was listed as a Wilton taxpayer, her property consisted of one dwelling house, two outbuildings (the barn and the woodshed), and 50 acres of land, all valued at something over $14,000.00.[14] As noted in the prologue, recent physical investigation has indicated that the barn was probably built before 1860, while the woodshed can only be dated to the late 19th or early 20th centuries.[15]

When the Burlinghams acquired the Webb house in 1931, they found it a "shambles."[16] Cora immediately set about an ambitious program of renovating and building extensive additions to the house, fixing up the barn, having a new sunken garden designed and installed, building a new tool house, surrounding her property with extensive and beautifully crafted dry stone walls, and constructing a terraced garden to the south of the main driveway. Many of these activities were initiated at more or less the same time in the 1930s, while others were projects of the 1940s. Meanwhile, their two young boys spent their weekends and the late spring season helping out in the garden, riding their ponies, skeet shooting, etc. During World War II, the field to the north of the house across from the Weir/Young house was given over to a large Victory Garden, a name that stuck even after vegetables were no longer grown there.[17] At some point, Cora painted the honey locust (Gleditsia triacanthos 'Moraine') on the west side of the south terrace (patio), which probably predated the Burlinghams' ownership and which still exists today.[18]

By the mid-1930s, the house had been extended to the south by the addition of a new dining room and kitchen. The additions to the house in the early and mid-1930s resulted in an entirely new south side to the house. At about the same time (ca. 1934–1938), Cora added the present stone terrace, constructed by the Knoche family, who were local masons. In 1938 she had New York City architect F. Nelson Breed, a neighbor in Wilton at 464 Nod Hill Road, design a greenhouse on the exterior south kitchen wall and a new doorway surround for the main entrance.[19] Before the greenhouse was constructed and for a time afterward, there was a pergola, probably for growing grapes, near the exterior south kitchen wall.[20] All of Cora's and Nelson Breed's additions and renovations to the house were designed in the Colonial Revival style. A photograph of the east facade of the house, taken probably in the 1940s, is illustrated in figure 112. In the foreground is the stone wall in front of the house (which apparently preceded Cora's stone walls) and the wooden gate leading into the driveway. Just behind the gate is a large tree, probably a sugar maple, which is now gone.[21] Several photographs of the south facade of the house show what appear to be wisteria vines climbing the posts of the porch.[22]

216

Figure 112   Webb/Burlingham house from the east. Photograph, ca. 1940s (WFNHS-HP No.
                    87).

217

The Sunken Garden

The next project was a small sunken garden between the house and the barn. To design this garden, begun in 1932, Cora turned to her architect's wife, Vera Breed. Descendant of a British governor of the Bahamas, Vera Poggi Breed (1890–1967), was born in Elizabeth, New Jersey, but was educated in Wales. When in Britain, she may have worked on some of Gertrude Jekyll's gardens. On her return to the United States in 1920, she looked for work with Ruth Dean, a New York City landscape architect who had a joint practice with her husband, architect Aymar Embury II. Dean advised Poggi to take the course in landscape architecture at Massachusetts State College (now the University of Massachusetts at Amherst), which Poggi did, completing the course in 1928–1929. She was then accepted in Ruth Dean's office. In 1931 Poggi married Nelson Breed and worked with him in a manner similar to that of Dean and Embury. At the beginning of a project, Nelson Breed would make a color rendering of the house he was designing, which would also include a general indication of the plantings. Vera would then take over and do the detailed landscape design. Plans for 51 projects by Vera Poggi Breed designed between 1927 and 1942 have survived; unfortunately, they do not include the Burlingham garden. Most of her projects were in Connecticut and New York, but she also designed a few gardens in the South and in California.[23]

The Burlingham sunken garden is a small secluded space of great charm. It was designed with curving flowerbeds backed by arborvitae and edged with dwarf boxwood. Although the original Breed plan for the garden has not survived, there are some photographs that show it at an early stage. Figure 113 is not dated, but all of the plants in the garden, especially the boxwood, look newly planted. The arborvitae, while tall, are less full than in later photographs. In 1956 the garden was published in *Treasury of American Gardens* by James M. Fitch and F. F. Rockwell (figure 114).[24] This autumn photograph shows seasonal plants that include what were then new large-flowered chrysanthemums: Huntsman, Magnolia, Lavender Lady and Bronze Pyramid. Bulbs were featured in the spring.[25]

After this garden was completed in 1940, Nelson Breed designed a stone toolshed for Cora.[26]

In 1969 Cora decided to have the planting of the sunken garden redesigned. Since Vera Breed had died, she went to Friede R. Stege, a landscape architect from New Canaan, Connecticut.[27] Stege's plan, shown in figure 115, is for planting only. The basic structure of the garden, including the boxwood edging, was left unchanged. The plan does not show any change from the original arborvitae, but the existing plants in their place today are dwarf Alberta spruce (*Picea glauca* var. *albertiana* 'Conica').[28] Although chrysanthemums are still featured (usually following *Dianthus barbatus*), there appears to be

218

Figure 113   Burlingham sunken garden. Photograph, ca. 1930s (WFNHS-HP No. 126).

Figure 114   Burlingham sunken garden. Photograph by Gottscho-Schleisner, ca. 1955 (From
                    Fitch and Rockwell, *Treasury of American Gardens,* 1956).

220

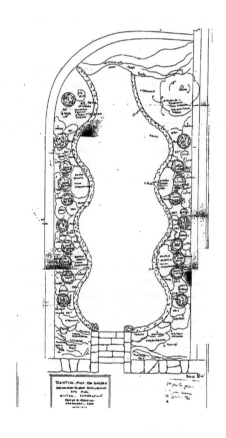

Figure 115   Friede R. Stege, Landscape Architect, "Planting Plan for Garden. Mr. and Mrs.
                  Charles Burlingham, Nod Hill, Wilton, Connecticut," May 1969 (Weir Farm
                  National Historic Site).

221

a much greater emphasis in 1969 on spring and early summer plants than previously. Plants on the Stege plan include Exbury and other types of azaleas, primroses, columbine, foxglove, and lupine together with many groups of iris. In figure 116, a photograph probably taken after 1969, Cora is holding a grandchild in the sunken garden with iris in the background. In the lower left-hand corner of the Stege plan near the driveway wall, a peony is indicated; a tree peony still exists in this location.

Cora's last gardener was Vinnie Marsili, now retired in Georgia. An interview with Marsili by the Weir Farm Heritage Trust itemizes some of his regular tasks, such as the removal of self-sown trees and shrubs, pruning of other trees and shrubs such as the boxwood, and the addition or replacement of new plants. Areas of the grounds besides the sunken garden are referred to, such as a rock garden by the rocks, plantings of pink thyme between the stones on the patio, etc.[29] Laura Radcliffe, a volunteer docent at the Weir Farm National Historic Site, noted that when she first visited the Burlingham property several years ago, it was late February and there were white snowdrops and yellow winter aconite *(Eranthis)* blooming through the snow in the front yard.[30] "Snow drops in front" was one of the items planted by Vinnie Marsili; another was an unspecified small yellow flower.

The "Great Wall of Cora"

Apparently, Mahonri Young liked to tease his sister-in-law, and the "Great Wall of Cora" was his name for the system of elegantly constructed dry stone walls that Cora Burlingham had local mason Joe Knoche design and build on the property. It is not yet clear whether Cora had a grand plan for the stone walls or whether they evolved incrementally, but they seem to have been completed by the late 1940s.[31] Joe Knoche and his men were one of Young's favorite subjects. He did numerous sketches of them, resulting in the etching illustrated in figure 117, which shows the construction of one of the walls to the north of the house. The north side of the toolshed is also visible. None of Young's Knoche sketches and etchings is dated, but they must have been done in the 1940s. Some of them show plowing or other gardening activities going on, possibly illustrating the Victory Garden located in this field. The "Great Wall of Cora" is one of the most distinctive features of the Burlingham grounds, providing an easily recognizable leitmotif, or "Cora signature," running throughout almost the entire extent of the property.

The Vegetable Gardens and South Terraces

Before World War II, Cora Weir Burlingham did not have a special interest in vegetable gardening. It was only with the advent of the war effort that she developed a large vegetable garden in the field to the north of the house. This plot measured about 150 feet long and 75 feet long.[32]

222

Figure 116   Cora with baby in the sunken garden. Photograph, ca. 1970 (WFNHS-HP No. 79).

Figure 117   Mahonri M. Young, "Joe Knoche Builds a New Stone Wall," n.d. (ca. 1940s). Etching (Museum of Art, Brigham Young University, Provo, Utah, No. 832040321).

224

The south terraces were one of the last of Cora's construction projects and seem to have been completed by about 1946 or 1947. They appear on an aerial photograph of May 1949 and show up very clearly on a September 1951 aerial (see figure 105). Joe Knoche and the "Knoche boys" constructed this feature as well.[33] It is unclear whether the terrace garden was preceded by another garden in the same location, or whether it was simply a replacement for the much larger Victory Garden in the north field, which was removed after World War II. It seems likely that a smaller garden closer to the house was desired for growing berries. A 1960 photograph of the terraces is illustrated in figure 118. These terraces appear to have been used primarily for growing raspberries, strawberries, and rhubarb, fruits that Cora especially liked.[34] However, other plants were undoubtedly grown there as well. A series of Burlingham family photographs dated 1963 definitely show irises in these terraces, as well as other plantings, including possibly herbs.[35] Today, stalks of asparagus still appear in the former asparagus beds.

Cora was a hands-on gardener, as can be seen in several photographs showing her working in the Victory Garden and the south terraces.[36] A 1939 drawing by Mahonri Young shows a plowed vegetable garden or field at the Burlingham property (figure 119). The World War II Victory Garden in the north field was quite extensive, and practically every kind of vegetable was grown there. Cora grew and canned beets, rhubarb, tomatoes, melons, squashes, and beans. Every year she bleached celery in the root cellar of the tool house, where turnips and other vegetables were kept in sand.[37]

Although after World War II large-scale vegetable gardening at the Burlingham property was phased out, Cora continued to have a small vegetable garden near the house. The Burlinghams never grew hay or any other field crop.[38]

Livestock and Pets

Although the Burlinghams did not farm, even to the extent that the Youngs did, they kept chickens during World War II and also had ponies for the boys. A photograph of Bill Carlin on a pony in the paddock behind the woodshed is illustrated in figure 120. Several dogs were also kept for a time in a large pen behind the house (figure 121).

Cora's Later Years

Cora was the person most directly responsible for preserving Weir Farm, even though public efforts on behalf of the property were most concentrated after her death in 1986. In 1969 she donated 37 acres of the Webb Farm land to the Nature Conservancy.[39] This is now part of the 113-acre Weir-Leary-

225

Figure 118   The Burlingham terraced garden. Photograph, October 1960 (WFNHS-HP No. 81).

Figure 119   Mahonri M. Young, Plowed field.   Crayon drawing, 1939 (Museum of Art, Brigham Young University, Provo, Utah, No. 832190159).

Figure 120   Bill Carlin on a pony in paddock by Burlingham woodshed. Photograph, ca. mid-
                    1930s (WFNHS-HP No. 143).

Figure 121   Burlingham and young families in dog pen at rear of Burlingham house.
                    Photograph, before 1940 (WFNHS-HP No. 125).

White Preserve.[40]   Cora was also instrumental in saving the pond and the land by the pond after developers had initially purchased it. She initiated petitions and neighborhood rallies and got Doris and Sperry Andrews involved.[41] (The full story of how Weir Farm was preserved will be outlined in chapter VI.) After the death of Charles Burlingham, Sr., in 1979, Cora did not want to stay in the house by herself and rented it to a family from New York City.[42]

SUMMARY

Over a period of slightly more than one hundred years, the Webb/Burlingham property evolved, especially under the ownership of Cora Weir Burlingham, from what was originally a working farm into an appealing country residence with gardens, stone walls, and terraces.

LANDSCAPE FEATURES AND CONDITIONS, CA. 1947

Methodology

The landscape conditions of the Burlingham Property in 1947 were documented using the same historic photographs, paintings, and written correspondence mentioned in the section on Methodology for the Weir Farm 1947 period plan. However, the 1949 aerial photograph, once again, was the primary source for this period for the location of buildings and the study of plant succession and other vegetation. Features such as the Victory Garden that were developed after 1919 and were no longer extant in 1947 are discussed in the text but do not appear on the period plan. Other sources are listed in exhibit 8.

Landscape Character

The landscape character of the Burlingham property and building complex in 1947 as shown in exhibits 6 and 18 was more cultivated in comparison to the landscape character of the Weir property at the same time. The immediate environs of the house were embellished with a flower garden and terraced garden that were still well maintained. These gardens perpetuated the gentleman's farm character of the property.

230

Major Landscape Developments

The major landscape developments existing on the Burlinghan property in 1947 (shown in exhibits 6 and 7) were the existence of several buildings, including the house, barn, woodshed, potting shed, and well; the extensive network of massive stone walls built by Cora; the existing of an ornamental garden area (the sunken garden to the immediate west side the house); and the terraced gardens located to the south side of the house.

Features No Longer Extant

Most of the structures, with the exception of the well, are still in existence today. The walls and the framework for the ornamental gardens remain; however, the plant materials in both gardens either no longer exist or, if existing, may not be the original plant materials of 1947. The pony paddock is no longer extant.

ENDNOTES TO CHAPTER IV

1.   Weir purchased only a portion of the Webb Farm, most of which remained in the Webb family. (There were several branches of the Webb family in the area.) Information, courtesy of Charles Burlingham, informal telephone interview with Cynthia Zaitzevsky, August 31, 1994.

2.   Maureen K. Phillips, "Weir Farm Historic Structure Report, Volume III: Burlingham Complex, Weir Farm National Historic Site, Wilton Connecticut" Draft Report (Boston: Building Conservation Branch, Cultural Resources Center, North Atlantic Region, National Park Service, U.S. Department of the Interior, 1994), 5.

3.   Ellen Paul, CGRS, "History and Documentation of Weir Farm" (1990), 6, 10–11.

4.   Doreen Bolger Burke, *J. Alden Weir: An American Impressionist* (Newark: University of Delaware Press, 1983), 175–184; Dorothy Weir Young, *The Life and Letters of J. Alden Weir* (New York: Kennedy Graphics, Inc., Da Capo Press, 1971), 169, 179.

5.   This is Weir's "Webb Farm," n.d. (Weir Farm Heritage Trust).

6.   Paul, "History and Documentation, 6, 7. Weir had just satisfied his 1886 mortgage on his first purchase.

7.   *Weir Farm National Historic Site, Wilton and Ridgefield, Connecticut. Draft General Management Plan: Environmental Impact Statement* (Boston: U.S. Department of the Interior, National Park Service, North Atlantic Region, Division of Planning, [May?] 1994), 3–12.

8.   J. Alden Weir to Dorothy Weir, March 25, 1915, AAA. See also Weir to Ella Baker Weir, April 23, 1915, AAA. Boughten apparently did not stay long after this, since Weir's letters in 1916 refer to the difficulty of getting good farmers. It was not until spring 1917 that he got "two good men for Branchville." See Weir to John Ferguson Weir, Spring 1917, AAA, Reel 125. These farmers also did not seem to stay long.

9.   Anna Weir Ely Smith, informal telephone interview with Cynthia Zaitzevsky, August 12, 1994.

10.   Paul, "History and Documentation," 7.

11.   Informal telephone interview with Charles Burlingham, by Cynthia Zaitzevsky, August 31, 1994.

12.   Weir Farm Heritage Trust, interview with Charlie Burlingham, March 17, 1989.

13.   Ibid.

14.   Wilton Town Clerk's Office, Tax Records, Grand List 1932. The items on Cora's tax list stayed virtually the same through at least 1959, except for 1940, when a third outbuilding (the toolshed) was added, and 1957, when a piece of land of 2.8 acres was sold. The assessed value naturally went up.

15.   Phillips, "Weir Farm Historic Structure Report, vol. III," 183–238.

16.   Weir Farm Heritage Trust, interview with Mahonri Sharp (Bill) Young, Charles Mahonri Lay, Mahonri M. Young II, and George Lay, August 7, 1989.

17.   Weir Farm Heritage Trust, interview with Charlie Burlingham, March 17, 1989.

18.   Weir Farm Heritage Trust, interview with Doris and Sperry Andrews, March 16, 1989; Draft General Management Plan," 6–10. The present whereabouts of the painting is unknown.

19.   Phillips, "Weir Farm Historic Structure Report, vol. III," 8–10. The F. Nelson Breed Papers are in the Southeastern Architectural Archive at Tulane University.

20.   Ibid., 9–10. See also WFNHS HP-No. 119.

21.   An earlier photograph, taken ca. 1933, showing part of the front of the house before the new front doorway surround, appears to shows the ground around the house and the driveway area newly graded. See WFNHS-HP No. 113, also figure 2 in Phillips, "Weir Farm Historic Structure Report, vol. III," 25.

22.   See, for example, WFNHS HP-Nos. 93, 124, and 144.

23.   Dona Caldwell, Biographical Sketch and List of Commissions, ms., Fairfield Historical Society, Fairfield, Connecticut, 1992. Copy Weir Farm National Historic Site. It is not known if the Nelson Breed Papers at Tulane include such a color rendering for the Burlingham House. They do include all of Breed's plans for the house, which will be used in the completed Historic Structure Report.

It is unclear just what Poggi's association with Jekyll might have been. Gertrude Jekyll, who died in 1932, did not employ assistants. (Information courtesy of Judith Tankard, Newton, Massachusetts, a Jekyll scholar.)

24.   James M. Fitch and F. F. Rockwell, *Treasury of American Gardens* (New York: Harper Brothers, 1956). There is no text other than the caption to the photograph, which is by Gottscho-Schleisner. Samuel Gottscho was an eminent architectural and landscape photographer some of whose records survive in private hands in Brooklyn, New York. (Information from The Catalog of Landscape Records in the United States, Wave Hill, The Bronx, New

York.) The photograph is also credited to *Flower Grower*. Vera Breed's name is not mentioned as the designer, but few of the gardens in the book are credited to landscape architects. Fletcher Steele, for example, designed at least three gardens in the book but is credited with only one—Naumkeag in Stockbridge, Massachusetts.

25.   Ibid.

26.   Phillips, "Weir Farm Historic Structure Report, vol. III," 239–255.

27.   No information is currently available about Friede R. Stege.

28.   "Weir Farm National Historic Site. Draft General Management Plan," 6–10.

29.   Connie Evans, interview with Vinnie Marsili, Weir Farm Heritage Trust.

30.   Laura Radcliffe to Minnie.Hollyman, Volunteer Coordinator, September 2, 1993, Weir Farm National Historic Site.

31.   Records, Weir Farm National Historic Site. A Knoche grandson still lives in the area. It is not known whether the firm is still in business or retains any business records.

32.   Informal telephone interview with Charles Burlingham, Cynthia Zaitzevsky, August 31, 1994.

33.   The west terraces of the Weir/Young grounds, thus far undated, could be compared with the Burlingham terraces to see if they might have been put in at the same time by the Knoches. Since Cora had an interest in "sprucing up" the Young place, this could have been done at her initiative (Weir Farm Heritage Trust, Interview with Charlie Burlingham, March 17, 1989.

34.   Informal telephone interview with Charles Burlingham, Cynthia Zaitzevsky, August 31, 1994.

35.   See WFNHS HP-Nos. 242-245.

36.   For example, WFNHS-HP No. 100 and WFNHS-HP No. 101.

37.   Weir Farm Heritage Trust, interview with Charlie Burlingham, March 17, 1989.

38.   Informal telephone interview with Charlie Burlingham, August 31, 1994.

39.   Paul, "History and Documentation," 7.

40.   "Weir Farm National Historic Site. Draft General Management Plan," 1-6, 1-7.

41.   Weir Farm Heritage Trust, interview with Doris and Sperry Andrews, March 16, 1989.

42.   Phillips, "Weir Farm Historic Structure Report," vol. III, 8.

CHAPTER V: THE DORIS AND SPERRY ANDREWS OWNERSHIP AND RESIDENCE, 1958-PRESENT

As the third generation of artist-residents of Weir Farm, Doris and Sperry Andrews have great respect for the history of its buildings and landscape. In the late 1980s, they were also active participants in the effort to preserve the site.

Sperry Andrews studied at the National Academy of Design in New York City, with which Weir was long associated and of which he was President from 1915 through 1917. He also studied at the Art Students League in New York City, where Mahonri Young taught. His work is in the collections of the American Academy and Institute of Arts and Letters, New York City; the Columbus Gallery of Fine Arts, Columbus, Ohio; the Wadsworth Athenaeum, Hartford, Connecticut; the National Academy of Design; and other museums.[1] Doris is also an artist, who does ink drawings and watercolors of architectural and still life subjects.[2]

The Andrews came to purchase the core area of Weir Farm because of their friendship with Mahonri Young during the last years of his life. In 1952 Fred Price, Sperry's art dealer in New York City, took him to see the J. Alden Weir Centennial Exhibition at the American Society of Arts and Letters, where he met Edward Hopper and Reginald Marsh. He also bought the catalogue for which Young had written the introduction. When he noticed that Young lived in Branchville, Sperry, who lived in Ridgefield, decided to call on him. With an artist friend, John Hubbard, Sperry went to the Young house and knocked on the door; from this developed a friendship of many years.[3]

By this time, Young's wife Dorothy had been dead for several years, and the couple's circle of artist friends, who had frequently visited the farm in earlier times, had also diminished. Although he continued to work and to find his studio a haven, Young, a convivial man, began to feel isolated and lonely.[4] In particular, he longed for another artist with whom to talk and paint. Sperry Andrews came frequently to paint at Weir Farm while Young was living, and sometimes the two would paint or sketch together in the orchard. Other times, they would go out in the car and sketch at other locations. By this time, Sperry, who also brought his painting class to Branchville once, was the only local artist who still came to visit Young and to paint on the grounds. In the mid-1950s, much of Young's time was spent writing his memoirs, which he worked on in the balcony study area in his studio.[5] When Sperry wanted to see Young or to paint on the grounds, he would go to the studio, call up, and ask Young: "Are you busy?" Young's invariable answer was: "I'm always busy, but come in anyway."[6]

After Young died on November 1, 1957, his children, Mahonri Sharp (Bill) Young and Agnes Young Lay, became his sole heirs. The Andrews made an offer for the house, outbuildings, and enough land to protect the core of the farm. They also asked for a right-of-way to the pond, but this part of the offer was not accepted. After the Andrews' purchase, the rest of the land was sold to developers, although, because of a zoning dispute, nothing was actually developed for many years. At Young's death, . the house and studios were filled with works of art—his own, Weir's, and other artists'. A decision was not made immediately about what to do with the art, and Young's children wanted to be sure it was safe. For about a year, the Andrews were the unofficial caretakers of the art, and then arrangements were made with Brigham Young University to acquire it.[7]

When the Andrews purchased the core area of the farm, the fields were still open, and large oak trees were left as shade for cows. The fishing bridge was also still intact, and Sperry used it to cross the wetland. Also extant was the old wagon trail, which went directly to the pond. The cows did not necessarily use the wagon trail but chose their own routes to the pond. The present fence surrounded the property but was in a more complete condition, and there was also a fence in front of the barn and around the tack house. In the Young vegetable garden there were still remnants of asparagus beds, a raspberry patch, and a row of Egyptian onions along the upper wall. The fence and gates of the Secret Garden were no longer extant (they probably came down sometime after Dorothy's death), but some of the plantings (roses, peonies) remained. The wooden canopy over the well near Pelham Lane, which lasted into the Young period (figure 79), was also gone when the Andrews came. At some point in the Young ownership, the neighbors had apparently became concerned about their children's safety, and the canopy was taken down. The other well behind the barn was still functioning and a source of "lovely Branchville water." In the late 1950s, the small town-owned cemetery was enclosed by a formal fence with gates, but this rotted away eventually and was never replaced. In the Weir barn, there were stalls for horses, cows, and donkeys; the cow stalls were whitewashed. The tack and harnesses were originally kept in the little tack house.[8]

Sperry Andrews also described the pond as having two tributaries feeding into it, which passed through a stone wall with a little arched hole. The stream was lined with rocks to improve the flow. The boathouse was built on a rock at its southern corner, and the boat, was under cover with a ramp on one side, where a person could open the door, climb into the boat, and row out into the pond. At its deepest point, near the dam, the water was about four-and-one-half feet deep. There were black bass in the pond and frogs. Sperry named the two parts of the pond "the great north bay" and "the great south bay."[9]

The Andrews' alterations to the Weir House, outbuildings, and landscape have been very minor. (They did make a number of interior remodellings to the caretaker's house.) Although initially they intended to let some of the outbuildings go, the only one they did not maintain was the wagon shed at the rear of the property. The foundations of this wagon shed still exist. On the main house, they added a

238

storm shelter to the south porch, probably shortly after they purchased the property (figure 122). The main house and other structures have been reroofed by the Andrews at various times. They have added no outbuildings. Sperry has never been interested in landscaping, so they have made no landscape changes to the property and have not maintained a garden.[10]

Sperry Andrews has painted the Weir Farm grounds over a period of almost forty years. Some of his more recent paintings of the property are illustrated in figures 123 through 126. Figure 123, "Weir Farm House," 1990, shows the northern elevation of the house from a vantage point along the path to the orchard. To the left is part of the barn and, at the far right, a corner of the Weir studio may be seen. Also visible in this painting are the hemlock in front of the eastern elevation of the house and the red oak in front of Weir's studio. Perhaps inspired by Weir's "The Laundry, Branchville" (figure 26), Sperry painted "The Laundry Line" in 1993 (figure 124), although this line is in a different location near the Young studio, which is also Sperry's workplace. In 1991 Sperry painted the evocative watercolor, "The Weir Pond" (figure 125), which shows an inlet of the pond seen through a screen of gray tree trunks (probably beech). Figure 126 is a 1989 painting showing trees among rocks in "The Weir Preserve" (a natural area 37 acres of which were originally owned by Weir but are not now part of the National Historic Site).

SUMMARY

Like the Youngs before them, the Andrews have been stewards of the property rather than reworkers of it. As a result, the most essential features of the Weir landscape have survived to the present without the imposition of later designs.

Figure 122   Southern elevation, Weir house. Photograph, after 1957 (WFNHS-HP No. 74).

igure 123   Sperry Andrews, "Weir Farm House," 1990. Oil on canvas (Collection, the
                   Artist).

Figure 124   Sperry Andrews, "The Laundry Line," 1993. Oil on canvas (Private Collection).

Figure 125   Sperry Andrews, "The Weir Pond," 1991. Watercolor (Collection, the Artist).

Figure 126   Sperry Andrews, "The Weir Preserve," 1990. Oil on canvas (Collection, the
                             Artist).

ENDNOTES TO CHAPTER V

1. "Sperry Andrews," in "Special Report: Nine Artists on Location at an American Impressionist's Historic Farm," *American Artist*, (May 1993) 57 (610): #26–27; *Selected Works by Sperry Andrews, Weir Farm Resident Artist (1957 to Present), September 19 - October 24, 1993* (Wilton, CT: Weir Farm National Historic Site, 1993).

2. Information, Weir Farm National Historic Site.

3. Weir Farm Heritage Trust, interview with Doris and Sperry Andrews, March 16, 1989, Branchville, CT; Doris and Sperry Andrews, interviewed by Connie Evans, 1991; Doris and Sperry Young, interviewed by Cynthia Zaitzevsky, with John Grove, Marie Carden, and Gay Vietzke, July 27, 1994, at the Weir House and grounds. A brief and very cryptic reference to Sperry is found in Price's memoirs. See Frederic Newlin Price, *Goodbye Ferargil* (New Hope, PA: The Huffnagle Press, 1958), np.

4. Mahonri M. Young to Jack Sears, July 13, 1956, Jack Sears Papers, Special Collections, Lee Library, Brigham Young University, Provo, Utah, hereafter cited as Sears Papers. In this letter, Young expresses his pleasure that his granddaughter Darcy Lay will be staying with him in New York City, while on work-study from Bennington College. He notes his lack of companionship since Dorothy's death.

5. Weir Farm Heritage Trust, interview with Doris and Sperry Andrews, March 16, 1989. The memoirs are in manuscript form in the Young Papers, Special Collections, Lee Library, Brigham Young University, Provo, Utah. It is difficult to tell if Young finished the memoirs because they are arranged topically rather than chronologically, but they are quite extensive. Further study of these memoirs may reveal mention of Doris and Sperry Andrews, but in general, Young concentrated on his earlier years rather than the period in which he was writing. (He also started on the memoirs long before he met the Andrews.) Selections of the early pages of the autobiography were reprinted in 1940. See Mahonri M. Young, "Notes at the Beginning: Being Excerpts from the Early Pages of a Projected Autobiography," *Mahonri M. Young: Retrospective Exhibition* (Andover, Massachusetts: Addison Gallery of American Art, Phillips Academy, 1940), 47–56.

6. Doris and Sperry Andrews, interviewed by Cynthia Zaitzevsky, with John Grove, Marie Carden, and Gay Vietzke, July 27, 1994.

7. Weir Farm Heritage Trust, interview with Doris and Sperry Andrews, March 16, 1989.

    In 1958 Mahonri S. Young and Agnes Young Lay sold the core property to the Andrews, and in two transactions in 1959, they sold other land to John R. Moore and Corinne T. Moore and to Clifford A. Winton and Wayne Hicklin. Some of these buyers were presumably developers. See Ellen Paul, CGRS, "History and Documentation of Weir Farm" (1990), 7.

8. Ibid.; Follow-up telephone interview with Doris Andrews by Cynthia Zaitzevsky, August 21, 1994.

9. Weir Farm Heritage Trust, interview with Doris and Sperry Andrews, March 16, 1989.

10.   Follow-up telephone interview with Doris Andrews by Cynthia Zaitzevsky, August 21, 1994.   For the alterations to the caretaker's house, see Maureen K. Phillips, "Weir Farm Historic Structure Report, Volume II, Caretaker's Buildings" (Boston: Building Conservation Branch, Cultural Resource Center, North Atlantic Region, National Park Service, U.S. Department of the Interior, 1994, Draft Report), 43–44.   Some exterior alterations were probably made at the same time but seem to be undocumented. (Ibid., 33).

CHAPTER VI: ROLE OF THE WEIR FARM HERITAGE TRUST AND THE ACQUISITION OF THE PROPERTY BY THE NATIONAL PARK SERVICE, 1989–1995

The effort to preserve Weir Farm, which resulted in its acquisition by the National Park Service in 1990, had its origins in the 1969 gift of 37 acres to the Nature Conservancy by Cora Weir Burlingham.

Cora was also the guiding spirit behind the movement to preserve the pond from developers. She initiated petitions and neighborhood rallies and involved Doris and Sperry Andrews in the effort. By late 1970, the various groups concerned with protecting the pond and Weir Farm from development organized the Citizens to Preserve the Weir Farm. Fortunately, the developers who purchased the pond from the Young heirs had another parcel that they developed first, and the pond was left alone for many years. In 1979–1980, the Task Force on the Preservation of Connecticut's Heritage named Weir Farm as one of three sites in the state that reflected its environmental, historical, and artistic heritage. In 1981 the Citizens to Preserve the Weir Farm, funded by corporate donations and the State of Connecticut Department of Environmental Protection, hired Terry Tondro, a Connecticut environmental lawyer to assess whether or not the undeveloped parcel could be preserved. Tondro's report was favorable.[1]

In the 1980s, the Ridgefield Preservation Trust did a survey of historic houses in the town, in the course of which this organization became very interested in the Weir house. In 1983 the Citizens to Preserve the Weir Farm and other interested groups sought assistance from the Trust for Public Land (TPL), a national land conservation organization. In 1985 Connecticut's Heritage Task Force identified Weir Farm as one of the top ten endangered sites in the state. After Cora's death in 1986, TPL purchased key acreage of Weir Farm as a temporary measure until a permanent management organization could be found. TPL served as a land broker and assembled and purchased the land in the expectation that Weir Farm would be protected by the State of Connecticut, with the aid of a newly formed land trust. In 1986 the state, with the assistance of State Senator John Matthews, appropriated funds to buy land at the site from TPL. Between 1988 and 1990, the Connecticut Department of Environmental Management purchased most of the site.[2]

In 1989 members of the Citizens to Preserve the Weir Farm formed the Weir Farm Heritage Trust to act as a grass-roots organization dedicated to preserving the property. The newly formed group was incorporated as a 501(c)(3) organization and received assistance and funding from TPL. In 1989-1990, the North Atlantic Region of the National Park Service, partially funded by TPL, conducted a study of the site to evaluate its feasibility and merit for inclusion within the National Park System and reported favorably. TPL then contacted United States Senator Joseph Lieberman, who in February 1990 introduced

247

the enabling legislation into Congress to make Weir Farm a National Historic Site.[3]

On October 31, 1990, President Bush signed a bill passed by Congress (P.L. 101-485, 104 stat. 1171) that would establish Weir Farm National Historic Site in order to preserve and interpret historically significant properties and landscapes associated with the life and work of J. Alden Weir. The National Park Service was charged in this legislation with preserving the site and maintaining "the integrity of a setting that inspired artistic expression." The Weir Farm Heritage Trust, still a private membership organization, has continued to function at the property through a cooperative agreement with the National Park Service. Indeed, the Trust managed the site until National Park Service staff arrived in January 1992. Once the preservation of Weir Farm was assured, the Trust assumed a primarily educational role, having as its mission the enhancement of public understanding of the site and the perpetuation of its artistic tradition.[4]

In 1992 the Connecticut Department of Environmental Protection donated its 52-acre parcel to the National Park Service. Doris and Sperry Andrews decided to sell the 2-acre historic core area to TPL at a fair-market value with an agreement of life tenancy, and in March 1993 TPL transferred this parcel to the National Park Service.[5]

Currently, the National Park Service owns 57 of the 238 acres that Weir purchased between 1882 and 1907. However, the site is part of nearly 300 acres of contiguous open space. It abuts the 113-acre Weir-Leary-White Preserve run by the Nature Conservancy, which includes Cora's original donation. In addition, there are 33 acres of Town of Ridgefield conservation land and 86 acres owned by the Connecticut Department of Transportation adjoining the site. To the northwest and southeast, there has been extensive residential development.[6]

In less than four years of full operation, the Weir Farm National Historic Site has undertaken several studies of which this report is one. Others include the General Management Plan, the Historic Furnishings Report, and the Historic Structure Report.[7] An important recommendation of the General Management Plan under its Preferred Alternative is to restore the landscape of the Weir Complex to its ca. 1940s appearance and to rehabilitate the landscape of the Burlingham complex to retain changes made by Cora Weir Burlingham after 1940.[8]

The Weir Farm Heritage Trust has been equally active, producing numerous programs, exhibitions, etc. Involvement on the part of the general public has also remained high. One example of a landscape project in which both a private group and the National Park Service have participated is described briefly here, because it concerns a part of the property, the Secret Garden, that has been discussed extensively

248

in earlier chapters.

By the time the National Park Service acquired the property in 1990, this garden had been neglected for decades. Through the interest of the Ridgefield Garden Club, preliminary restoration plans were made in 1991 by landscape architect Rudy Favretti. In 1992 the Garden Club of America awarded the Ridgefield Garden Club $5000.00 for the project. In 1994 the Olmsted Center for Landscape Preservation of the National Park Service, located at the Frederick Law Olmsted National Historic Site in Brookline, Massachusetts, further documented the garden through archaeological investigation and study of historic photographs.[9] (In 1992, the Olmsted Center had carried out a hazardous tree stabilization and shrub rejuvenation project at Weir Farm as well as preparing a grounds maintenance plan for the site.[10]) Dr. Peter del Tredici of the Arnold Arboretum identified the perennials that appear in the historic photographs of the garden, many of which are illustrated in chapter II of this report. In the spring of 1994, the Olmsted Center prepared a historic landscape assessment report on the Weir Garden and a series of plans.[11] In March 1994, 25 trees were removed from the area, and the box and privet plants were pruned to 8 inches in height.[12] One of the plans in the Olmsted Center report, which documents the remaining historic features, missing historic features, etc., of the garden, has already been illustrated in figure 52. Figure 127 is the Olmsted Center's planting plan for the garden. At the present time (June 1995), the Ridgefield Garden Club is implementing the Olmsted Center's plan.

The early 1990s, when Weir Farm became a National Historic Site, have seen an unprecedented growth of interest in historic landscapes and the rapid development of new technologies to study and preserve them. Especially in recent years, the National Park Service has pioneered the study and treatment of cultural landscapes, a circumstance that should greatly benefit Weir Farm, which has an unusual mix of landscapes. Here, gardens and designed features are found side by side with former agricultural lands and wild natural areas. However, the greatest significance of the Weir Farm landscape is that, for almost forty years, it was an inspiration to the imagination and creativity of J. Alden Weir, one of the nation's great turn-of-the-century painters. This tradition has been continued, first by sculptor Mahonri M. Young, who, between 1931 and 1957, drew dozens of sketches of the landscape, and by artists Sperry and Doris Andrews, who have lived and worked at the site since 1958.

249

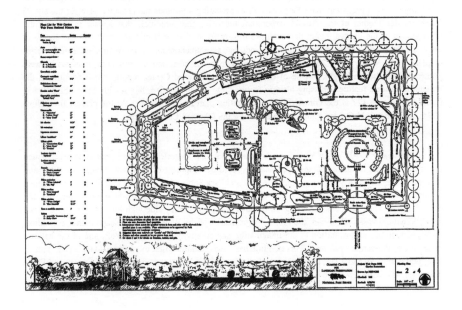

Figure 127   Planting plan, Weir garden.   Olmsted Center for Landscape Preservation,
                    November 1994 (Olmsted Center).

ENDNOTES TO CHAPTER VI

1.   "Chronology: Key Activities and Events Leading up to the Creation of Weir Farm National Historic Site," n.d., Weir Farm National Historic Site. Weir Farm Heritage Trust, interview with Doris and Sperry Andrews, March 16, 1989.

2.   Ibid.; "Weir Farm National Historic Site. Draft General Management Plan/Environmental Impact Statement" (Boston: U.S. Department of the Interior, National Park Service, North Atlantic Region, Division of Planning, 1994), 1-3.

3.   Ibid.

4.   Ibid.

5.   Ibid.; "Draft General Management Plan," 1-3, 1-7; Weir Farm Heritage Trust, interview with Doris and Sperry Andrews, March 16, 1989.

6.   "Draft General Management Plan," 1-3-1-7.

7.   "Draft General Management Plan;" David H. Wallace, Staff Curator, "Historic Furnishings Report, Weir Farm, Weir Farm National Historic Site, Wilton, Connecticut," draft (Harpers Ferry: Division of Historic Furnishings, Harpers Ferry Center, National Park Service, 1994); Maureen K. Phillips, "Weir Farm Historic Structure Report, Volume II, Caretaker's Buildings, Weir Farm National Historic Site," draft (Boston: Building Conservation Branch, Cultural Resources Center, North Atlantic Region, National Park Service, U.S. Department of the Interior, 1994); and Maureen K. Phillips, "Weir Farm Historic Structure Report, Volume III, Burlingham Complex, Weir Farm National Historic Site," draft (Boston: Building Conservation Branch, Cultural Resources Center, North Atlantic Region, National Park Service, U.S. Department of the Interior, 1994.) Volume I of the Weir Farm Historic Structure Report, which deals with the Weir house and studios is scheduled to appear in June 1995.

8.   "Draft General Management Plan," 2-6.

9.   Olmsted Center for Landscape Preservation, "Historic Landscape Assessment of Weir Garden, Weir Farm National Historic Site," prepared for Weir Farm National Historic Site in collaboration with the Ridgefield Garden Club, April 1994.

10.   Olmsted Center for Landscape Preservation, "1992 Annual Report" (Boston: U.S. Department of the Interior, National Park Service, Cultural Landscape Program, North Atlantic Region in partnership with the Frederick Law Olmsted National Historic Site, 1993), 8.

11.   "Historic Landscape Assessment of Weir Garden, Weir Farm National Historic Site."

12.   Ibid., 9, 11.

CHAPTER VII: EXISTING CONDITIONS

INTRODUCTION

A study and analysis of the existing conditions at Weir Farm was undertaken as part of this report to provide an inventory of existing field conditions and to aid park managers in making decisions concerning the future use of the property. The following sections explain and outline the existing conditions of the Weir Farm National Historic Site. The first section of this chapter provides a general description of the site, as well as descriptions of the natural features such as landforms, slopes, vegetation, soils, and hydrology. The second section of this chapter is a detailed inventory of existing conditions, which illustrates graphically the significant features (natural and manmade) of the site. The third section of this chapter describes and graphically depicts the general evolution of the site from 1919 to 1947 (the two periods of significance outlined in previous chapters) through to the present day.

Methodology

The base information utilized for all plans in this section is from an aerial photograph which was flown on December 21, 1992 (exhibit 9), and a topographic survey (4/15/93) compiled from this aerial photograph by Eastern Topographics, Wolfeboro, New Hampshire (exhibit 10). The aerial photograph is a winter photograph that indicates buildings and roads, open fields and waterbodies, stone walls, and vegetative cover. This aerial was the sole source used to compile the topographic site survey (exhibit 10). No field work was used to supplement this survey, however, the ground control necessary to tie the aerial to the ground plane was performed by the National Park Service. This survey indicates all buildings and structures, roads and drives, one-foot contours, spot elevations, exposed bedrock, ponds and standing water, stream flow and wet areas, and tree canopy cover with individual trees over 12-inch caliper noted. The Weir Farm property boundary was added to the topographic survey by Child Associates, Inc., interpreted from information provided by the National Park Service. The following plans of natural features, exhibits 11, 12, 13, and 14 are graphic interpretations of information gleaned from other sources, which are noted on the plans and in the text description for each plan. The detailed existing conditions plans, exhibits 15, 16, and 17, were developed using supplemental information gained from field reconnaissance conducted by Child Associates, Inc., on May 27, 1993, and May 2, 1994, and from the National Park Service-Weir Farm National Historic Site staff.

Subsequent to the preparation of the Draft Cultural Landscape Report, the National Park Service acquired Lot 18, a 3-acre lot located just east of Nod Hill Road along the Southern Property Boundary. Since this was a recent acquisition, Lot 18 is not shown on the Existing Conditions Plans which follow in this section.

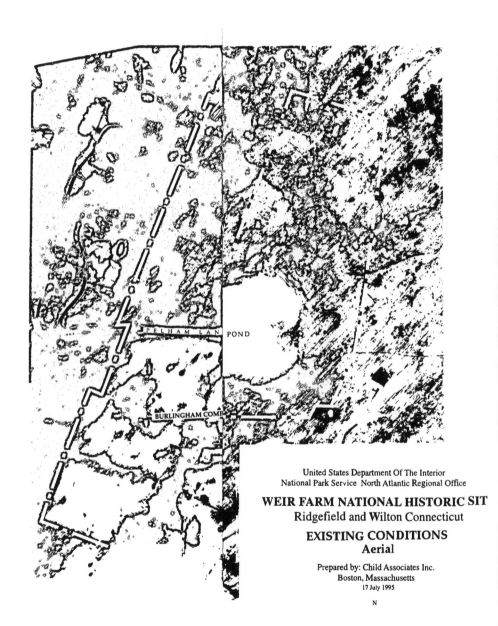

POND

PELHAM LANE

BURLINGHAM COMP

United States Department Of The Interior
National Park Service North Atlantic Regional Office

WEIR FARM NATIONAL HISTORIC SIT
Ridgefield and Wilton Connecticut

EXISTING CONDITIONS
Aerial

Prepared by: Child Associates Inc.
Boston, Massachusetts
17 July 1995

N

United States Department Of The Interior
National Park Service North Atlantic Regional Office

WEIR FARM NATIONAL HISTORIC SIT
Ridgefield and Wilton Connecticut
EXISTING CONDITIONS
Aerial

Prepared by: Child Associates Inc.
Boston, Massachusetts
17 May 1995

N

0   100   200   400
SCALED IN FEET

POND

BURLINGHAM COMPLEX

NOD HILL ROAD

Sources:

TOPOGRAPHIC WORKSHEET

OF THE

WEIR FARM NATIONAL HISTORIC SITE
RIDGEFIELD and WILTON, CT

FOR

CHILD ASSOCIATES, INC.
BOSTON, MA

BY

EASTERN TOPOGRAPHICS
WOLFEBORO, NH

SCALE: 1"= 40'   CONTOUR INTERVAL: 1'

PHOTO DATE: 21 DEC 92
COMPILATION DATE: 15 APR 93

GROUND CONTROL BY: CULTURAL RESOURCES CENTER
NPS/NARO at LOWELL, MA

ANY USER SHOULD DETERMINE THE SUITABILITY
OF THIS AERIAL MAPPING FOR HIS INTENDED USE
AND ASSUME ALL RISK AND LIABILITY IN CONNECTION
THEREWITH.

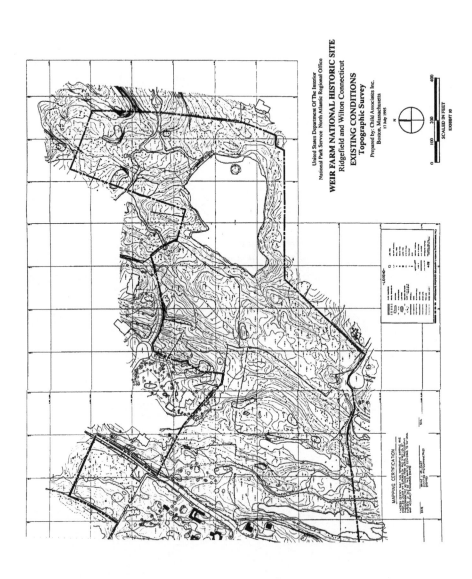

United States Department Of The Interior
National Park Service North Atlantic Regional Office

WEIR FARM NATIONAL HISTORIC SITE

Ridgefield and Wilton Connecticut

EXISTING CONDITIONS

Topographic Survey

Prepared by: Child Associates Inc.
Boston, Massachusetts

17 July 1995

SCALED IN FEET

0   100   200   400

EXHIBIT 10

EXISTING CONDITIONS AND NATURAL FEATURES

General Description

Weir Farm is a 60–acre site located in southwestern Connecticut, in the towns of Ridgefield and Wilton. The town line runs east-west through the center of the site. The area is suburban in nature, with one or two local farms still in use. The site is abutted by relatively new residential uses to the north, east, and southeast, and the Weir Nature Preserve to the west and southwest. The main vehicular access to the site, Nod Hill Road, is a two-lane rural road that runs north-south. Pelham Lane, another rural two-lane road, comes from the west along the town line until it meets and ends at Nod Hill Road. The site includes woodlands, open fields/meadows, wet areas, stone walls, a 3.6-acre pond, and three clusters of buildings: the Weir complex, the Burlingham complex, and the caretaker's complex. The Weir complex is west of Nod Hill Road and north of Pelham Lane, and the Burlingham complex is west of Nod Hill Road and south of Pelham Lane. The caretaker's complex is located east of Nod Hill Road. A more detailed description of the existing conditions is outlined later in this chapter.

Landform Analysis

The Landform Analysis Plan (exhibit 11) diagrams the site's basic natural land features. Topographic elevation, severe slopes, and exposed bedrock combine to define the geologic and landform character of the site. These characteristics were derived from spotgrades, contours, and exposed bedrock mapped on the survey by Eastern Topographics (04/15/93). The plan indicates the relative elevations of the site in 20-foot intervals, severe slopes over 30%, and exposed bedrock locations. A site section is shown at the top of the plan to indicate the extent of elevation change throughout the site.

There is a 100-foot change in elevation within the site. The highest area of the site is located at the west side of the site along a ridge on which Nod Hill Road and the Weir and Burlingham complexes are located. Land elevations fall off slowly on the west side of the ridge, but drop off quickly on the east side. The land is consistently undulating while continuing to fall steadily in elevation toward the east. The Weir and Burlingham buildings are sited 80 feet above the surface of the pond.

Severe slopes on the site tend to occur in narrow bands running in a northerly direction. Though these bands exist throughout the site, the greatest concentration can be found around the pond and just north of the pond along a drainage ravine. The most severe slope found on the site runs parallel to and just east of Nod Hill Road.

259

650 –

600

550

W - E SECTION

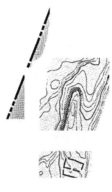

Sources:

- Eastern Topographic Survey 4/15/93
  (1' contour, bedrock)

Note: Features on this plan that do not appear on the
photogrammetric survey prepared by Eastern
Topographic were added manually.

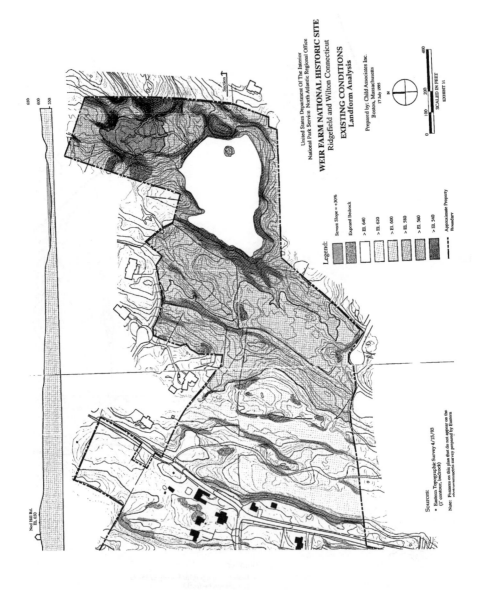

United States Department Of The Interior
National Park Service North Atlantic Regional Office

WEIR FARM NATIONAL HISTORIC SITE
Ridgefield and Wilton Connecticut
EXISTING CONDITIONS
Landform Analysis

Prepared by: Child Associates Inc.
Boston, Massachusetts
17 July 1995

Legend:

	Severe Slope = +30%
	Exposed Bedrock
	> El. 640
	> El. 620
	> El. 600
	> El. 580
	> El. 560
	> El. 540
- - -	Approximate Property Boundary

N

0   100   200   400
SCALED IN FEET
EXHIBIT 11

Sources:
• Eastern Topographic Survey 4/15/93
  (3' contour, bedrock)

Note: Features on this plan that do not appear on the photogrammetric survey prepared by Eastern

Section →

Nod Hill Rd.
El. 650

650
600
550

Elongated formations of exposed bedrock exist on the site, rising just above the surface of the surrounding grade. They can be found along ridges and in small knolls in three areas of the site: the ridge line along Nod Hill Road, the center of the site, and in larger masses in the northeast corner of the site. The most visible area of exposed bedrock can be found between Weir's studio and the barn.

Slope Analysis

The Slope Analysis Plan (exhibit 12) was derived using the survey by Eastern Topographics (04/15/93). Using the one-foot contours on the plan, slope percentages were calculated. The site slope conditions were then divided into four categories: 0–8%, 8–15%, 15–30%, and greater than 30%. The criteria for slope percentage intervals was established to reveal basic site slope characteristics. These characteristics influence the constructability of future paths, roads, parking, and building foundations.

As seen on the plan, slope variation occurs randomly throughout the site, with no slope category dominating one particular area. Direction is the most prominent slope characteristic with long narrow bands of the steepest slopes running in a northeast/southwest direction. Approximately 50% of the site is comprised of relatively flat land (0–8% slope) that runs in a similar direction, but in wider bands. These flat bands tend to occur in lowland/wetlands and on the highest ridge along Nod Hill Road.

Vegetation Analysis

The primary objective of the Vegetation Analysis Plan (exhibit 13) is to show areas of existing tree coverage and canopies, open space areas, and the location of trees over 12-inch caliper, which reveal vegetation age and pattern. The three major forest types are classified by dominant vegetation and soil condition, as described in "An Ecological Survey of Weir Farm":[1] the mixed oak forest, sugar maple-white ash forest, and the red maple forest. These are indicated in exhibit 13.

1.   The mixed oak forest is represented on the site by the existence of one subtype or subcategory of vegetation: the oak–maple leaved viburnums, which are the most dominant forest types on the site, and can be found in the well-drained areas at the center of the site, northwest of the Weir buildings and north and east of the pond. Trees classified as part of the mixed oak forest and oak–maple-leaved viburnum subcategory found in these areas include: red oak, black birch, red maple, with some sugar maple, striped maple, white ash and flowering dogwood.[2]

United States Department Of The Interior
National Park Service North Atlantic Regional Office

WEIR FARM NATIONAL HISTORIC SITE
Ridgefield and Wilton Connecticut

EXISTING CONDITIONS
Slope Analysis

Prepared by: Child Associates Inc.
Boston, Massachusetts
17 July 1995

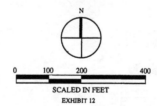

SCALED IN FEET
EXHIBIT 12

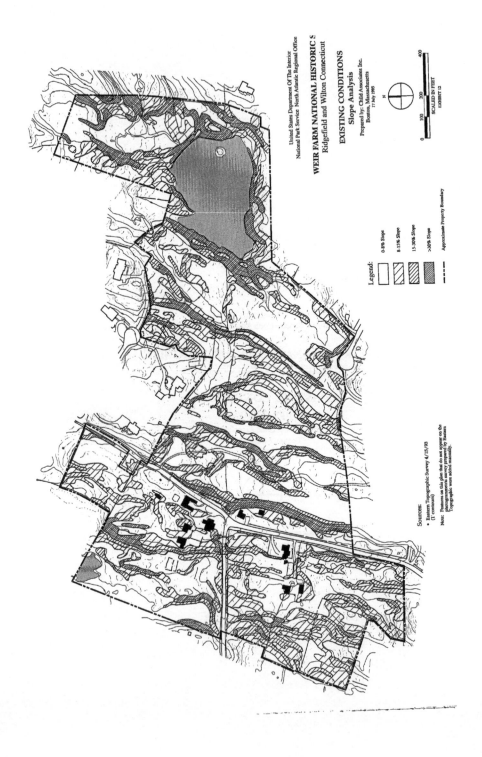

United States Department Of The Interior
National Park Service North Atlantic Regional Office

WEIR FARM NATIONAL HISTORIC S
Ridgefield and Wilton Connecticut

EXISTING CONDITIONS
Slope Analysis

Prepared by: Child Associates Inc.
Boston, Massachusetts
17 July 1995

N

0   100   200   400

SCALED IN FEET

EXHIBIT 12

Legend:

0-8% Slope

8-15% Slope

15-30% Slope

>30% Slope

Approximate Property Boundary

Sources:
• Eastern Topographic Survey 4/15/93
  (1' Contours)

Note: Features on this plan that do not appear on the
      photogrammetric survey prepared by Eastern
      Topographic were added manually.

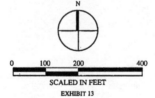

United States Department Of The Interior
National Park Service North Atlantic Regional Office

EIR FARM NATIONAL HISTORIC SITE
Ridgefield and Wilton Connecticut

EXISTING CONDITIONS
Vegetation Analysis

Prepared by: Child Associates Inc.
Boston, Massachusetts
17 July 1995

N

```
0      100     200            400
```
SCALED IN FEET
EXHIBIT 13

United States Department Of The Interior
National Park Service North Atlantic Regional Office

WEIR FARM NATIONAL HISTORIC SITE
Ridgefield and Wilton Connecticut

EXISTING CONDITIONS
Vegetation Analysis

Prepared by: Child Associates Inc.
Boston, Massachusetts
17 July 1995

Legend:

- Tree Cover
- Open Space (Meadow, Lawn, Garden, Wetland, Roads & Parking)
- Tree over 12" caliper

MAJOR FOREST TYPES

- Mixed Oak Forest
  1. Oak - Maple Laurel Viburnum Type
- Sugar Maple - White Ash Forest
  1. Maple - Ash - New York Fern Type
- Red Maple Forest
  1. Red Maple - Sweet Pepperbush Forest
  2. Red Maple - Spicebush Forest
  3. Rattlesnake Thicket
- Other

- - - Approximate Property Boundary

N

SCALED IN FEET
0   100   200   400

EXHIBIT 13

Sources:
- Eastern Topographic Survey 4/15/93
  (Tree Cover and Mature Tree Location)
- Ecological Survey of Weir Farm 1991 D.E.P.
  (Forest Communities)

Note: Features on this plan that do not appear on the ——

?

The sugar maple–white ash forest has one subtype or subcategory of vegetation represented on the site: the maple-ash-New York fern type. This subcategory of vegetation can be found in moist soils on lower slopes, east of the Burlingham property across Ned Hill Road and in the pond's southwest watershed. Trees found in these areas include sugar maple, white ash with limited red maple, red oak, and black cherry. This forest subcategory also has a well-developed shrub layer.[3]

The red maple forest has three subtypes or subcategories of vegetation represented on the site: red maple-sweet pepperbush forest, red maple-spicebush forest and buttonbush thickets. These subcategories, or forest subtypes, can be found in the many wet depressions and drainageways of the site. Trees found in these areas include red maple, yellow birch, black gum and some hemlocks. This forest type also has a well-developed shrub layer.[4]

Open space areas shown on the Vegetation Analysis Map are comprised of meadows and mowed fields (some of which, as outlined in previous chapters, were formerly cultivated fields), lawn areas, paved roads and driveways, and wetland areas. The open space wetland areas consisting of understory or shrub and herbaceous vegetation will be described further in the following soils and hydrology section.

Tree coverage occurs over 75% of the site, with the central and eastern portions of the site being almost entirely wooded. The majority of open space occurs at the highest portion of the site, near the Weir and Burlingham buildings. Trees larger than 12-inch caliper tend to occur along walls, roads, and hedgerows and in groupings found in steep and wet areas of the site. Larger trees were probably able to develop in these areas because they were outside the areas disturbed by cultivation.

Soils and Hydrology

Because wetland areas and certain soil types are interrelated, the soil and hydrologic conditions of the site were mapped together (exhibit 14). Five major soil types and various hydrologic features such as waterbodies, streams, and wetland areas are found on the site and shown on the Soils and Hydrology Map. The description of the five major soil types was taken from the Soil Conservation Service (SCS) survey for Fairfield County, Connecticut. Descriptions of soils from other noted sources vary slightly. Hydrologic information was taken from the Weir Farm NPS Wetlands Map and Assessment by Carl Melberg, Resource Management, February 5, 1993, and Eastern Topographics survey (04/15/93). It should be noted that a resource evaluation project to be completed by the fall of 1994 and conducted by the National Park Service and Soil Conservation Service will evaluate the site's natural resources, including

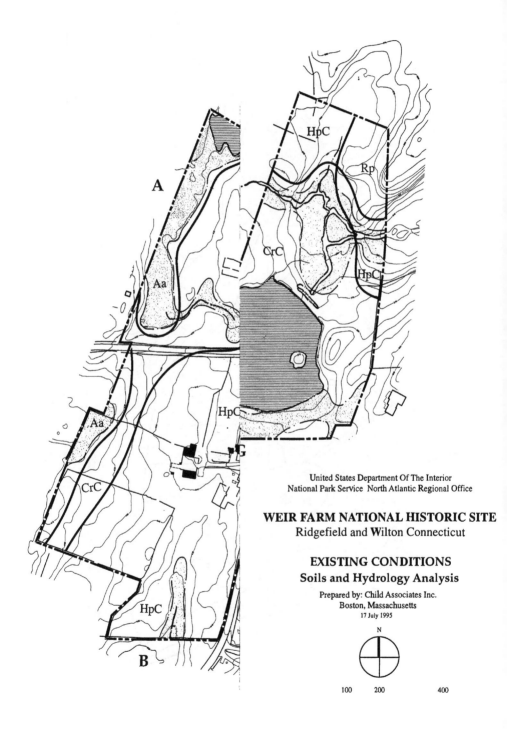

A

B

United States Department Of The Interior
National Park Service North Atlantic Regional Office

WEIR FARM NATIONAL HISTORIC SITE
Ridgefield and Wilton Connecticut

EXISTING CONDITIONS
Soils and Hydrology Analysis

Prepared by: Child Associates Inc.
Boston, Massachusetts
17 July 1995

N

100   200   400

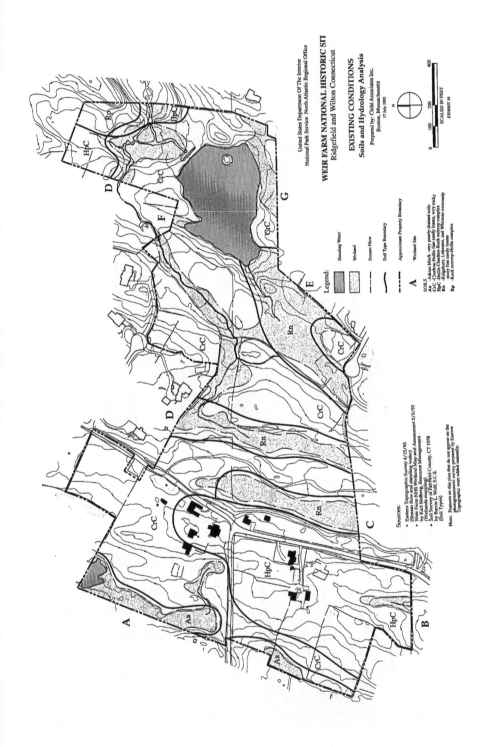

United States Department Of The Interior
National Park Service North Atlantic Regional Office

WEIR FARM NATIONAL HISTORIC SIT
Ridgefield and Wilton Connecticut

EXISTING CONDITIONS
Soils and Hydrology Analysis

Prepared by: Child Associates Inc.
Boston, Massachusetts
17 July 1995

N

0   100   200   400

SCALED IN FEET

EXHIBIT 14

Legend:

	Standing Water
	Wetland
----	Stream Flow
----	Soil Type Boundary
—·—·—	Approximate Property Boundary
A	Wetland Site

SOILS
Aa -Adrian Muck - very poorly drained soils
CrC -Charlton-Hollis fine sandy loams, very rocky
HpC -Hollis-Charlton-Rock outcrop complex
Re -Ridgebury, Leicester, and Whitman extremely
      stony fine sandy loams
Rp -Rock outcrop-Hollis complex

Sources:
• Eastern Topographic Survey 4/15/93
  (Stream flow and standing water)
• Weir Farm NHS Wetland Map and Assessment 2/5/93
  by Karl Malberg, Resource Management
  (Wetlands mapping)
• Soil Survey of Fairfield County, CT 1978
  by Barrie L. Wolf, S.C.S.
  (Soil Types)

Note: Features on this plan that do not appear on the
  photogrammetric survey prepared by Eastern
  Topographic were added manually.

water quality, and assess the potential impacts of existing and proposed actions on those resources.

The soils of the site have been derived solely from glacial till. These are generally rocky and have little organic accumulation in the upper layers.[5] The five major soil types are indicated on exhibit 14 and described briefly below.

CrC-Charlton-Hollis is a fine sandy loam and very rocky with 3 to 15 percent slopes. It consists of gently sloping and well drained and somewhat excessively drained soils on hills and ridges. They have an undulating topography marked with exposed bedrock, a few drainageways, and a few small wet depressions. This very strongly acid to medium acid soil is the dominant soil type on the site. It can be found throughout the northwest, central, and eastern portions of the site.[6]

HpC-Hollis-Charlton-rock outcrop complex is very similar to the Carlton-Hollis complex and consists of gently sloping and sloping soils on hills and ridges. It makes up the ridge along Nod Hill Road and at the Weir and Burlingham building areas.[7]

Rn-Ridgebury, Leicester and Whitman is an extremely stony, fine sandy loam. It consists of poorly drained and very poorly drained soils in depressions and drainageways on uplands and in valleys. Outcroppings typically cover 5 to 35 percent of the surface. The areas are irregularly shaped or long and narrow. Slopes range from 0 to 8 percent, but are typically less than 3 percent. This strongly acid to slightly acid soil makes up the majority of the drainageways and wetland areas at the central portion of the site.[8]

Aa-Adrian Muck is a poorly drained soil with a water table at the surface most of the year. It can be found in two depressed areas at the most western edge of the site.[9]

Rp-rock outcrop-Hollis complex is found typically on hills and ridges. It consist of gently sloping to steep, somewhat excessively drained soils and areas of exposed bedrock. This complex can be found at the northeasternmost corner of the site.[10]

Standing water exists in pond form on two areas of the site. A portion of a small pond can be found at the northwesternmost corner of the site behind the Weir buildings. However, the most dominant hydrologic feature of the site is a 3.6-acre manmade pond located at the eastern end of the site. A 200-foot earthern dam constructed at the northwest end of the pond contains water from the surrounding watershed and the stream located at the pond's southwestern banks. A small island exists at the pond's eastern edge.

Several wetland areas occur on the site as shown on exhibit 14 and described herein from The Weir Farm NPS Wetlands Assessment by Carl Melberg. They include the following.

Wetland Site A is located just to the west of the Weir house and is hydrologically supported by runoff from the surrounding landscape. This wetland is connected vegetatively to a much larger wetland system to the west. During periods of precipitation and spring high water, the two wetlands will have a hydric connection. This entire wetland complex after passing through several open water areas, discharges into the Norwalk River.[11]

Wetland Site B is located west of Nod Hill Road, southwest of the Burlingham House. This area is a seasonal wet meadow dominated by emergent vegetation that becomes dry enough during the summer months to mow. This finger-shaped area collects adjacent runoff, forming a swale configuration. The water from this area flows to the south connecting to the same system as Wetland C.[12]

Wetland Site C is located due east of Nod Hill Road. It runs in a north-south direction parallel to the road and is situated at the upper end of a fairly large watershed. This wetland is composed of three distinct zones. The most northerly zone is emergent wetland that is supported by runoff from adjacent lands. This emergent wetland changes further south or downslope into a broad-leaved deciduous wetland that then changes further into open water extending south off the property, through a constricted outlet culvert at a private residential access road. From this point south, the drainage is confined to a narrow streambed. This complex system eventually connects to the Norwalk River.[13]

Wetland Site D is part of a wetland complex that connects to a major stream. This wetland is adjacent to Wetland C, likewise extending in a north-south direction; however, it is associated with another watershed. This wetland makes up the upper reaches of this watershed, which is within the NPS boundary. The section of the wetland adjacent to Wetland C is open water surrounded by a riparian zone supporting wetland vegetation. This wetland area contributes water in a northerly direction to the NPS boundary. At this point, the wetland system gets narrower and turns eastward becoming part of a major watercourse. This watercourse contributes water to two drainage systems. The majority of the water from this system bypasses the pond and flows northeasterly off the property. The balance of the water connects with Wetland E and flows into the pond.[14]

274

Wetland Site E is part of the watershed associated with Wetland D. The wetland has its source just south of Tall Oaks Drive. Water from the wetland flows slowly east, supplying water to the pond. Wetland D connects to Wetland E vegetatively and hydrologically during high water.[15]

Wetland Site F is immediately adjacent to the pond. This wetland is regulated and maintained by pond elevation. Prior to the pond excavation by Weir, this wetland may have been a natural drainage for this area.[16]

Wetland Site G forms the inlet to the pond from the southeast. The wetland is supported by down-gradient seepage from the south. This seepage originates from the open water area west of Thunder Lake Road at the junction of Tall Oaks Drive. Emergent vegetation dominates this wetland.[17]

DETAILED EXISTING CONDITIONS INVENTORY

The objective of the detailed existing conditions plans (exhibits 15, 16, and 17) was to locate, identify, and define site features that contribute to the existing character of the site. The following summarizes the existing features of the site by area.

Weir Complex

This zone comprises the area north of Pelham Lane and west of Nod Hill Road. Five main structures exist in this area. The Weir house is located at the corner of Pelham Lane and Nod Hill Road. North of the Weir house lie the Weir barn and tack house, the Weir studio and garden shed, and the Young studio. Approximately 100 feet north of the Weir barn are the former ice house and a small shed. Two wells exist in this area. One is located west of the Weir house along Pelham Lane and consists of a stone structure about six feet square and four feet high. The other well is located north of the Weir barn along Nod Hill Road and is enclosed in a small woodshed.

Stone walls define two grass terraces occurring between the Weir house and the two studio buildings. Stone animal enclosures exist in the wooded area just west of the Young studio. Stone walls are found along Pelham Road, Nod Hill Road, enclosing the cemetery, and along the property lines to the north.

United States Department Of The Interior
National Park Service .North Atlantic Regional Office

WEIR FARM NATIONAL HISTORIC SITE
Ridgefield and Wilton Connecticut

DETAILED EXISTING CONDITIONS
Plan A

Prepared by: Child Associates Inc.
Boston, Massachusetts
17 July 1995

N

0   50   100   200

SCALED IN FEET

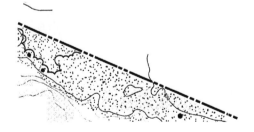

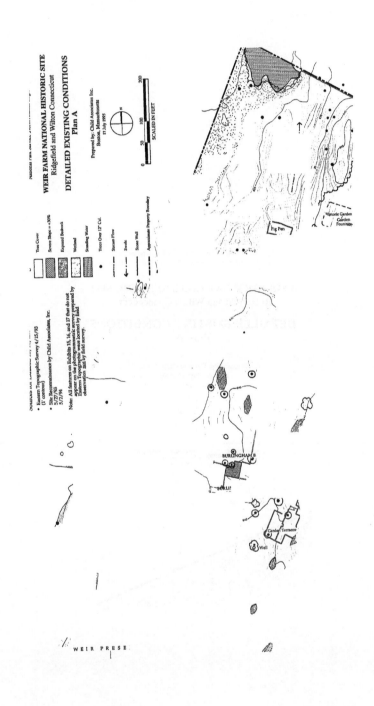

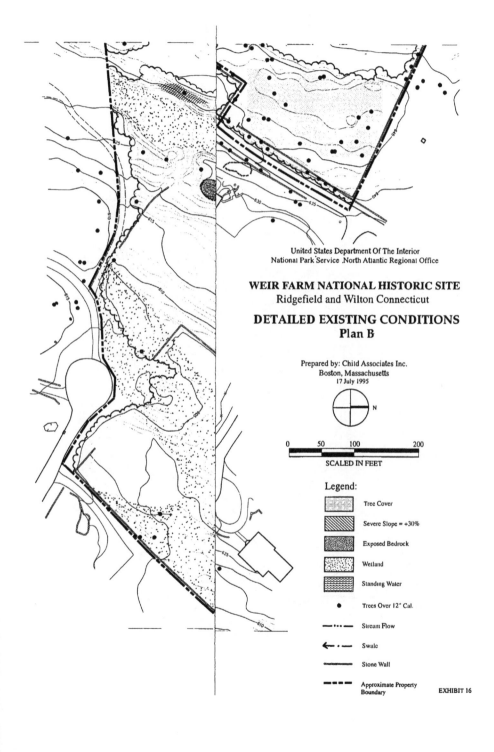

United States Department Of The Interior
National Park Service ,North Atlantic Regional Office

WEIR FARM NATIONAL HISTORIC SITE
Ridgefield and Wilton Connecticut

DETAILED EXISTING CONDITIONS
Plan B

Prepared by: Child Associates Inc.
Boston, Massachusetts
17 July 1995

N

0	50	100		200

SCALED IN FEET

Legend:

Tree Cover

Severe Slope = +30%

Exposed Bedrock

Wetland

Standing Water

●   Trees Over 12" Cal.

— • • • —   Stream Flow

⬅ — • —   Swale

〰〰〰   Stone Wall

▬ ▬ ▬ ▬   Approximate Property Boundary

EXHIBIT 16

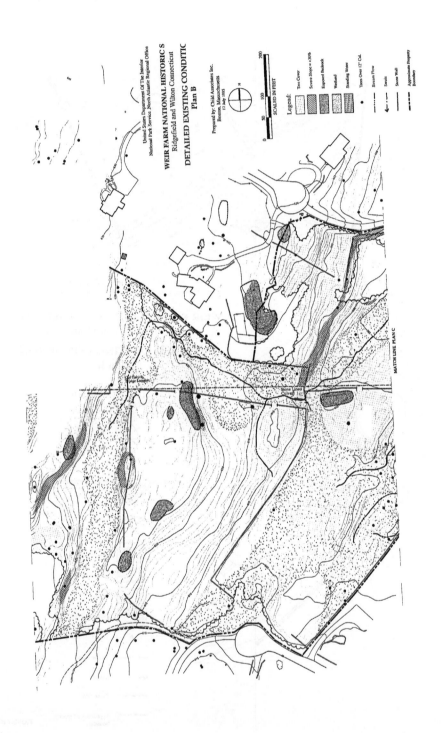

United States Department Of The Interior
National Park Service North Atlantic Regional Office

WEIR FARM NATIONAL HISTORIC S
Ridgefield and Wilton Connecticut
DETAILED EXISTING CONDITIC
Plan B

Prepared by: Child Associates Inc.
Boston, Massachusetts
17 July 1995

| | |
| 0 | 50 | 100 | 200 |
SCALED IN FEET

Legend:

Tree Cover
Severe Slope > 30%
Exposed Bedrock
Wetland
Standing Water
Trees Over 12" Cal.
Stream Flow
Swale
Stone Wall
Approximate Property Boundary

MATCH LINE PLAN C

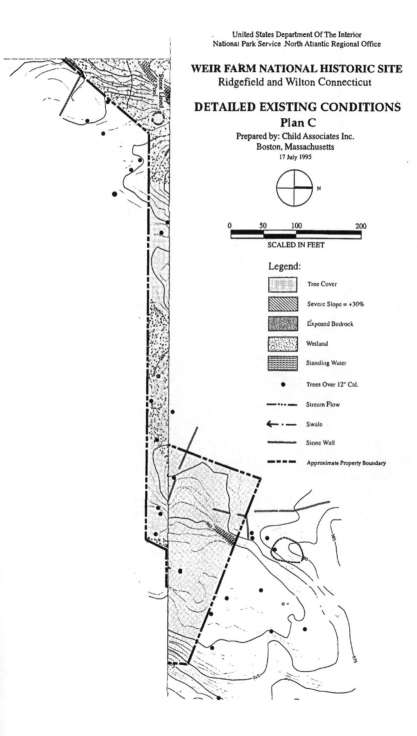

United States Department Of The Interior
National Park Service .North Atlantic Regional Office

WEIR FARM NATIONAL HISTORIC SITE
Ridgefield and Wilton Connecticut

DETAILED EXISTING CONDITIONS
Plan C
Prepared by: Child Associates Inc.
Boston, Massachusetts
17 July 1995

N

0	50	100		200

SCALED IN FEET

Legend:

Tree Cover

Severe Slope = +30%

Exposed Bedrock

Wetland

Standing Water

● Trees Over 12" Cal.

—— ··· —— Stream Flow

◄— · —— Swale

Stone Wall

— — — — Approximate Property Boundary

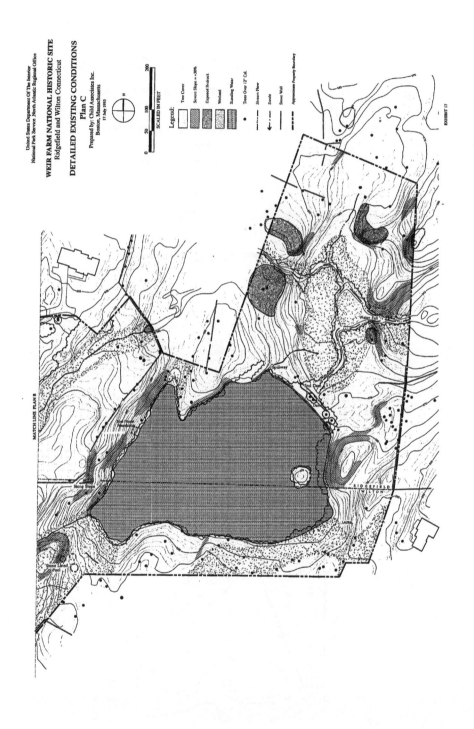

United States Department Of The Interior
National Park Service, North Atlantic Regional Office

WEIR FARM NATIONAL HISTORIC SITE
Ridgefield and Wilton Connecticut

DETAILED EXISTING CONDITIONS
Plan C

Prepared by: Child Associates Inc.
Boston, Massachusetts
17 July 1995

0   50   100   200
SCALED IN FEET

Legend:

▢	Tree Cover
▨	Severe Slope = >30%
▦	Exposed Bedrock
▦	Wetland
▦	Standing Water
•	Trees Over 12" Cal.
- - -	Stream Flow
←·-	Swale
—	Stone Wall
-··-	Approximate Property Boundary

EXHIBIT 17

The eastern portion of this area, where the buildings occur, is fairly open with sporadic canopy trees. Remnants of a historical formal garden are found in the area just north of the two studio structures. These remnants include the base of a stone fountain surrounded by unusually old boxwood shrubs and other very old garden plant materials. Seven existing apple trees or remnants are found north of the ice house structure. The locations of the apple trees have been recorded and the remnants have been propagated and removed due to their deteriorated condition.

The western portion of this area is heavily wooded with a wetland area along the western property boundary that flows north to a pond, of which a small portion lies on the Weir property.

Burlingham Complex

This zone comprises the area south of Pelham Lane and west of Nod Hill Road. Three main buildings occur in this area. The Burlingham house is located just west of Nod Hill Road and has a small toolshed behind. One-hundred-twenty feet to the west of the house is the Burlingham barn, and just south of the barn is the woodshed/garage. A driveway turns off Nod Hill Road south of the Burlingham house to the area between the barn and the woodshed/garage.

A sunken garden is located west of the Burlingham house and north of the driveway. This garden is defined by a stone retaining wall on four sides. The plants that remain are the evergreen plants (cedar, boxwood) that formed the structural planting components of the garden. A stone wall runs parallel to the driveway on the south side. The wall is broken opposite the house by a wood gate flanked by two crabapple trees. South of this wall lies a series of terraces defined by stone walls. Southwest of the terraces is an enclosed well structure.

The remainder of this area is essentially a series of meadows/fields separated by stone walls and vegetation. Stone walls occur along the entire length of Pelham Lane and Nod Hill Road. Remnants of an apple orchard appear along the southern property boundary. Two causeways lead from the western edge of the site across a wet area to the Weir Nature Preserve.

This area is essentially open, other than vegetation occurring along the stone walls, some of which containing large canopy trees.

Caretaker's Complex

This zone contains the area east of Nod Hill Road and west of Weir Pond. Two buildings occur in this area southeast of the intersection of Pelham Lane and Nod Hill Road: a house structure currently being referred to as the "caretaker's house" and south of this is the "caretaker's garage." A stone wall runs north-south just east of these structures to Nod Hill Road and then runs parallel to the road northeast to the northern property boundary. Directly across Nod Hill Road from the Weir house this wall is broken by stone steps that descend to a series of stone terraces.

East of the caretaker's buildings and below the stone wall, there is a very steep slope with a wet area at the base, running parallel to Nod Hill Road, draining from north to south. A stone and earthen causeway crosses the wet area near the southern property line. A trail begins at the north part of the site at the eastern edge of Nod Hill Road, winds south along the eastern edge of the wetland, and runs offsite at the southern property line. Between the trail and the wetland, remnants of stone foundations occur that supported some type of structure. Neither type nor use of the structure has been determined, but it was probably a farm-related outbuilding.

Central Area

A path diverges from this main trail approximately where the trail meets the town line. This path winds its way eastward to the pond area. At its beginning it emerges through an opening in a stone wall, flanked by two large canopy trees, a 24-inch caliper hickory and a 28-inch caliper London plane tree. Immediately after passing through the wall, the path crosses another wet area that has remnants of a wooden bridge. The path continues east through a wooded area, then along a small stream that is lined with stones and is actually culverted through a stone wall. The path proceeds east to the pond.

This entire central area has numerous stone walls and rock outcroppings. While the majority of the area is wooded, much of it is of relatively new growth, with the larger trees occurring in wet, steep, or rocky areas.

Pond Area

This area comprises the pond and the entire eastern portion of the site. The pond is approximately

3.6 acres in size. A small island (1,800–2,000 sq. ft.) exists near its eastern shore. Two dams occur on the northeast edge of the pond. The first dam is approximately 200 feet in length and consists of large rocks and earth. The second dam is approximately 15 to 20 feet behind the first and is approximately 80 feet long. This dam is poured concrete with stone set into it. The spillway for the pond is located at the northern edge of the first dam.

A foundation of a preexisting boathouse exists along the western shore of the pond. Southwest of this, stone steps ascend a steep slope to an overlook area consisting of large rocks and a stone bench. The area along the western shore of the pond is heavily wooded and contains some very large caliper trees.

The wet area southwest of the pond is the inlet for the pond. This area is very rocky and contains manmade stone features including walls and stone-lined pools. A significant amount of rusted barbed wire fencing is also found in this area.

South and east of the pond is also heavily wooded with a extensive amount of mountain laurel as understory vegetation. Selective clearing of some of this area from the adjacent residences is evident.

Northeast of the pond (north of the two dam structures) is a very heavily wooded area with steep slopes and larger rock outcroppings. This area contains a stream fed by both the pond from the south and another stream from the west. A waterfall exists where these two streams meet. Large specimen canopy trees occur in this area. Marked trails from the adjacent town conservation area wind through this area as well as around the pond.

Site Evolution

The Site Evolution Comparison Inventory Plan (exhibit 18) is a figure/ground comparison of the two periods of significance, 1919 and 1947, and the existing conditions today. For more detailed information for the period 1919, refer to chapter II, and for the period 1947, refer to chapters III and IV. The existing conditions for Weir Farm is outlined in detail earlier in this chapter.

The intent of this exhibit is to illustrate, in a general way, the evolution and development of the site from 1919 to present. Indicated in the diagrams are the extent of property ownership at that time, buildings, roads, and tree cover. The current property ownership is indicated on all plans for reference.

285

Legend:

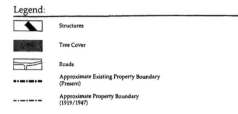

(filled structure symbol)	Structures
(tree cover symbol)	Tree Cover
(roads symbol)	Roads
▪▪▬▪▬▪▪	Approximate Existing Property Boundary (Present)
▬▪▬▪▬▪▬	Approximate Property Boundary (1919/1947)

Sources:

- Eastern Topographic Survey 4/15/93 (5' contour)
- Historic Aerials: 1939 - C-19
  10/20/41 - GA W9 65
  12/4/49 - 5 72 -65 1M
- WFHS Land Ownership Maps NPS (Park Boundaries)
- Historic Photographs
- Historic Paintings, Etchings, Sketches
- Interviews

United States Department Of The Interior
National Park Service North Atlantic Regional Office

WEIR FARM NATIONAL HISTORIC SITE
Ridgefield and Wilton Connecticut

SITE EVOLUTION
Comparison Inventory: 1919, 1947, 1994

Prepared by: Child Associates Inc.
Boston, Massachusetts
17 July 1995

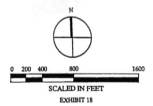

0	200	400	800	1600

SCALED IN FEET

EXHIBIT 18

1919

1947

1994

1919

This plan represents approximately 238 acres of property, most of which extends to the east and west of the current property ownership. Most of the current buildings existed, except for the caretaker's garage and the Young studio. Nod Hill Road and Pelham Lane existed, although neither were paved.

Approximately 50% of the property was forested at this time with the majority of the open space areas occurring west of Nod Hill Road and just east of the Weir complex. Selected areas had been cleared in the eastern part of the site.

1947

This plan also represents approximately 238 acres of land, all of which is shown on the 1919 plan. (References have indicated that an additional 9 1/2 acres was bought by Dorothy Weir Young in 1932. It is unclear exactly where these parcels were located.) All of the major buildings existed during this period, with the Young studio being built in 1932, and the caretaker's garage built sometime prior to 1947. Nod Hill Road and Pelham Lane both existed.

The tree cover significantly increased over this period, with the majority of the open space being located in the vicinity of the building areas. Selected clear areas still existed in the eastern property area, as well as the western area.

1994

The property line shown is the current ownership of 60 acres. The previously owned areas shown on the period plans is predominantly new residential subdivision developments (most of which were developed in the late 1970s), except for what is now the Weir Preserve, west of the Burlingham property.

The amount of open space has been reduced significantly since 1919, with the meadow area on the Burlingham property and the core area of the Weir Complex being the only open space areas remaining.

ENDNOTES TO CHAPTER VII

1.   An Ecological Survey of Weir Farm, Wilton/Ridgefield, CT., author unknown.

2.   Ibid.

3.   Ibid.

4.   Ibid.

5.   Ibid.

6.   U.S. Department of Agriculture, Soil Conservation Service, "Nontechnical Soils Description Report for Description Survey Area—Fairfield County, Connecticut," December 17, 1992, 1-2.

7.   Ibid., 2.

8.   Ibid., 2.

9.   Ibid., 1.

10.   Ibid., 2.

11.   Memorandum from Carl Melberg, Division of Cultural Resource Management, to Regional Coordinator, Water Resource Program, North Atlantic Regional Office, National Park Service, subject: Weir Farm National Historic Site Wetlands Map and Assessment, February 5, 1993.

12.   Ibid.

13.   Ibid.

14.   Ibid.

15.   Ibid.

16.   Ibid.

17.   Ibid.

CONCLUSION

Between 1882 and 1957, a span of 75 years, the American Impressionist painter, J. Alden Weir and the American realist sculptor and graphic artist Mahonri M. Young lived and worked at Weir Farm. Their artist friends also painted and sketched at the farm. In addition, Weir's first wife, Anna Baker Weir, who was initially his art student, his second wife, Ella Baker Weir, and his three daughters, Caroline, Dorothy (later Mrs. Mahonri M. Young), and Cora practiced a variety of arts and crafts at the Weir and Burlingham properties. Since 1958, Sperry and Doris Andrews have also lived and practiced their art at Weir Farm, adding up to a period of more than 110 years of continuous artistic activity in this one location.

To many members of the Weir family, from Weir's first wife, Anna, to Cora Weir Burlingham, gardening was an important aspect of life at Weir Farm. The property was farmed continuously probably for at least a century before Weir's purchase, until farming was gradually phased out after the death of Dorothy Weir Young in 1947. Agricultural activities at the site were painted and sketched first by Weir and then by Young between the early 1880s until about 1955. Weir Farm was thus a rare example of an informal artists' colony that was at the same time a working farm.

The intimate agricultural landscape of Weir Farm, captured in many paintings by J. Adlen Weir and other artists, is now very rare. This landscape is now preserved for future generations under the auspices of the National Park Service in partnership with the Weir Farm Heritage Trust. The information presented in this report will be used to guide the management of the site in a manner that respects the tradition of artists working on the site and the spirit of creativity inspired by the landscape at Weir Farm.

RECOMMENDATIONS FOR FURTHER RESEARCH

CHAPTER I

More information could be sought about Weir's projected Adirondack house in Keene Valley, New York, in the Adirondacks. Mr. Robin Pell, who lives in what is known locally as "Weir's studio" in Keene Valley, was contacted, but neither he nor his landlord, Mr. Howard Bushman-Kelly, had definitive information. Professor Richard Plunz of Columbia University's Department of Architecture is writing a book about Keene Valley and could also be contacted.

The handwriting on the 1895 herbarium pages should be compared with known examples of Weir's and Ella Weir's handwriting.

Archaeological investigation may be advisable on some parts of the site, particularly the site of the former fishing bridge.

CHAPTER II

The C. E. S. Wood Papers at the Huntington Library, San Marino, California, should be studied, especially the additional papers that have been acquired recently.

CHAPTER III

The Mahonri M. Young Papers in Special Collections, Lee Library, Brigham Young University, Provo, Utah, should be studied more completely than was possible in the time available for this project.

The Jack Sears Papers in Brigham Young's Special Collections should also be completely studied.

An attempt should be made to find out which artists from the Century Club and the Art Students League visited the Youngs and whether their art includes paintings or drawings showing the farm, the pond, etc.

An attempt should also be made to contact Spiro Anaganos, Young's assistant, who was living in San Francisco in 1989.

A Mr. Rodier, who is a friend of the Andrews, did landscape work on the property when Young was building the studio. He is now 82 years old.

Sally Iselin and her husband, the late sculptor Lewis Iselin, were friends of the Youngs. She lives in New York City.

CHAPTERS I, II, III, AND IV

The assistance of Dr. Peter Del Tredici of the Arnold Arboretum would be highly desirable in identifying trees from some of the historical photographs. His assistance was invaluable in the preparation of the Cultural Landscape Report for the Frederick Law Olmsted National Historic Site.

CHAPTER V

Sperry Andrews should be asked about the sketches or paintings of the farm he did while Young was still alive.

CHAPTERS II, III, IV, AND V

A Mr. Bill De Forest, who was born in 1900 and remembers Weir, lives on Nod Hill Road. He has been interviewed previously by the Weir Farm Heritage Trust but was not asked anything about the landscape. His wife's father, whose last name was Fuller, worked for Weir as a farmer and lived in the caretaker's house. Mr. De Forest could, of course, also be asked about all subsequent periods.

Members of the Gully, Knoche, Webb, and Beers families should also be interviewed.

We are very grateful to all the family members and others who have been interviewed for this project either in person or over the telephone. Their input has been invaluable. However, we have had to ask them to rely on memory alone for the very specific visual information we need for this project. If at all practical, we feel that some sort of informal workshop that brings all of these people together at the site to look at old photographs and to walk on the grounds would help to resolve many questions that we still have.

GENERAL

We also recommend that at some point an agricultural historian be asked to look at some of the historic photographs, Weir paintings and Mahonri Young drawings, as well as at the property itself, to try to understand more completely the agricultural activities at the site.

Further physical investigation of the stone wall on the east side of Nod Hill Road adjacent to the Weir house, especially the stone caps and the steps in this wall, and of the stone steps near the picnic table would also be helpful. Nothing has been located in the documentation that explains these features.

LIST OF REPOSITORIES CONSULTED AND OUTCOMES

CONNECTICUT

Weir Farm National Historic Site, Ridgefield and Wilton

The archives at the site include: copies of land, deed, and probate records; photographs; slides of Weir art works; reports, etc., prepared since the NPS ownership; and other records.

Yale University Archives, New Haven

Contains the John Ferguson Weir Papers. Gay Vietzke has studied this collection and shared her notes with us. The letters relating to Weir Farm appear to be the same as those microfilmed by the Archives of American Art, although Bob Brown of the Archives believes that the family added more materials when the gift to Yale was made.

BOSTON AND CAMBRIDGE, MASSACHUSETTS

Archives of American Art, Boston

Within the past year, all of the Archives' microfilm has been given to the Fine Arts Department of the Boston Public Library except for items with publication restrictions. All of the microfilm relating to Weir is now at the Boston Public Library except for Reel 533, which is restricted.

Fine Arts Department, Boston Public Library, Copley Square, Boston

The other eight microfilm reels relating to Weir and the Weir family are here. David Wallace took excellent notes on these. I read through key reels again but did not pick up any additional documents relating to the farm. However, it was sometimes helpful to have the entire letter, rather than extracts.

299

Also, the references to farming are clearer if you know whether the letter was written in Ridgefield or Windham.

BRIGHAM YOUNG UNIVERSITY, PROVO, UTAH

Lee Library

Special Collections has four sets of papers relevant to the project:

(1)   The Weir Family Papers. Read in full. This collection overlaps to some extent with the microfilm of the Archives of American Art, but there is much information on other members of the family.

(2)   The Dorothy Weir Young Papers. Not read. The finding aid indicated that nearly all of this collection consists of drafts of her book, so time was not spent on it.

(3)   The Mahonri M. Young Papers. Read selectively. This consists mostly of sections of his draft autobiography, not all of which is relevant to the project. Young's arrangement was topical, and the pieces on Weir and Dorothy Weir were helpful in preparing chapter III. Further exploration of this collection would be valuable. It is large, and the finding aid is only in draft form.

(4)   The Jack Sears Papers. Read one box out of four. A reference to this collection was found (on the last day of research) in the Hinton dissertation listed in the Bibliography. It turned out to be extremely valuable for Chapter III. Box 1 contained letters from Young to Sears, a boyhood friend, dating from 1932 through 1956. There is no finding aid to this collection, and valuable material may well be in the other boxes. The Weir, Young, and Sears Papers all include photographs, mostly snapshots of people.

The stack section of the library has a copy of the Hinton dissertation and a master's thesis on Young's early work (see Bibliography).

Museum of Art

Contains in storage:

(1) Works of art by Weir. All of these seem to be well known, but it was helpful to see some of the originals.

(2) Works of art by Dorothy Weir Young. Only one of these was looked at, since the computer listing indicated that nearly all were still lifes.

(3) Approximately 7000 works of art by Mahonri M. Young. Several hundred drawings, watercolors, and prints were examined. Photographs were made of about 60 Branchville and Windham drawings, not duplicating the ones previously made for David Wallace.

It should be cautioned that the titles given to Young's drawings, etc., are not very accurate. In most cases, they are not Young's titles but are ones given to the works of art by a previous curator or cataloguer. Some are a little fanciful: i.e., "Red Village," for the buildings on the farm. A search was done on the computer for works with "Branchville" in the title, but this did not pick up everything relevant. I requested several other drawings with rural sounding titles that could be views of Weir Farm and found other things that way. However, a number were of Windham, Danbury, or elsewhere.

(3) Curator's office. Dawn Phewsey kindly gave me xeroxes of some articles, clippings, etc., from her files.

FRICK MUSEUM, NEW YORK CITY

A telephone inquiry was made to the Frick Art Reference Library, which holds Theodore Robinson's diaries. I was referred to Sona Johnston, Associate Curator of Painting and Sculpture at the Baltimore Museum of Art, who is editing the diaries. She said she believed that there were a number of references to Weir, but she has not yet gotten back to me.

301

List of Repositories Consulted and Outcomes

HUNTINGTON LIBRARY, SAN MARINO, CALIFORNIA

A telephone inquiry was made to Peter Blodgett, Curator of Western Historical Manuscripts, who responded by sending detailed listings of the C. E. S. Wood Collection. The Wood Papers are not on microfilm, although several of them are quoted in Dorothy Weir Young's book. I was also told that the library had recently acquired a large additional collection of Wood Papers, which includes a number of letters from Weir to Wood. The new acquisition is still being catalogued but will be ready for scholars "in the near future."

BIBLIOGRAPHY

BOOKS AND EXHIBITION CATALOGS

Bailey, Liberty Hyde. *The Standard Cyclopedia of Horticulture.* New York: MacMillan, 1928 edition.

Benes, Peter, ed. *The Farm: Proceedings of the 1986 Dublin Seminar for New England Folklife.* Boston: Boston University, 1988.

Burke, Doreen Bolger. *J. Alden Weir: An American Impressionist.* Newark: University of Delaware Press, 1983.

Connecticut and American Impressionism. Storrs: The William Benton Museum of Art, The University of Connecticut, 1980.

Cox, Madison. *Artists' Gardens: From Claude Monet to Jennifer Bartlett.* Photographs by Erica Lennard. New York: Harry N. Abrams, Inc., 1993.

Curry, David Park. *Childe Hassam: An Island Garden Revisited.* Denver: Denver Art Museum/W. W. Norton & Company, 1990.

Dorothy Weir Young, 1890–1947. New York: The Cosmopolitan Club, n.d. (ca. 1948). Introduction by Mahonri M. Young.

Duncan Phillips: Centennial Exhibition, June 14 to August 31, 1986. Washington, DC: The Phillips Collection, 1986.

Fitch, James M., and F. F. Rockwell. *Treasury of American Gardens.* New York: Harper & Brothers, 1956.

303

Gerdts, William H. *American Impressionism*. New York: Abbeville Press, 1984.

Goodrich, Lloyd. *Albert P. Ryder*. New York: Braziller, 1959.

J. Alden Weir: A Place of His Own. Storrs: The William Benton Museum of Art, The University of Connecticut, Storrs, 1991.

Keeney, Elizabeth. *The Botanizers: Amateur Scientists in 19th-Century America*. Chapel Hill: University of North Carolina Press, 1992.

Mahonri M. Young: Retrospective Exhibition. Introduction by Frank Jewett Mather, Jr. Andover, MA: Addison Gallery of American Art, Phillips Academy, 1940.

McSpadden, J. Walker. *Famous Painters of America*. New York: Dodd, Mead and Co., 1916.

Morgan, Keith N. *Charles A. Platt: The Artist as Architect*. Cambridge, MA: M.I.T. Press, 1985.

Pierson, William H., Jr. *American Buildings and Their Architects: The Colonial and Neoclassical Styles*. Garden City, NY: Doubleday & Company, 1970.

Price, Frederic Newlin. *Goodbye Ferargil*. New Hope, PA: The Hufnagle Press, 1958.

Reynolds, Donald Martin. *Masters of American Sculpture: The Figurative Tradition from the American Renaissance to the Millennium*. New York: Abbeville Press, Publishers, 1993.

Roth, Leland M. *McKim, Mead and White, Architects*. New York: Harper and Row, 1983.

Thaxter, Celia. *An Island Garden*. Illustrated by Childe Hassam. Ithaca, New York: Bullbrier

Press, 1985, reprint of 1894 edition.

Young, Dorothy Weir. *The Life and Letters of J. Alden Weir.* New York: Kennedy Graphics, Inc., Da Capo Press, 1971.

ARTICLES

Cummings, Hildegard. Home Is the Starting Place: J. Alden Weir and the Spirit of Place. *J. Alden Weir: A Place of His Own* Storrs: The William Benton Museum of Art, The University of Connecticut, 1991, 15–36.

Goodwin, Alfred Henry. An Artist's Unspoiled Country Home. *Country Life in America* (October 1905) (816): #625–630.

Hinton, Wayne K. Mahonri Young and the Church: A View of Mormonism and Art. *Dialogue*, 35–43.

IFAR Reports. Special Issue: Losses at Brigham Young University. (June 1988) (96): Entire issue. Copy at Weir Farm National Historic Site.

Larkin, Susan. The Cos Cob Clapboard School. In *Connecticut and American Impressionism.* Storrs: The William Benton Museum of Art, The University of Connecticut, 1980, 82–99.

———. A Curious Aggregation: J. Alden Weir and His Circle. In *J. Alden Weir: A Place of His Own.* Storrs: The William Benton Museum of Art, The University of Connecticut, 1991, 59–77.

Mahonri Young's Sculpture Preserves His Mormon Past. *Life* (February 17, 1941) 10(7): 76, 79.

Mormon Artist. *Newsweek*, Vol. XVI, no. 13, (September 23, 1940) 16(13): 58.

Bibliography

Wheelwright, Robert. Charles Downing Lay, September 3, 1877–February 15, 1956. A Biographical Minute. *Landscape Architecture* Vol. XLVI, no. 3, (April 1956) 46(3): 162-164

NEWSPAPER ARTICLES

In Grateful Remembrance for Winged Deliverance. *The Deseret News,* Salt Lake City, Christmas edition. 1924. 16.

Famous Artist Predicts End of Modernism: Mahonri Young Arrives to Visit Salt Lake, His Birthplace. *Salt Lake Tribune,* May 3, 1936.

ORAL HISTORIES

Young, Mahonri Mackintosh. The Reminiscences of Mahonri Young. New York: Columbia University Oral History Research Office, 1958. Typescript, copy at Weir Farm National Historic Site..

REPORTS

Carden, Marie L., Architectural Conservator, Richard C. Crisson, Historical Architect, and Maureen K. Phillips, Architectural Conservatory, with Stephen Pisani, Contributor. Weir Farm Historic Structure Reports, Weir Farm National Historic Site, Ridgefield and Wilton, Connecticut, Volume I (Carden, Crisson and Pisani), The Site and the Weir Complex; Volume II-A (Phillips and Carden), Weir Farm Outbuildings; Volume II-B (Phillips), Weir Farm Outbuildings: Caretaker's House. Caretaker's Garage; and Volume III (Phillips), Burlingham Complex. Lowell, Massachusetts: Building Conservatory Branch, Northeast Cultural Resources Center, National Park Service U. S. Department of the Interior, 1995.

Chronology: Key Activities and Events Leading Up to the Creation of Weir Farm National Historic Site, n.d. Weir Farm National Historic Site.

Olmsted Center for Landscape Preservation. Historic Landscape Assessment of Weir Garden, Weir Farm National Historic Site. Prepared in Cooperation with the Ridgefield Garden Club for the Weir

Farm National Historic Site. Brookline, MA: Frederick Law Olmsted National Historic Site, April 1994.

Paul, Ellen, CGRS. History and Documentation of Weir Farm. Wilton, CT: 1990.

Ransom, David F., consultant. National Register of Historic Places Inventory-Nomination Form for the J. Alden Weir Farm in Ridgefield, Connecticut. January 16, 1983. Weir Farm National Historic Site.

Wallace, David H. Historic Furnishings Report, Weir Farm, Weir Farm National Historic Site, Wilton, Connecticut, Draft Report. Harpers Ferry, VA: Division of Historic Furnishings, Harpers Ferry Center, National Park Service, 1994. Final draft report pending.

Weir Farm National Historic Site, Wilton and Ridgefield, Connecticut. Draft General Management Plan. Environmental Impact Statement. Boston: United States Department of the Interior, National Park Service, North Atlantic Region, Division of Planning, 1994.

THESES AND DOCTORAL DISSERTATIONS

Hinton, Wayne K. A Biographical History of Mahonri M. Young, A Western American Artist. A dissertation presented to the Department of History, Brigham Young University, in partial fulfillment of the requirements for the degree Doctor of Philosophy, April 1974. Provo, UT: Lee Library, Brigham Young University.

Hopkin, Elizabeth B. A Study of the Philosophical and Stylistic Influence of Jean-François Millet on Mahonri M. Young from 1901-27. A thesis presented to the Department of Art, Brigham Young University, in partial fulfillment of the requirements for the degree Master of Arts, April 1990. Provo, UT: Lee Library, Brigham Young University.

UNPUBLISHED PAPERS

Caldwell, Dona. Vera Poggi Breed (Mrs. Nelson Breed), 1890-1967. Fairfield, CT: Fairfield Historical Society.

APPENDIX

CORRESPONDENCE FROM MAHONRI M. YOUNG AND BILL YOUNG'S MARK-UP PLAN

August 23, 1994

MAHONRI M. YOUNG

KELLIS POND LANE, R.D.1
WATER MILL, NEW YORK, 11976

August 23, 1994

Dear Mr. Grove,

My father has asked me to respond to your letter of Aug.
12 regarding information on Weir Farm ca. 1947.

Based on my recollections from summers spent on the farm
in the fifties, I have come up with the information noted directly
on the 1"=100' site plan (enclosed).

We question whether the chicken house (as it was in our day)
was originally an icehouse. It appears inappropriate for that
use. To my recollection, the icehouse was a circular pit in the
grounddcovered by a circular windowless shed and roof at approx.
location 6 on the map.

You should also check with Doris and Sperry Andrews and
their children. Although their residency dates from 1958 (not
1957 as given in some printed material), I doubt that any changes
of significance were made by my grandfather between Dorothy's
death in 1947 and his own death in 1957 (except for removing
the railing around the front porch of the main house). The
Andrews' recollections of the property in the late fifties would
probably reflect thevconditions of a decade earlier.

My cousin Charlie Lay and his sister Darcy might also have
relevant recollections. The three Weir grandchildren are probably
the best living source on information on the Burlingham property.

Please feel free to contact me if you wish further details.
I can be reached at 516-537-3091 until Sept. 12 and at
613-789-5714 from Sept. 14.

Sincerely,

Lightning Source UK Ltd.
Milton Keynes UK
UKHW010906271218
334508UK00013B/1158/P

9 781528 525664